Vocational Guidance of Elementary Schools

Vocational Guidance of Elementary Schools

Gautam Sinha

RANDOM PUBLICATIONS
NEW DELHI - 110 002 (INDIA)

Vocational Guidance of Elementary Schools

ISBN 978-93-51112-97-6

Published in 2014 in India by

RANDOM PUBLICATIONS

4376-A/4B, Gali Murari Lal, Ansari Road
New Delhi-110 002
Phone: +9111-43580356, 23289044
E-mail: randomexports@gmail.com; sales@randompublications.com;
info@randompublications.com

Type Setting by: Friends Media, Delhi-110089
Printed at : Thomson Press (India) Ltd

Preface

For their educational, social, and career success in the twenty-first century, students will require effective work habits and the ability to make sound decisions, solve problems, plan effectively, work independently, communicate well, research, evaluate themselves realistically, and explore new educational and career opportunities. A carefully planned guidance and career education program, beginning in the elementary grades and continuing through secondary school, will help students acquire these skills. Students must learn and develop skills at school that will help them become more independent and responsible individuals. They must be able to apply what they learn in school to other areas of their lives. They must learn to work cooperatively and productively with a wide range of people, to set and pursue education and career goals, to evaluate their achievement of these goals, and to assume their roles as responsible citizens. A comprehensive guidance and career education program will provide students with an understanding of the concepts in the three areas of learning in the program (student development, interpersonal development, and career development) and with many opportunities to practise new skills in structured and supportive settings. It will allow them to learn from their experiences and accomplishments, and to apply their skills and knowledge in the classroom, in the school with their peers and teachers, and in the community. It will also involve parents, community partners, teachers, teacher-advisers, guidance counsellors, and community mentors in the program. The guidance and career education program will help students relate what they learn in school to the community, understand and value education, recognize the learning opportunities available to them, make choices from among those opportunities, and adapt to changing circumstances. It will help them make transitions throughout their lives – from family to school, from school to school, from school to work, and from school to lifelong learning.

Through learning activities that emphasize managing time, completing tasks, setting goals, resolving conflicts, volunteering, collaborating, and cooperating, students will learn self-discipline, personal and social responsibility, and respect for others from diverse cultures. Students will learn to set and achieve learning goals both inside and outside school, manage their own learning, and acquire the habits and skills necessary for success both inside and outside school. As students develop the ability to understand how they learn, recognize areas that need improvement, set goals for improvement, monitor their own learning, and become independent learners, they are acquiring the basic habits and skills they will require for lifelong learning. Students will learn to demonstrate self-discipline, take responsibility for their own behaviour, acquire the knowledge and skills required for getting along with others both within and beyond the school, and choose ways of interacting positively with others in a variety of situations. They will also learn about thoughtful and non-violent problem resolution, social responsibility, working cooperatively with others, and caring about others. Students will learn how to make informed and appropriate choices to ensure their successful transition from elementary to secondary school and from secondary school to further education, training, and work. This involves the acquisition of the knowledge and skills required to make informed and responsible decisions at key transition points throughout elementary and secondary school and in preparation for leaving secondary school. Students will also assess their interests, competencies, and achievements; explore and evaluate education and career opportunities; make appropriate choices from among those opportunities; collect and interpret information; set goals; and create and evaluate plans for the future.

This book provides information on currently available career guidance materials and resources for the elementary and middle/ junior high school levels.

I thank all members of my team who have helped in the preparation of the book. My special thanks go to "Random Publications" who have published the book.

—*Gautam Sinha*

Contents

1

Introduction

The Nature and Meaning of Guidance

Vocational guidance is one of the basic pillars in the life of contemporary societies as this process continues throughout the individual life, starting as he joins kindergarten and continues throughout his shift to the stages of general education, graduation in higher education stages, embarking on practical life till his pension.

Guidance process has an important and constructive impact on the individual life as it helps him achieve harmony between the various factors of his personality, tendencies and preparedness and the reality of life. This helps him develop and grow in various psychological, social and economic aspects and consequently assist in achieving prosperity and progress of the society in which he lives.

The Concept of Guidance

It is a process to guide the individual to the various paths through which he is able to discover and utilize his potentials and capabilities, tendencies and desires to lead a pleasant life and contributes to the happiness of his society. The need for vocational guidance has grown as a result of the greater variety of jobs and skills required in modern society, and greater awareness of how widely people differ in interests and abilities.

Whatever a person's work, a high degree of efficiency is usually important. To achieve this, individuals have to be satisfied with their jobs. The choice of a vocation affects not only the quality of their work but also their relationships with others and their usefulness to the community.

Young people need help in finding their real interests and capabilities. They need help in making a realistic, as opposed to fanciful, choice of a career. And they need guidance in planning for a well-rounded education as well as for specific training for a particular vocation. Adults, too, are often in need of vocational guidance. A person may realize, after months or even years in a particular occupation, that he or she is unsuited to the work and unhappy in it. Circumstances may force a person to leave one kind of job and seek another. After retirement from a job, older persons often find they still need to work. Women who leave work to have children often need or want to reenter the job market when their children reach school age. Immigrants need help in adjusting to jobs in their new homeland. Disabled persons require help in training for and adjusting to jobs.

Vocational guidance usually covers six areas: (1) studying or surveying the various kinds of occupations; (2) determining aptitudes; (3) choosing a vocation; (4) preparing for work in the chosen vocation; (5) finding a job; (6) adjusting to and gaining competence in the job.

For young people, vocational guidance may be spread over a period of years. Specific guidance may start in the seventh or eighth grade, where students may read books and watch films and videotapes that deal with careers. They may visit factories, farms, stores, or other places of work such as hospitals, courtrooms, and airports.

In high school, a student may decide upon an occupation with the help of a counsellor. The student may take vocational education courses, such as auto mechanics or bookkeeping, or take part in career-related activities offered by such organizations as 4-H clubs, the school newspaper, or the school art club. Vocational guidance counsellors may help the student find a part-time job. Young people who are leaving school may be helped in finding and adjusting to full-time jobs. Many colleges and universities have guidance and testing programmes, often as part of their job-placement services.

General Objectives of Guidance:

- To guide trainees in various psychological, moral, social, educational and occupational aspects in order to become active members in the nation building process.
- To discuss the personal, social or educational problems encountered by the trainees during their study and work towards finding appropriate solutions which enable them to progress in their study.

- To work towards discovering the skills, capabilities and tendencies of distinct or ordinary trainees and help them invest their skills.
- To encourage trainees to learn and give them an insight into the training unit system and help them utilize available programmes.
- To help trainees select the specialization and occupation which meet the society requirements.
- To guide trainees in cooperation with the students tutor and solve their problems and participate in various councils and committees.

History and Development of Guidance

The history of school counselling around the world varies greatly based on how different countries and local communities have chosen to provide academic, career, college readiness, and personal/social skills and competencies to K-12 children and their families based on economic and social capital resources and public versus private educational settings in what is now called a school counselling programme.

United States

Early Years: In the United States, the school counselling profession began as a vocational guidance movement at the beginning of the 20th century. Jesse B. Davis is considered the first to provide a systematic school guidance programme. In 1907, he became the principal of a high school and encouraged the school English teachers to use compositions and lessons to relate career interests, develop character, and avoid behavioural problems. Many others during this time did the same. For example, in 1908, Frank Parsons, "Father of Vocational Guidance" established the Bureau of Vocational Guidance to assist young people in making the transition from school to work.

From the 1920s to the 1930s, school counselling and guidance grew because of the rise of progressive education in schools. This movement emphasized personal, social, moral development. Many schools reacted to this movement as anti-educational, saying that schools should teach only the fundamentals of education. This, combined with the economic hardship of the Great Depression, led to a decline in school counselling and guidance. In the 1940s, the U.S. used psychologists and counsellors to select, recruit, and train military personnel. This propelled the counselling movement in schools by providing ways to test students and meet their needs. Schools accepted these military tests openly. Also, Carl Rogers' emphasis on helping relationships during this time influenced the profession of school counselling.

1950s and 60s

In the 1950s the government established the Guidance and Personnel Services Section in the Division of State and Local School Systems. In 1957, the Soviet Union launched Sputnik I. Out of concern that the Russians were beating the U.S. in the space race, which had military implications, and that there were not enough scientists and mathematicians, the American government passed the National Defence Education Act, which spurred a huge growth in vocational guidance through large amounts of funding. Since the 1960s, the profession of school counselling has continued to grow as new legislation and new professional developments were established to refine and further the profession and improve education. On January 1, 2006, congress officially declared February 6–10 as National School Counselling Week.

The 1960s was also a time of great federal funding in the United States for land grant colleges and universities interested in establishing and growing what are now known as Counsellor Education programmes. School counselling began to shift from a focus exclusively on career development to a focus on student personal and social issues paralleling the rise of social justice and civil rights movements in the United States. It was also in the late 60s and early 1970s that Norm Gysbers began the work to shift from seeing school counsellors as solitary professionals into a more strategic and systemic goal of having a comprehensive developmental school counselling programme for all students K-12. His and his colleagues' work and research evidence showing strong correlations between fully implemented school counselling programmes and student academic success was critical to beginning to show an evidence base for the profession especially at the high school level based on their work in the state of Missouri.

1980s and 90s

But school counselling in the 1980s and early 1990s in the United States was not seen as a player in educational reform efforts buffeting the educational community. The danger was the profession becoming irrelevant as the standards-based educational movement gained strength in the 1990s with little evidence of systemic effectiveness for school counsellors. In response, Campbell & Dahir (1997) consulted widely with school counsellors at the elementary, middle, and high school levels and created the ASCA National Standards for School Counselling with three core domains (Academic, Career, Personal/Social), nine standards, and specific competencies and indicators for K-12 students.

The publication of the ASCA standards in 1997 ushered in a unique period of professionalization and strengthening of school counselling identity, roles, and programmes. A year later, the first systemic meta-analysis of school counselling was published and gave the profession a wake-up call in terms of the need to focus on outcome research and the small set of methodologically accurate school counselling outcome research studies in academic, career, and personal/social domains.

National Centre for Transforming School Counselling

Also in the late 1990s, a former mathematics teacher, school counsellor, and administrator, Pat Martin, was hired by The Education Trust to work on a project focusing the school counselling profession on helping close achievement gaps hindering the life successes of children and adolescents, including children and adolescents of colour, poor and working class children and adolescents, bilingual children and adolescents and children and adolescents with disabilities.

Martin's project developed focus groups of K-12 students, parents, guardians, teachers, building leaders, and superintendents and interviewed professors of school counselling in Counsellor Education programmes. She hired a school counsellor educator from Oregon State University, Dr. Reese House, and they co-created what became the National Centre for Transforming School Counselling at The Education Trust in 2003.

Their foci included (1) changing how school counselling was taught at the graduate level in Counsellor Education programmes and (2) changing the practices of K-12 school counsellors in districts throughout the USA to teach school counsellors prevention and intervention skills to help close achievement and opportunity gaps for all students. The NCTSC focus groups found what Hart & Jacobi (1992) had indicated—too many school counsellors were working as gatekeepers for the status quo instead of advocates for equity. Too many school counsellors were using inequitable practices and unwilling to challenge them, which kept students from nondominant backgrounds from the advanced coursework (honours, AP, IB courses) and academic, career, and college readiness skills needed to successfully graduate from high school and pursue rigorous post-secondary options including college.

They found funding for $500,000 grants for six different Counsellor Education/School Counselling programmes in rural and urban settings, to transform their School Counsellor Education programmes to focus teaching school counsellor candidates advocacy, leadership, teaming and collaboration, equity assessment using data, and culturally competent programme counselling and coordination beginning in 1998. By 2008, NCTSC consultants had also worked in over 100 districts around the United States including most major cities to help transform the work of school counsellors to help close gaps and challenge inappropriate policies and procedures through the use of data and assessing equity.

Practitioners, too, jumped on board the school counselling transformation train. In 2008, Rowman Littlefield Education published The New School Counsellor: Strategies for Universal Academic Achievement. The text, written by Rita Schellenberg, a practicing school counsellor and counsellor educator, describes the new vision for school counselling and guides school counsellors and pre-service school counsellors through accountable, data-driven programming. Schellenberg introduces Standards Blending, a crosswalking strategy that hold the potential to be culturally sensitive and effective in enhancing academic achievement and closing the achievement gap.

Recent History

In 2002, the American School Counsellor Association released the ASCA National Model framework for school counselling programmes, written by Dr. Trish Hatch and Dr. Judy Bowers, comprising some of the top school counselling components in the field into one model—the work of Norm Gysbers, Curly & Sharon Johnson, Robert Myrick, Dahir & Campbell's ASCA National Standards, and the skill-based focus for closing gaps from the Education Trust's Pat Martin and Reese House into one document. ASCA also developed the RAMP (Recognized ASCA Model Programmes) Awards to honour school counselling programmes that have fully implemented the ASCA National Model with demonstrable evidence of success for K-12 students. In 2003, the Centre for School Counselling Outcome Research was developed as a clearinghouse for evidence-based practice with regular research briefs disseminated and original research projects developed and implemented with founding director Jay Carey. One of the research fellows, Tim Poynton, developed the EZAnalyze software programme for all school counsellors to use as free-ware to assist in using data-based interventions.

In 2004, the ASCA Code of Ethics was substantially revised to focus on issues of equity, closing gaps, and ensuring all students received access to a K-12 school counselling programme. Pat Martin left the Education Trust and moved to the College Board. She hired School Counsellor Educator Dr. Vivian Lee and they developed an equity-focused entity on school counsellors and college counselling, the National Office for School Counsellor Advocacy (NOSCA). NOSCA developed scholarships for research on college counselling by K-12 school counsellors and how it is taught in School Counsellor Education programmes. They also created Advocacy Awards to focus on best practices in college counselling programmes in K-12 schools that show effective school counselling practices in creating college-going cultures with demonstrated results in ensuring high rates of college admissions for large percentages of students of nondominant backgrounds.

In 2008, The first NOSCA study was released by Jay Carey and colleagues focusing on innovations in selected College Board "Inspiration Award" schools where school counsellors collaborated inside and outside their schools for high college-going rates and strong college-going cultures in schools with large numbers of students of nondominant backgrounds. Also in 2008, the American School Counsellor Association released School Counselling Competencies focused on assisting school counselling programmes to effectively implement school counselling programmes based on the ASCA Model.

The ASCA Model encourages professional school counsellors to use crosswalking strategies and to create action plans and results reports that demonstrate "how" school counsellors are making a difference in the lives of students. In 2008, Dr. Rita Schellenberg introduced *Standards Blending* as a crosswalking strategy to aid in aligning school counselling more directly with the academic achievement mission of schools. Scholars have identified *Standards Blending* as a promising approach for enhancing academic achievement and closing the achievement gap. At the same time, Dr. Schellenberg introduced the School Counselling Operational Plan for Effectiveness (SCOPE) and the School Counselling Operational Report of Effectiveness (SCORE), a data reporting system to demonstrate accountable practices and programme outcomes. The SCOPE and SCORE are designed to simplify the task of creating action plans and results reports with immediate access to the ASCA and core academic standards, data sources, and data analysis tools. The most recent version of the ASCA National Model was published in 2012.

The history of the profession continues shifting as more students, parents, guardians, teachers, building leaders, and government officials learn of changes in the profession, and as the evidence base and equity-building skills of school counsellor candidates and school counsellors in K-12 schools develop through the dissemination of results and successful outcomes of increased student academic, career, college, and personal/social competencies including reduced achievement and opportunity gaps for all students.

Other Countries

A balanced, comprehensive school counselling programme provides services to promote student success. It involves school counsellors working in conjunction with parents, teachers and other school personnel and community agencies. Many developmental concepts that must be covered through a comprehensive programme can be incorporated into other classroom studies, giving the school counsellor more opportunities for direct counselling, prevention, and remediation functions.

It is important that a comprehensive school counselling programme provide a range of services in order to address the needs of all students. Counsellors should strive to balance their time among all these services, based on the unique needs of their school community. By developing and implementing a comprehensive school counselling plan, school counsellors can establish services and activities that allow them to spend most of their time providing direct services to children.

In the United States, the school counselling profession began as a vocational guidance movement at the beginning of the 20th century. In 1907, Jesse B. Davis became the principal of a high school and encouraged the school English teachers to use compositions and lessons to relate career interests, develop character, and avoid behavioural problems. From that grew systematic guidance programmes which later evolved into comprehensive school counselling programmes that address three basic domains: academic development, career development, and personal/social development.

Educational and Other Forms of Guidance

Education in its general sense is a form of learning in which the knowledge, skills, and habits of a group of people are transferred from one generation to the next through teaching, training, or research. Education frequently takes place under the guidance of others, but may also be autodidactic. Any experience that has a formative effect on the way one thinks, feels, or acts may be considered educational.

Type of Education

Figure: *School children line, in Kerala, India*

Education can take place in formal or informal educational settings.

Formal Education

Systems of schooling involve institutionalized teaching and learning in relation to a curriculum, which itself is established according to a predetermined purpose of the schools in the system. Schools systems are sometimes also based on religions, giving them different curricula.

Curriculum

In formal education, a curriculum is the set of courses and their content offered at a school or university. As an idea, curriculum stems from the Latin word for *race course*, referring to the course of deeds and experiences through which children grow to become mature adults. A curriculum is prescriptive, and is based on a more general syllabus which merely specifies what topics must be understood and to what level to achieve a particular grade or standard.

Figure: *School children in Durban, South Africa.*

An academic discipline is a branch of knowledge which is formally taught, either at the university–or via some other such method. Each discipline usually has several sub-disciplines or branches, and distinguishing lines are often both arbitrary and ambiguous. Examples of broad areas of academic disciplines include the natural sciences, mathematics, computer science, social sciences, humanities and applied sciences. Educational institutions may incorporate fine arts as part of K-12 grade curricula or within majors at colleges and universities as electives. The various types of fine arts are music, dance, and theater.

Curriculum

In formal education, a curriculum is the planned interaction of pupils with instructional content, materials, resources, and processes for evaluating the attainment of educational objectives. Other definitions combine various elements to describe curriculum as follows:

- All the learning which is planned and guided by the school, whether it is carried on in groups or individually, inside or outside the school. (John Kerr)
- Outlines the skills, performances, attitudes, and values pupils are expected to learn from schooling. It includes statements of desired pupil outcomes, descriptions of materials, and the planned sequence that will be used to help pupils attain the outcomes.

- The total learning experience provided by a school. It includes the content of courses (the syllabus), the methods employed (strategies), and other aspects, like norms and values, which relate to the way the school is organized.
- The aggregate of courses of study given in a learning environment. The courses are arranged in a sequence to make learning a subject easier. In schools, a curriculum spans several grades.
- Curriculum can refer to the entire programme provided by a classroom, school, district, state, or country. A classroom is assigned sections of the curriculum as defined by the school. For example, a fourth grade class teaches the part of the school curriculum that has been designed as developmentally appropriate for students who are approximately nine years of age.

Etymology

As an idea, curriculum came from the Latin word which means *a race* or *the course of a race* (which in turn derives from the verb "currere" meaning *to run/to proceed*). As early as the seventeenth century, the University of Glasgow referred to its "course" of study as a *curriculum*, and by the nineteenth century European universities routinely referred to their curriculum to describe both the complete course of study (as for a degree in Surgery) and particular courses and their content. By the beginning of the twentieth century, the related term *curriculum vitae* ("course of one's life") became a common expression to refer to a brief account of the course of one's life.

A curriculum is prescriptive, and is based on a more general syllabus which merely specifies what topics must be understood and to what level to achieve a particular grade or standard. Curriculum has numerous definitions, which can be slightly confusing. In its broadest sense a curriculum may refer to all courses offered at a school. This is particularly true of schools at the university level, where the diversity of a curriculum might be an attractive point to a potential student. A curriculum may also refer to a defined and prescribed course of studies, which students must fulfill in order to pass a certain level of education. For example, an elementary school might discuss how its curriculum, or its entire sum of lessons and teachings, is designed to improve national testing scores or help students learn the basics. An individual teacher might also refer to his or her curriculum, meaning all the subjects that will be taught during a school year. On the other hand, a high school might refer to a curriculum as the courses required in order to receive one's diploma. They might also refer to curriculum in exactly the same way as the elementary school, and use curriculum to mean both individual courses needed to pass, and the overall offering of courses, which help prepare a student for life after high school.

Beliefs

Some of the beliefs that result in very difficult or living is a question that sometimes occupies curriculum designers. Traditionally high school prepared students for college. Those students who did not intend to go to college often dropped out of high school. During the middle of the 20th century it was believed that high school was valuable for all students so the high schools began tracking students. Some took more rigorous classes to prepare for college while others took a general track. Later high schools added courses to prepare for vocations that did not require college. Now high school is desired for all students.

- Should curriculum be designed as pieces or as a whole? One concern in the 1990s and after is the fragmented curriculum. This has resulted from adding courses and content without aligning them to what is already being taught. The curriculum today has many pieces, but seems not to have a wholeness about it. For example, even in the primary grades, there may be classes in phonetics, reading, language arts, and writing. This is very fragmented as reading and writing are part of the whole system of communicating with symbols.
- What is a good balance between academic achievement and developmentally appropriate curriculum is an ongoing question. Academic achievement sets levels of standards to meet in certain grade levels which is advocated by those who believe all students should attain the same skills; however, those who are aware of developmental stages and the problems of late development believe that levels of standards should be more flexible and compared over multiage levels.
- Should it be a spiral or mastery curriculum is a major design question. The American curriculum has been a spiral curriculum in which many ideas are introduced at each grade and then repeated at following grades to add depth of understanding.

The Outcome Based curriculum advocated by Spady used a different approach, that of mastery. For this, the students study a topic in depth until it is mastered. The question of "what is mastery?" has been discussed by many curriculum committees as they implement this type of curriculum.

Traditional Points of View of Curriculum

In the early years of the 20th century, the traditional concepts held of the "curriculum is that it is a body of subjects or subject matter prepared by the teachers for the students to learn." It was synonymous to the "course of study" and "syllabus".

Robert M. Hutchins views curriculum as "permanent studies" where the rules of grammar, rhetoric and logic and mathematics for basic education are emphasized. Basic education should emphasize 3 Rs and college education should be grounded on liberal education. On the other hand, Arthur Bestor as an essentialist, believes that the mission of the school should be intellectual training, hence curriculum should focus on the fundamental intellectual disciplines of grammar, literature and writing. It should also include mathematics, science, history and foreign language.

This definition leads us to the view of Joseph Schwab that discipline is the sole source of curriculum. Thus in our education system, curriculum is divided into chunks of knowledge we call subject areas in basic education such as English, Mathematics, Science, Social Studies and others. In college, discipline may include humanities, sciences, languages and many more. To Phenix, curriculum should consist entirely of knowledge which comes from various disciplines.

Thus curriculum can be viewed as a field of study. It is made up of its foundations (philosophical, historical, psychological, and social foundations); domains of knowledge as well as its research theories and principles. Curriculum is taken as scholarly and theoretical. It is concerned with broad historical, philosophical and social issues and academics.

Progressive Points of View of Curriculum

On the other hand, to a progressivist, a listing of school subjects, syllabi, course of study, and list of courses of specific discipline do not make a curriculum. These can only be called curriculum if the written materials are actualized by the learner. Broadly speaking, curriculum is defined as the total learning experiences of the individual. This definition is anchored on John Dewey's definition of experience and education. He believed that reflective thinking is a means that unifies curricular elements. Thought is not derived from action but tested by application. Caswell and Campbell viewed curriculum as "all experiences children have under the guidance of teachers." This definition is shared by Smith, Stanley and shores when they defined "curriculum as a sequence of potential experiences set up in schools for the purpose of disciplining children and youth in group ways of thinking and acting."

Marsh and Willis on the other hand view curriculum as all the "experiences in the classroom which are planned and enacted by teacher, and also learned by the students.

Historical Conception

File: Curriculum Concept.svg In *The Curriculum*, the first textbook published on the subject, in 1918, John Franklin Bobbitt said that curriculum, as an idea, has its roots in the Latin word for *race-course*, explaining the curriculum as the course of deeds and experiences through which children become the adults they should be, *for success in adult society*. Furthermore, the curriculum encompasses the entire scope of formative deed and experience occurring in and out of school, and not only experiences occurring in school; experiences that are unplanned and undirected, and experiences intentionally directed for the purposeful formation of adult members of society. (cf. image at right.) To Bobbitt, the curriculum is a social engineering arena. Per his cultural presumptions and social definitions, his curricular formulation has two notable features: (i) that scientific experts would best be qualified to and justified in designing curricula based upon their expert knowledge of what qualities are desirable in adult members of society, and which experiences would generate said qualities; and (ii) curriculum defined as the deeds-experiences the student *ought to have* to become the adult he or she *ought to become*.

Hence, he defined the curriculum as an ideal, rather than as the concrete reality of the deeds and experiences that form people to who and what they are. Contemporary views of curriculum reject these features of Bobbitt's postulates, but retain the basis of curriculum as the course of experience(s) that forms human beings into persons. Personal formation via curricula is studied at the personal level and at the group level, i.e. cultures and societies (e.g. professional formation, academic discipline via historical experience). The formation of a group is reciprocal, with the formation of its individual participants.

Although it formally appeared in Bobbitt's definition, curriculum as a course of formative experience also pervades John Dewey's work (who disagreed with Bobbitt on important matters). Although Bobbitt's and Dewey's idealistic understanding of "curriculum" is different from current, restricted uses of the word, curriculum writers and researchers generally share it as common, substantive understanding of curriculum.

Primary and Secondary Education

A curriculum may be partly or entirely determined by an external, authoritative body (e.g., the National Curriculum for England in English schools).

In the U.S., each state, with the individual school districts, establishes the curricula taught. Each state, however, builds its curriculum with great participation of national academic subject groups selected by the United States Department of Education, e.g. National Council of Teachers of Mathematics (NCTM) for mathematical instruction. In Australia each state's Education Department establishes curricula with plans for a National Curriculum in 2011. UNESCO's International Bureau of Education has the primary mission of studying curricula and their implementation worldwide.

Curriculum means two things: (i) the range of courses from which students choose what subject matters to study, and (ii) a specific learning programme. In the latter case, the curriculum collectively describes the teaching, learning, and assessment materials available for a given course of study.

Currently, a spiral curriculum is promoted as allowing students to revisit a subject matter's content at the different levels of development of the subject matter being studied. The constructivist approach proposes that children learn best via pro-active engagement with the educational environment, i.e. learning thru discovery.

Crucial to the curriculum is the definition of the course objectives that usually are expressed as *learning outcomes'* and normally include the programme's assessment strategy. These outcomes and assessments are grouped as units (or modules), and, therefore, the curriculum comprises a collection of such units, each, in turn, comprising a specialised, specific part of the curriculum. So, a typical curriculum includes communications, numeracy, information technology, and social skills units, with specific, specialized teaching of each. A core curriculum is a curriculum, or course of study, which is deemed central and usually made mandatory for all students of a school or school system.

However, this is not always the case. For example, a school might mandate a music appreciation class, but students may opt out if they take a performing musical class, such as orchestra, band, chorus, etc. Core curricula are often instituted, at the primary and secondary levels, by school boards, Departments of Education, or other administrative agencies charged with overseeing education.

In the United States, the Common Core State Standards Initiative promulgates a core curriculum for states to adopt and optionally expand upon. This coordination is intended to make it possible to use more of the same textbooks across states, and to move toward a more uniform minimum level of educational attainment.

Higher Education

Figure: *Core curriculum has typically been highly emphasized in Soviet and Russian universities and technical institutes. In this photo, a student has come to the university's main class schedule board on the first day of classes to find what classes he – and all students in his specialization (sub-major) – will attend this semester.*

Many educational institutions are currently trying to balance two opposing forces. On the one hand, some believe students should have a common knowledge foundation, often in the form of a core curriculum; on the other hand, others want students to be able to pursue their own educational interests, often through early speciality in a major, however, other times through the free choice of courses. This tension has received a large amount of coverage due to Harvard University's reorganization of its core requirements.

An essential feature of curriculum design, seen in every college catalogue and at every other level of schooling, is the identification of prerequisites for each course. These prerequisites can be satisfied by taking particular courses, and in some cases by examination, or by other means, such as work experience. In general, more advanced courses in any subject require some foundation in basic courses, but some coursework requires study in other departments, as in the sequence of math classes required for a physics major, or the language requirements for students preparing in literature, music, or scientific research. A more detailed curriculum design must deal with prerequisites within a course for each topic taken up. This in turn leads to the problems of course organization and scheduling once the dependencies between topics are known.

United States

Core Curriculum: At the undergraduate level, individual college and university administrations and faculties sometimes mandate core curricula, especially in the liberal arts. But because of increasing specialization and depth in the student's major field of study, a typical core curriculum in higher education mandates a far smaller proportion of a student's course work than a high school or elementary school core curriculum prescribes. Amongst the best known and most expansive core curricula programmes at leading American colleges are that of Columbia College at Columbia University, as well as the University of Chicago's. Both can take up to two years to complete without advanced standing, and are designed to foster critical skills in a broad range of academic disciplines, including: the social sciences, humanities, physical and biological sciences, mathematics, writing and foreign languages.

In 1999, the University of Chicago announced plans to reduce and modify the content of its core curriculum, including lowering the number of required courses from 21 to 15 and offering a wider range of content. When *The New York Times*, *The Economist*, and other major news outlets picked up this story, the University became the focal point of a national debate on education. The National Association of Scholars released a statement saying, "*It is truly depressing to observe a steady abandonment of the University of Chicago's once imposing undergraduate core curriculum, which for so long stood as the benchmark of content and rigor among American academic institutions.* Simultaneously, however, a set of university administrators, notably then-President Hugo Sonnenschein, argued that reducing the core curriculum had become both a financial and educational imperative, as the university was struggling to attract a commensurate volume of applicants to its undergraduate division compared to peer schools as a result of what was perceived by the pro-change camp as a reaction by "the average eighteen-year-old" to the expanse of the collegiate core. Further, as core curricula began to be diminished over the course of the twentieth century at many American schools, several smaller institutions became famous for embracing a core curriculum that covers nearly the student's entire undergraduate education, often utilizing classic texts of the western canon to teach all subjects including science. St. John's College in the United States is one example of this approach. Concordia University, Irvine (California) has also implemented a similar classical core curriculum starting in the fall of 2010.

Distribution Requirements

Some colleges opt for the middle ground of the continuum between specified and unspecified curricula by using a system of distribution requirements. In such a system, students are required to take courses in particular fields of learning, but are free to choose specific courses within those fields.

Open Curriculum

Other institutions have largely done away with core requirements in their entirety. Brown University offers the "New Curriculum," implemented after a student-led reform movement in 1969, which allows students to take courses without concern for any requirements except those in their chosen concentrations (majors), plus a single writing course. In this vein it is certainly possible for students to graduate without taking college-level science of mathematics or math courses, or to take only science or math courses. Amherst College requires that students take one of a list of first-year seminars, but has no required classes or distribution requirements. Others include Evergreen State College, Hamilton College, and Smith College. Wesleyan University is another school that has not and does not require any set distribution of courses. However, Wesleyan does make clear "General Education Expectations" such that if a student does not meet these expectations, he/she would not be eligible for academic honours upon graduation.

2

Curriculum Theory

Curriculum theory (CT) is an academic discipline devoted to examining and shaping educational curricula. Within the broad field of curriculum studies, CT includes both the historical analysis of curriculum and ways of viewing current educational curriculum and policy decisions. There are many different views of CT including those of Herbert Kliebard and Michael Stephen Schiro, among others.

Kliebard takes a more historical approach to examining the forces at work that shape the American curriculum, as he describes those forces between 1893 and 1958. Schiro takes a more philosophical approach as he examines the curriculum ideologies (or philosophies) that have influenced American curriculum thought and practice between ca 1890-2007. Kliebard discusses four curriculum groups that he calls humanist (or mental disciplinarians), social efficiency, developmentalist (or child study), and social meliorists. Schiro labels the philosophies of these groups the scholar academic ideology, social efficiency ideology, learner-centred ideology, and social reconstruction ideology.

One of the common criticism of curriculum of broadfield curriculum is that it lays more emphasis on mental discipline and education. "Mental disciplinarians" and Humanists believe in all students' abilities to develop mental reasoning and that education was not intended for social reform in itself but for the systematic development of reasoning power. Good reasoning power would lead to the betterment of society. Harris described the subjects to be taught as the "five windows" into the soul of the student: "grammar, literature and art, mathematics, geography, and history" and prescribed it in that order to be taught

(Kliebard,2004,p. 15). Some critics view this group as having too much emphasis on the "classics" as determined by the dominant groups in a society (and particularly in history by the Committee of Five and Committee of Ten in the late 19th century). In today's society this group is may be seen as having a cultural bias toward the upper class, as well as, the Caucasian majority in the United States.

Social Meliorism

Social meliorists believe that education is a tool to reform society and create change of the better. This socialization goal was based on the power of the individual's intelligence, and the ability to improve on intelligence through education. An individual's future was not predetermined by gender, race, socio-economic status, heredity or any other factors. "The corruption and vice in the cities, the inequalities of race and gender, and the abuse of privilege and power could all be addressed by a curriculum that focused directly on those very issues, thereby raising a new generation equipped to deal effectively with those abuses" (Kliebard,2004, p. 24). Some critics contend that this group has goals that are difficult to measure and a product that has slow results.

John Dewey's Curriculum Theory

John Dewey felt that the curriculum should ultimately produce students who would be able to deal effectively with the modern world. Therefore, curriculum should not be presented as finished abstractions, but should include the child's preconceptions and should incorporate how the child views his or her own world. Dewey uses four instincts, or impulses, to describe how to characterize children's behaviour. The four instincts according to Dewey are social, constructive, expressive, and artistic. Curriculum should build an orderly sense of the world where the child lives. Dewey hoped to use occupations to connect miniature versions of fundamental activities of life classroom activities. The way Dewey hoped to accomplish this goal was to combine subject areas and materials. By doing this, Dewey made connections between subjects and the child's life. Dewey is credited for the development of the progressive schools some of which are still in existence today.

Social Efficiency Educators

"Social efficiency educators" such as theorists Ross, Bobbitt, Gilbreth, Taylor, and Thorndike were aiming to design a curriculum that would optimize the "social utility" of each individual in a society.

By using education as an efficiency tool, these theorists believed that society could be controlled. Students would be scientifically evaluated (such as IQ tests), and educated towards their predicted role in society. This involved the introduction of vocational and junior high schools to address the curriculum designed around specific life activities that correlate with each student's societal future. The socially efficient curriculum would consist of minute parts or tasks that together formed a bigger concept. This educational view was somewhat derived with the efficiency of factories which could simultaneously produce able factory workers. Critics believe this model has too much emphasis on testing and separating students based on the results of that testing

Culturally and Ethnically Diverse Curriculum

Gay (2001) & Villegas & Lucas (2002) discuss the need for educators and institutions to be responsive to the needs of students in US high school and primary education. This is further discussed by authors such as Suleiman (2001) & Taylor & Whittaker (2003) identify curriculum as an important element in the negative schooling experiences of minority students because a traditional curriculum does not adequately represent their history (Said & Richardson 2007). Nieto (1999, 97) supports this concern for students who do not belong to the dominant group and seem to have challenging curriculum experiences that conflict with their personal cultural identity and their wider community reference groups. This view is also supported by Jabbar & Hardaker (2012) who mention that within curriculum development to much time is spent discussing what students do not have as opposed to skills and history that they come equipped with.

It is within this context that Gay (2001), Villegas & Lucas (2002) and Jabbar & Hardaker(2012) provide frameworks that help prepare academics and teachers to develop curriculum that supports ethnic and cultural diversity that focuses on understanding the learner and developing curricula and practice that is consistent and thoughtful.

Developmentalism

Developmentalists focus attention to the development of children's emotional and behavioural qualities. One part of this view is using the characteristics of children and youth as the source of the curriculum. Some critics claim this model is at the expense of other relevant factors. One example of an extreme Hall advocated differentiated instruction based on native endowment and even urged separate schools for "dullards" in the elementary grades.

Reconceptualized Curriculum

In the late 1960s a group of curriculum theorists suggested that the field of curriculum had devolved into a mechanistic approach to content creation. This group made up of Apple, McClintock, Pinar and others created other ways of thinking about curriculum and its role in the academy, in schools, and in society in general.

Preschools

The term preschool refers to a school for children who are not old enough to attend kindergarten. It is a nursery school. Preschool education is important because it can give a child the edge in a competitive world and education climate. While children who do not receive the fundamentals during their preschool years will be taught the alphabet, counting, shapes and colours and designs when they begin their formal education they will be behind the children who already possess that knowledge. The true purpose behind kindergarten is "to provide a child-centred, preschool curriculum for three to seven year old children that aimed at unfolding the child's physical, intellectual, and moral nature with balanced emphasis on each of them."

This period of education is very important in the formative years of the child. Teachers with special skills and training are needed at this time to nurture the children to develop their potentials.

Preschool Education

Preschool education (or infant education) is the provision of learning to children before the commencement of statutory and obligatory education, usually between the ages of three and five, depending on the jurisdiction. In some places, such as the United States, preschool precedes Kindergarten and the normal primary school system. In others, including much of Europe, preschool and Kindergarten programmes are the same early childhood education programmes. Preschool programmes may be part of or separate from child care services needed by working parents. They may be government-run programmes or private ventures. Some countries provide significant subsidies to pay for the costs of the programmes.

In the United Kingdom nursery school (or 'playgroup') is the form of preschool education. In the United States the terms 'preschool' and 'Pre-K' are used, while "nursery school" is an older term. Preschool work is organized within a framework that professional educators create. The framework includes structural (administration, class size, student–teacher ratio, services, etc.), process (quality of classroom environments, teacher-child interactions, etc.), and alignment (standards, curriculum, assessments) components that are associated with each individual unique child that has both social and academic outcomes. At each age band, an appropriate curriculum should be followed. For example, it would be normal to teach a child how to count to 10 after the age of four. Arguably the first pre-school institution was opened in 1816 by Robert Owen in New Lanark, Scotland. The Hungarian countess Theresa Brunszvik followed in 1828. In 1837, Friedrich Fröbel opened one in Germany, coining the term "kindergarten".

Developmental Areas

The areas of development which preschool education covers varies from country to country. However, the following main themes are represented in the majority of systems.

- Personal, social, economical, and emotional development
- Communication, including sign language, talking and listening
- Knowledge and understanding of the world
- Creative and aesthetic development
- Educational software
- Mathematical awareness and development
- Physical development
- Physical health
- Playing
- Teamwork
- Self-help skills
- Social skills
- Scientific thinking
- Creative arts
- Literacy
- Speaking ability is started too.

Allowing preschool aged children to discover and explore freely within each of these areas of development is the foundation for developmental learning. While the National Association for the Education of Young Children (NAEYC) and the National Association of Child Care Professionals (NACCP) have made tremendous strides in publicizing and promoting the idea of developmentally appropriate practice, there is still much work to be done. It is widely recognized that although many preschool educators are aware of the guidelines for developmentally appropriate practice, putting this practice to work effectively in the classroom is more challenging. The NAEYC published that although 80% of Kindergarten classrooms claim to be developmentally appropriate, only 20% actually are.

Age and Importance

It is well established that the most important years of learning are begun at birth. During these early years, a human being is capable of absorbing more information at a time than they will ever be able to again. The environment of the young child influences the development of cognitive skills and emotional skills due to the rapid brain growth that occurs in the early years. Studies have shown that high quality/ or any high rated preschools have a long term effect in improving the outcomes of a child, especially a disadvantaged child.

However, some more recent studies dispute the accuracy of the earlier results which cited benefits to preschool education, and actually point at preschool being detrimental to a child's cognitive and social development. A study by UC Berkeley and Stanford University on 14,000 Kindergarteners revealed that while there is a temporary cognitive boost in pre-reading and math, preschool holds detrimental effects on social development and cooperation. The Universal Preschool movement is an international effort to make access to preschool available to families in a similar way to compulsory primary education. Various jurisdictions and advocates have differing priorities for access, availability and funding sources. There has been a shift from preschools that operated primarily as controlled play groups to educational settings in which children learn specific, if basic, skills. It examines several different perspectives on teaching in kindergarten, including those of the developmentally appropriate practice, the academic approach, the child-centred approach, and the Montessori approach to the curriculum.

Gratuity

The gratuity of infant education has been established in some countries, as Spain, beginning in the second cycle (from three to six years), but extending to the first cycle (from birth to three years). It is when children develop through all areas. This is true for other countries like Portugal.

Role in Cultural Transmission

Preschool education, like all other forms of education, is intended by the society that controls it to transmit important cultural values to the participants. As a result, different cultures make different choices about preschool education. Despite the variations, there are a few common themes. Most significantly, preschool is universally expected to increase the young child's ability to perform basic self-care tasks such as dressing, feeding, and toileting.

In Japan, development of social skills and a sense of group belonging are major goals for preschools. Class sizes tend to be large, up to 40 students per class, to decrease the role of the teacher's personality and increase the likelihood of peer interactions. Because exclusion from the group is extremely undesirable, a wide range of behaviours is tolerated. For example, a young child who is standing near the class during an exercise session is deemed to be participating in the group activity and belonging to the group, even if he does not engage in any of the exercises. Children are expected to be learn how to work harmoniously in large and small groups, and to develop the praiseworthy qualities of childhood, such as cooperativeness, kindness, and social consciousness.

Because the most important goal for preschools is to provide children with the rich social environment that increasingly isolated nuclear families are unable to provide at home, unstructured, lightly supervised time to play freely with other children is valued. Teachers take a hands-off approach to most disputes between children, including physical fighting, as well as to children's choices to participate or to move to another activity. Most behavioural problems are believed to be due to the disruptive child's inappropriately expressed emotional need to be dependent, resulting in gentle care and careful attention to accepting the child, rather than a biological problem to be treated medically or a willfully chosen behaviour to be punished. Consistent with the social belief that success is a result of hard work rather than inborn talent, teachers are expected to minimize innate differences between children by encouraging and praising perseverance in less-capable children and suppressing or ignoring high-performing children. Although a wide variety of attitudes and educational philosophies exist in Japanese preschools, most preschools focus on age-appropriate personal development, such as learning empathy, rather than academic programmes. Academic programmes tend to be more common among Westernized and Christian preschools in Japan.

In China, a vast and varied country, the preschool programmes are highly variable. Some amount to little more than babysitting services, and others are university-run programmes with high-quality curricula. Some are showpieces designed to impress foreign visitors, and others have very limited facilities and resources. The qualifications of staff members and their beliefs about early childhood education are also highly variable. Many are associated with an employer, and some provide overnight care during the week, frequently reserving these slots for parents who work at night or in jobs requiring travel. However, a few themes are common to most Chinese preschools: Chinese parents' traditional concerns about spoiling their children have intensified since the introduction of the one-child policy: Only children are widely seen as lonely, selfish, and prone to anti-social behaviours. Parents, however, feel somewhat reluctant to discipline their only children, thinking it may cause resentment and ultimately an unwillingness to care for the parents in their old age.

Teachers, therefore, are seen as professionals whose primary responsibility is to counteract the parents' natural tendency to indulge their children and the unfortunate effects of the one-child policy, and thus produce well-behaved children who benefit society. Because parents worry about their children's health, Chinese society provides significant, visible health care through the preschools, such as on-site nurses to examine children after a weekend at home. Children are taught to behave as part of an orderly, regimented collective that is obedient to its leader. For example, children eat meals silently and sit quietly for long periods of time during the school day while the teacher reads or instructs them. Unlike the Japanese programmes, group dynamics are authoritarian and vertical, with the relationship between the teacher and the children more important than the relationships between the children. Teachers intervene very early to stop inappropriate behaviour before it escalates to disruption, usually by verbally criticizing the child's behaviour. Positive reinforcement through publicly praising examples of proper behaviour is typical. Programmes permit little unstructured time and emphasize academic development. For example, a lesson may have children use building blocks to construct pre-determined structures exactly matching a printed diagram, rather than to build anything they wish. Academic progress and good public speaking skills are valued, as parents believe this will result in the child being economically successful later in life. Parents in Taiwan have similar attitudes in many respects, and many of the concerns and goals related to child rearing in the modern era echo those found in ancient Confucian writings. In the United States, preschool education emphasizes the basic American values of individual liberty and self-determination. Rather than the teacher leading all children through a specific activity, the children are frequently permitted to choose from a wide variety of activities in a learning centre model. During these times, a few children may choose to be painting, a few children may be playing house, a few children may be playing with puzzles, and a few more may be listening to the teacher read a storybook aloud. Different learning centre activities are offered in each session.

Children are assumed to be more different than similar, with each child having particular strengths and weaknesses that must be encouraged or ameliorated by the teachers. A typical belief is that children's play is their work, and by allowing the child to select the type of play, then the child will meet his or her individual developmental needs. Preschools also model the rule of law and American ideas about justice, such as the idea that everyone is innocent until proven guilty. Teachers actively intervene in disputes between children and encourage them to "use your words" rather than to engage in physical aggression. Children may be punished with a time out or a requirement to apologize or make reparations for misbehaviour, such as taking a toy from another child, but the teachers assist them through a process of "defending" themselves (by explaining what happened) before the teacher imposes a punishment.

The development of self-expressive language skills, so that the child can describe an experience to an adult, is emphasized through both informal interactions with the teachers and through structured group activities like show and tell exercises. The equipment and facilities available to a preschool vary depending on the wealth of the area, but they generally have more and fancier supplies than other cultures. As most programmes are not subsidized by government funds, preschools are often expensive compared to the average worker's income, and the staff is typically poorly paid. However, student-teacher ratios are lower than in other cultures, with about 15 students per group seen as ideal. Parents and teachers also see preschool teachers as being extensions of or partial substitutes for the parents, and consequently emphasize personal relationships and consistent expectations at home and at school. Children in North Korea are taught to enjoy military games and to hate the *miguk nom*, or "American bastard".

History of Preschool in the United States

Head Start, the first publicly funded preschool programme, was created in 1965 by President Johnson. The federal government helped create this half-day programme for preschool children from low-income families. Head Start began as a summer pilot programme that included an education component, nutrition and health screenings for children, and support services for families (CPE, 2007). In the 1960s only ten percent of the nations three and four year olds were enrolled in a classroom setting. Due to a large amount of people interested, and a lack of funding for Head Start, during the 1980s a handful of states started their own version of a programme for students from low-income families. The positive success and effects of preschool meant many state leaders were showing interest in educational reform of these young students (CPE, 2007). By 2005 sixty-nine percent, or over 800,000, four year-old children nationwide participated in some type of state preschool programme (CPE, 2007). The yearly increase in enrollment of preschool programmes throughout the years is due to an increase of higher maternal employment rates, national anti-poverty initiatives, and research showing the link between early childhood experiences and the brain development of young children. These factors have caused the rate of attendance in preschool programmes to grow each year (CPE, 2007). It is important one note that Head Start was the first publicly funded preschool programme and not necessarily the first preschool programme. It should also be stressed that Head Start programmes are not the same as preschool programmes in the private sector. Head Start is a federally funded programme with specific federal guidelines that they must adhere to. Preschools in the private sector do not have to adhere to these same federal guidelines and they do not receive the same public and federal funding.

In most states, there are multiple preschool or Pre-K options for young children. Parents have the choice of sending their child to a federally funded Head Start programme, if their income is at the poverty level, state-funded preschool, government-funded special education programmes, and for-profit and not-for-profit providers (Levin & Schartz, 2007), including those that accept government subsidies that help low income parents pay.

In his February 2013 State of the Union address, President Obama outlined a proposal for working with states to ensure accessible universal Pre-K for all four-year-olds. The White House later clarified saying Pre-K would be guaranteed for four-year-olds whose families earn 200% of the federal poverty level or less. Many states have already implemented this sort of system; Florida currently enrolls 76% of all four-year-olds in its universal preschool education, but with no barriers, income or otherwise, to entry. In order for states to receive money for Pre-K, the president's plan stipulates that programmes must meet state-level standards for early learning, employ qualified teachers for all preschool classrooms, maintain small class sizes, and create a plan to implement comprehensive data and assessment systems. When Obama released his FY 2014 budget on 10 April 2013 he stated that his universal Pre-K plan would be funded through a 94 cent tobacco tax, with the administration planning on paying $75 billion over the span of ten years in grants and $750 million in development grants to improve quality in existing programmes. The federal share of funding would be 90 percent in the first year, slowly declining to about 25 percent after a decade.

Methods of Preschool Education

Some preschools have adopted specialized methods of teaching, such as Montessori, Waldorf, Head Start, HighScope, Reggio Emilia approach, Bank Street, Forest kindergartens, and various other pedagogies which contribute to the foundation of education.

In the United States, most preschool advocates support the National Association for the Education of Young Children's Developmentally Appropriate Practices.

Funding for Preschool Programmes

While a majority of American preschool programmes remain tuition-based, support for some public funding of early childhood education has grown over the years. As of 2008, 38 states and the District of Columbia invested in at least some pre-kindergarten programmes, and many school districts were providing preschool services on their own, using local and federal funds.

The benefits and challenges of a public preschool are closely tied to the amount of funding provided. Funding for a public preschool can come in a variety of sources. According to Levin and Schwartz (2007) funding can range from federal, state, local public allocations, private sources, and parental fees (p. 4). The problem of funding a public preschool occurs not only from limited sources but from the cost per child. The average cost across the 48 states is $6,582 (Levin and Schwartz, 2007). There are four categories that determine the costs of public preschools: personnel ratios, personnel qualifications, facilities and transportation, and health and nutrition services. According to Levin and Schwartz (2007) these structural elements depend heavily on the cost and quality of services provided (p. 14). The main personnel factor related to cost is the qualifications each preschool require for a teacher. Another determinate of cost is the length of a preschool day. The longer the session, the more increase in cost. Therefore, the quality of programme accounts presumably for a major component of cost (Levin and Schwartz, 2007).

Collaboration has been a solution for funding issues in several districts. Wilma Kaplan, principal, turned to collaborating with the area Head Start and other private preschool to fund a public preschool in her district. "We're very pleased with the interaction.

It's really added a dimension to our programme that's been very positive" (Reeves, 2000). The National Head Start Bureau has been looking for more opportunities to partner with public schools. Torn Schultz of the National Head Start Bureau states, "We're turning to partnership as much as possible, either in funds or facilities to make sure children get everything necessary to be ready for school" (Reeves, 2000, p. 6). The goal for funding is to develop a variety of sources that provide for all children to benefit from early learning within a public preschool.

Special Education in Preschool

In the United States, students who may benefit from special education receive services in preschools. Since the inception of the Individuals with Disabilities Education Act (IDEA) Public Law 101-476 in 1975 and its amendments, PL 102-119 and PL 105-17 in 1997, the educational system has moved away from self-contained classrooms and progressed to inclusion.

As a result, there has been a need for special education teachers to practice in various settings in order to assist children with special needs, particularly by working with regular classroom teachers when possible to strengthen the inclusion of children with special needs.

As with other stages in the life of a child with special needs, the Individualized Education Plan (IEP) or an Individual Family Service Plan (IFSP) is an important way for special education teachers, regular classroom teachers, administrators and parents to set guidelines for a partnership to help the child succeed in preschool.

Primary Schools

Figure: *Primary school in open air. Teacher (priest) with class from the outskirts of Bucharest, around 1842.*

Primary (or elementary) education consists of the first 5–7 years of formal, structured education. In general, primary education consists of six or eight years of schooling starting at the age of five or six, although this varies between, and sometimes within, countries. Globally, around 89% of primary-age children are enrolled in primary education, and this proportion is rising.

Under the Education For All programmes driven by UNESCO, most countries have committed to achieving universal enrollment in primary education by 2015, and in many countries, it is compulsory for children to receive primary education. The division between primary and secondary education is somewhat arbitrary, but it generally occurs at about eleven or twelve years of age. Some education systems have separate middle schools, with the transition to the final stage of secondary education taking place at around the age of fourteen. Schools that provide primary education, are mostly referred to as *primary schools*. Primary schools in these countries are often subdivided into infant schools and junior school.

In India, compulsory education spans over twelve years, out of which children receive elementary education for 8 years. Elementary schooling consists of five years of primary schooling and 3 years of upper primary schooling. Various states in the republic of India provide 12 years of compulsory school education based on national curriculum framework designed by the National Council of Educational Research and Training.

Primary Education

Primary education is the first stage of compulsory education. It is preceded by pre-school or nursery education and is followed by secondary education. In North America, this stage of education is usually known as elementary education and is generally followed by middle school.

In most countries, it is compulsory for children to receive primary education although it is permissible for parents to provide it. The major goals of primary education are achieving basic literacy and numeracy amongst all pupils, as well as establishing foundations in science, mathematics, geography, history and other social sciences. The relative priority of various areas, and the methods used to teach them, are an area of considerable political debate.

Typically, primary education is provided in schools, where the child will stay in steadily advancing classes until they complete it and move on to high school/secondary school. Children are usually placed in classes with one teacher who will be primarily responsible for their education and welfare for that year. This teacher may be assisted to varying degrees by specialist teachers in certain subject areas, often music or physical education. The continuity with a single teacher and the opportunity to build up a close relationship with the class is a notable feature of the primary education system. Traditionally, various forms of corporal punishment have been an integral part of early education. Recently this practice has come under scrutiny, and in many cases been outlawed, especially in Western countries.

Australia

In Australia, students undertake preschool then 13 years of schooling before moving to vocational or higher education. Primary schooling for most children starts after they turn 5 years old. In most states, children can be enrolled earlier at the discretion of individual school principals on the basis of intellectual giftedness. In Victoria, New South Wales, Northern Territory, ACT and Tasmania students then move through Kindergarten/Preparatory School/Reception and Years 1 to 6 before starting high school. In Queensland, South Australia and Western Australia students do Year 7 while still enrolled at primary school, although most governmental primary schools are moving to a K to 6 structure to line up with the other states in order to ensure that Year 7 students are able to undertake laboratory practical components of the national syllabus.

- Pre-School/Kindergarten: 4-5 year olds
- Prep./Reception/Kindergarten: 5-6 year olds
- Grade/Year 1: 6–7 years of age
- Grade/Year 2: 7-8 year olds
- Grade/Year 3: 8-9 year olds
- Grade/Year 4: 9-10 year olds
- Grade/Year 5: 10-11 year olds
- Grade/Year 6: 11-12 year olds
- Grade/Year 7: 12-13 year olds (WA, SA, QLD)

Brazil

- Year 1: 6 year olds (former pre-school)
- Year 2: 7 year olds
- Year 3: 8 year olds
- Year 4: 9 year olds
- Year 5: 10 year olds
- Year 6: 11 year olds
- Year 7: 12 year olds
- Year 8: 13 year olds
- Year 9: 14 year olds
- Year 10: 15 year olds (optional)
- Year 11: 16 year olds (optional)
- Year 12: 17 year olds (optional)

Burma

Canada:

- Pre-kindergarten (Pre-K) or Early Childhood Education (ECE) (Ages 3-4) *
- Primary (Kindergarten) (Ages 4–5) *
- Grade 1 (Ages 5–7)
- Grade 2 (Ages 6–8)
- Grade 3 (Ages 7–9)
- Grade 4 (Ages 8–10)
- Grade 5 (Ages 9–11)
- Grade 6 (Ages 10–12)

- Grade 7 (Ages 12–13) ** Quebec, 1e secondaire
- Grade 8 (Ages 13–14) ** Quebec, 2e secondaire
- Grade 9 (Ages 14–15) ** Quebec, 3e secondaire
- Grade 10 (Ages 15–16) ** Quebec, 4e secondaire
- Grade 11 (Ages 16–17) ** Quebec, 5e secondaire
- Grade 12 (Ages 17–18) (except Quebec) **

* students in the Prairie Provinces are not required by statute to attend pre-kindergarten or kindergarten ** Quebec only goes up to grade 11 then students are required to go to CÉGEP before University

Denmark

In Denmark, 9 years of primary school (*Folkeskole*) are compulsory.

Kindergarten (optional): 5–6 years

- 0th grade: 5–7 years
- 1st grade: 6–8 years
- 2nd grade: 7–9 years
- 3rd grade: 8–10 years
- 4th grade: 9–11 years
- 5th grade: 10–12 years
- 6th grade: 11–13 years
- 7th grade: 12–14 years
- 8th grade: 13–15 years
- 9th grade: 14–16 years

10th grade (optional): 15–18 years

Estonia

In Estonia, 9 years of primary school (*Põhikool* or "basic school") are compulsory. The first three grades of primary school are called *Algkool* which can be translated as "beginning school" and can be confused with primary school. In some low density population areas Algkool is the only school available and students enter primary school in bigger towns.

- 1st grade: 7–8 years
- 2nd grade: 8–9 years
- 3rd grade: 9–10 years
- 4th grade: 10–11 years

- 5th grade: 11–12 years
- 6th grade: 12–13 years
- 7th grade: 13–14 years
- 8th grade: 14–15 years
- 9th grade: 15–16 years

Finland

9 years of primary school (Peruskoulu) are compulsory.

- Kindergarten (optional): 6–7 years
- 1st grade: 7–8 years
- 2nd grade: 8–9 years
- 3rd grade: 9–10 years
- 4th grade: 10–11 years
- 5th grade: 11–12 years
- 6th grade: 12–13 years
- 7th grade: 13–14 years
- 8th grade: 14–15 years
- 9th grade: 15–16 years
- 10th grade (optional): 16–17 years

France

Education is mandatory from 6 years old to 16 years old. Grade is determined by the age on September 1 (year ends around July 5th). Free public and free private education is offered from 3 years old (sometimes 2 years old). Home education is allowed. Occasionally classes are of a double level to make up the number of pupil per class, usually to 29.

Pré-élémentaire (day care)

- garderie (day care)
- crèche (0–4 years old)
- Élémentaire

École maternelle (pre-school)

- très petite section (2 years old) (rare)
- Cycle I

    petite section (3 years old)
    moyenne section (4 years old)
    grande section (5 years old) (September - January)

- Cycle II

    grande section (5 years old) (February - July)

    École primaire (primary/elementary)

- CP (cours préparatoire) (6 years old) (may be tried a second time (7 years old) if reading and writing are not learned the first time)
- CE1 (cours élémentaire 1) (7 years old)

Cycle III

- CE2 (cours élémentaire 2) (8 years old)
- CM1 (cours moyen 1) (9 years old)
- CM2 (cours moyen 2) (10 years old)

Secondary

- Collège (11 - 15/16 years old - junior high school) *Brevet* diploma
- Lycèe (15/16 – 19 years old - senior high school) *Baccalauréat* diploma supérieur

Premier cycle (17-... years old) - Second cycle (20-... years old) - Troisième cycle (22-... years old)

Collège and *Lycée* are usually separate establishments, with large communes having a *collège*, while the *Lycée* are usually in the larger towns and cities.

Germany

The first school for German children is called Grundschule. It takes usually four years, the pupils are between six and ten years old. The education consists of learning to read, write, basic math and general knowledge.

In some schools, a first foreign language is introduced, usually English. In the final year of primary school, children receive a recommendation as to which further school they can attend.

- Kindergarten: 3–6 years
- Grade 1: 6–7 years
- Grade 2: 7–8 years
- Grade 3: 8–9 years
- Grade 4: 9–10 years
- Grade 5: 10–11 years (Berlin and Brandenburg only)
- Grade 6: 11–12 years (Berlin and Brandenburg only)

Depending on the recommendation they received from their teacher, children proceed to their mandatory secondary education in either Hauptschule (Grades 5-9, sometimes 10th grade is added which is then called "Werkrealschule"), Realschule (Grades 5-10), or Gymnasium (Grades 5-12). Upon the successful completion of Grades 11 and 12 in the Gymnasium, students receive the Abitur, a diploma with the permission to enter post-secondary education (similar to the A-level or High School Diploma). The Abitur will not be received at the end of Haupt- and Realschule, but graduating students are eligible to enter the 11th Grade of the Gymnasium if they wish to obtain the Abitur.

Hungary

Primary School education for children in Hungary takes 8 years.

- 1st grade: 6–7 years
- 2nd grade: 7–8 years
- 3rd grade: 8–9 years
- 4th grade: 9–10 years
- 5th grade: 10–11 years
- 6th grade: 11–12 years
- 7th grade: 12–13 years
- 8th grade: 13–14 years

Iceland

In Iceland, 10 years of primary school (*Grunnskóli*) are compulsory.

Primary school teaching in Iceland consists of 10 grade levels. These are:

- 1st grade: 6–7 years
- 2nd grade: 7–8 years
- 3rd grade: 8–9 years
- 4th grade: 9–10 years
- 5th grade: 10–11 years
- 6th grade: 11–12 years
- 7th grade: 12–13 years
- 8th grade: 13–14 years
- 9th grade: 14–15 years
- 10th grade: 15–16 years

India

The National Council of Educational Research and Training (NCERT) is the apex body for school education in India. The NCERT provides support and technical assistance to a number of schools in India and oversees many aspects of enforcement of education policies. In India, the various bodies governing school education system are:

- The state government boards, in which the majority of Indian children are enrolled.
- The Central Board of Secondary Education (CBSE) board.
- The Council for the Indian School Certificate Examinations (CISCE) board.
- The National Institute of Open Schooling.
- International schools affiliated to the International Baccalaureate Programme and/or the Cambridge International Examinations.
- Islamic Madrasah schools, whose boards are controlled by local state governments, or autonomous, or affiliated with Darul Uloom Deoband.
- Autonomous schools like Woodstock School, Auroville, Patha Bhavan and Ananda Marga Gurukula.

Primary school teaching in India consists of 12 grade (Standard) levels. These are:

- Kindergarten: nursery - 3 years, Lower Kindergarten (LKG) -4 years, Upper Kindergarten (UKG) - 5 years.
- 1st Standard: 6 years
- 2nd Standard: 7 years
- 3rd Standard: 8 years
- 4th Standard: 9 years
- 5th Standard: 10 years
- 6th Standard: 11 years
- 7th Standard: 12 years
- 8th Standard: 13 years
- 9th Standard: 14 years
- 10th Standard: 15 years
- 11th Standard: 16 years
- 12th Standard: 17 years

Iran

Ireland: Primary school teaching in Ireland consists of 8 class levels. These are:

- Junior Infants (4–5 years)
- Senior Infants (5–6 years)
- 1st class (Rang a haon, 6–7 years)
- 2nd class (Rang a dó, 7–8 years)
- 3rd class (Rang a trí, 8–9 years)
- 4th class (Rang a ceathair, 9–10 years)
- 5th class (Rang a cúig, 10–11 years)
- 6th class (Rang a sé, 11–12 years)

Junior and Senior infants correspond to Kindergarten.

The subjects mainly taught in primary school are:

- English (Béarla, Spellings are taught more in Primary education, not taught in Secondary although if you make a spelling mistake in Secondary English work, you would be corrected)
- Maths (Mata)
- Irish (Gaeilge)
- Modern European language (i.e. French or/and German) (Very rarely)
- History (Stair)
- Geography (Tíreolaíocht/Tír Eolas, direct translation "Country-science/Country information")
- Science (Eolaíocht)
- PE (Physical Education), (Corpoideachas, direct translation "Body education"
- Art (Ealaín)
- Drama (Drámaíocht)
- Music (Ceol)
- SPHE (Social, Personal, Health Education), (OSPS, Oideachas Sóisialta, Pearsanta, Sláintiúil)
- Religion (Reiligiún/Creideamh)

Primary school teaching in Ireland consists of 8 class levels. These are:

- 1st year (12-13 years)
- 2nd year (13-14 years)
- 3rd year (14-15 years)
- 4th year (15-16 years)
- 5th year (16-17 years)
- 6th year (17-18 years)

The content of the Religion course taught depends on the management of the school. Many schools are managed and owned by the Roman Catholic Church, with a lesser number belonging to the Church of Ireland and to the Multi Denominational Group Educate Together and a handful run by other religions such as Muslims. Each school body decides on the emphasis of its religious instruction. In Catholic schools 2nd and 6th class prepare children for Holy Communion and Confirmation respectively. In the Church of Ireland this preparation is done when the pupil is aged about 14 years, and is in secondary school.

Children may start at primary school at any age between four and six years of age. Most children finish primary school at or around twelve years of age.

Italy

Primary school teaching in Italy consists of 5 grades. Before the First Grade, there is the kindergarten (*scuola dell'infanzia* in Italian), which is not compulsory.

Elementary

- First Grade (6–7 years)
- Second Grade (7–8 years)
- Third Grade (8–9 years)
- Fourth Grade (9–10 years)
- Fifth Grade (10–11 years)

Schools used to have a six day school week, Monday to Saturday. Lately, as of 2008, most elementary and middle schools have reduced the school week to five days, with high schools remaining with six.

Israel

Japan: Kindergartens nursery schools are private institutions and attendance is not mandatory.

- Nursery School / Kindergarten (Junior): 3-4 year olds
- Nursery School / Kindergarten (Intermediate): 4-5 year olds
- Nursery School / Kindergarten (Senior): 5-6 year olds
- Elementary School Grade 1: 6-7 year olds
- Elementary School Grade 2: 7-8 year olds
- Elementary School Grade 3: 8-9 year olds
- Elementary School Grade 4: 9-10 year olds
- Elementary School Grade 5: 10-11 year olds
- Elementary School Grade 6: 11-12 year olds
- Middle School Grade 1: 12-13 year olds
- Middle School Grade 2: 13-14 year olds
- Middle School Grade 3: 14-15 year olds
- High School Grade 1: 15-16 year olds
- High School Grade 2: 16-17 year olds
- High School Grade 3: 17-18 year olds

English has become a compulsory subject at primary schools in Japan, since April 2011 in order to compete with other Asian countries in English proficiency; Japanese students have among the lowest English TOEFL scores in Asia.

Malaysia

Primary education is compulsory in Malaysia. Children spend 6 years in primary schools. In 6th year, students sit for a national standardized test known as the Ujian Pencapaian Sekolah Rendah (UPSR, Primary School Achievement Test).

Level One

- Standard 1 : age 7-8
- Standard 2 : age 8-9
- Standard 3 : age 9-10

Level Two

- Standard 4 : age 10-11
- Standard 5 : age 11-12
- Standard 6 : age 12-13 (UPSR: Ujian Pencapaian Sekolah Rendah or Primary School Achievement Test)

After completing Standard 6, students will go on to secondary schools.

Lower Secondary

- Form 1 : age 13
- Form 2 : age 14
- Form 3 : age 15 (PMR: Penilaian Menengah Rendah or Lower Secondary Assessment)

Upper Secondary

- Form 4 : age 16
- Form 5 : age 17 (SPM: Sijil Pelajaran Malaysia or Malaysian Certificate of Education)
- Form 6 (Lower): age 18(optional)
- Form 6 (Upper): age 19 (optional)

Next, the students will be moving on into universities or college

Netherlands

Children in the Netherlands must be at least four years old to enter primary education. Almost all 4-year-olds (99.3%) in the Netherlands indeed attend primary school, although this is not *compulsory* until children reach the age of 5. Primary school is free of charge. In most schools, children are grouped by age in mixed ability classes, with one teacher for all subjects. Primary school consists of 8 groups (thus 8 years of schooling). During the first two years (both kindergarten), children receive an average of 22 hours of education, during the last 6 years children receive an average of 25 hours per week. Schools are open 5 days a week, but all children have a half day on Wednesdays (ending at noon). At the end of primary school, in group 8, schools advice on secondary school choice. Most schools use a national test to support this advice, for instance the 'Citotoets', a test developed by the Central Institute for Test development.

- group 1: age 4-5 (kindergarten)
- group 2: age 5-6 (kindergarten)
- group 3: age 6-7 (school curriculum starts with writing, reading, etc.)
- group 4: age 7-8
- group 5: age 8-9
- group 6: age 9-10
- group 7: age 10-11
- group 8: age 11-12 (last school year with advice on secondary school choice)

Poland

Primary School:

- 0th - 6–7 years old
- 1st - 7–8 years old
- 2nd - 8–9 years old
- 3rd - 9–10 years old
- 4th - 10–11 years old
- 5th - 11–12 years old
- 6th - 12–13 years old

Middle School:

- 1st 13–14 years old
- 2nd 14–15 years old
- 3rd 15–16 years old

Secondary School:

- 1st 16–17 years old (Vocational School, Liceum and Technikum)
- 2nd 17–18 years old (Vocational School, Liceum and Technikum)
- 3rd 18–19 years old (Vocational School, Liceum and Technikum)
- 4th 19–20 years old (only in Technikum)

Higher education: 18 and over Children may end their schooling after passing secondary school if desired.

Portugal

In Portugal, the primary education (*ensino primário*) is known as the 1st cycle of the basic education (*1° ciclo do ensino básico*). It includes the first four years of compulsory education (*1ª classe*, *2ª classe*, *3ª classe* and *4ª classe*), their pupils being children between six and ten years old. After the education reform of 1986, the former primary education became part of the basic education (*educação básica*).

Basic education now includes:

- 1st cycle (*1° ciclo*) - former primary education
    - 1st year (6–7 years old)
    - 2nd year (7–8 years old)
    - 3rd year (8–9 years old)
    - 4th year (9–10 years old)
- 2nd cycle (*2° ciclo*) - former preparatory education

  - 5th year (10–11 years old)
  - 6th year (11–12 years old)
- 3rd cycle (*3º ciclo*) - former preparatory education (continuation)
  - 7th year (12–13 years old)
  - 8th year (13–14 years old)
  - 9th year (14–15 years old)

Singapore

Primary education in Singapore, normally starting at age seven, is a four-year *foundation stage* (Primary 1 to 4) and a two-year *orientation stage* (Primary 5 to 6). Primary education is compulsory and fees are low at public schools, there are also other fees per student to help cover miscellaneous costs. During the foundation stage, all students are taught English Language as a first language, a mother tongue as a second language and Mathematics. Science is introduced from Primary 3 onwards. In addition to these examinable subjects, lessons in Civics and Moral Education, arts and crafts, music, health education, social studies and physical education are conducted at various levels. Students are also introduced to project work, receive pastoral care and career guidance, and are to participate in Co-Curricular Activities and Community Involvement Programmes. In the orientation stage, weaker students are banded based on their abilities in the four examinable subjects. Known as "Subject-based Banding", they take individual subjects either at the standard or foundation level. Conversely, higher mother tongue is offered for higher ability students.

Sri Lanka

Sweden:

- Pre-school class (not compulsory), age 6
- *Grundskola*
  - *Lågstadie*
    - Year 1, age 7
    - Year 2, age 8
    - Year 3, age 9
  - *Mellanstadie*
    - Year 4, age 10
    - Year 5, age 11
    - Year 6, age 12

- o *Högstadie*
- – Year 7, age 13
- – Year 8, age 14
- – Year 9, age 15
- • *Gymnasieskola* (not compulsory), age 16-18

Gymnasieskola is not compulsory but most common. What you wish to read is your choice, if you have the right grades for your wanted education. If there are more people who wish to read than spots, the ones with the highest grades are accepted. This is either a preparation for University or for work.

During the year before children start compulsory school, all children are offered a place in a pre-school class (*förskoleklass*), which combines the pedagogical methods of the pre-school with those of compulsory school. Between ages 7 and 15, children attend compulsory comprehensive school (*grundskola*), divided in three stages. The vast majority of schools in Sweden are municipally run, but there are also independent schools. The education in independent schools has many objectives in common with the municipal school, but it can have an orientation that differs from that of the municipal schools.

Syria

9 years of primary school are compulsory.

Kindergarten (optional): 5–6 years

- 1st grade: 6–7 years
- 2nd grade: 7–8 years
- 3rd grade: 8–9 years
- 4th grade: 9–10 years
- 5th grade: 10–11 years
- 6th grade: 11–12 years
- 7th grade: 12–13 years
- 8th grade: 13–14 years
- 9th grade: 14–15 years

Tunisia

Main article (Education in Tunisia)

In Tunisia pre-school education (3–6 years) is optional and provided primarily in three settings:

Kindergartens:socio-educational institutions that come under the supervision of Ministry of culture.

Kouttabs:religious institutions also cater for children between 3 and 5 years of age. Their task is to initiate them into learning the Quran as well as reading, writing, and arithmetic. They are under the supervision of the Ministry of Religious Affairs

Preparatory year: It is also an integral part of basic education but it is not compulsory. It is supervised by the Ministry of Education and is provided in public, private and quasi-public primary schools

9 years of basic education are compulsory.

Kindergarten (optional): 5–6 years

1st grade: 6–7 years

2nd grade: 7–8 years

3rd grade: 8–9 years

4th grade: 9–10 years

5th grade: 10–11 years

6th grade: 11–12 years

7th grade: 12–13 years

8th grade: 13–14 years

9th grade: 14–15 years

Ukraine

United Kingdom: Primary education is provided by state schools run by the government and by independent fee-paying schools. In the state system children are either educated in separate infant and junior schools or in a combined primary school. Schools in the private sector providing primary education are generally known as preparatory schools or prep schools. In the private sector the transfer to the final stage of education sometimes takes place at 14.

England

Children start school either in the year or the term in which they reach five depending upon the policy of the Local Education Authority. All state schools are obliged to follow a centralised National Curriculum. The primary school years are split into Key Stages:

- Nursery, age 1 to 4
- Reception, age 4 to 5

- Year 1, age 5 to 6
- Year 2, age 6 to 7
- Year 3, age 7 to 8
- Year 4, age 8 to 9
- Year 5, age 9 to 10
- Year 6, age 10 to 11

At the end of Key Stage 2 in Year 6 all children in state primary schools are required to take National Curriculum tests in reading and mathematics also called SATs. All state primary schools are under the jurisdiction of the Department for Children, Schools and Families and are required to receive regular inspections by the Office for Standards in Education (OFSTED). Private schools are inspected by the Independent Schools Inspectorate.

They then change schools to go to secondary school.

- Year 7, age 11 to 12
- Year 8, age 12 to 13
- Year 9, age 13 to 14
- Year 10, age 14 to 15
- Year 11, age 15 to 16
- Year 12, (6th form) 16 to 17
- Year 13 (6th form) 17 to 18

Northern Ireland

Children start school either in the year or the term in which they reach four. All state schools are obliged to follow a centralised National Curriculum. The primary school years are split into Key Stages:

- Primary education
  - o Primary school
    - – Foundation Stage
    - – Primary 1, age 4 to 5
    - – Primary 2, age 5 to 6
    - – Key Stage 1
    - – Primary 3, age 6 to 7
    - – Primary 4, age 7 to 8
    - – Key Stage 2
    - – Primary 5, age 8 to 9

- Primary 6, age 9 to 10
- Primary 7, age 10 to 11 (Transfer procedure exams to determine secondary school placement.)

At the end of Key Stage 2 in P7, all children are offered the voluntary Eleven Plus (also called the *transfer procedure*) examinations, though the parents of thirty percent of children elect not to, and send their kids to secondary schools instead of grammar schools.

All state primary schools are under the jurisdiction of the Department of Education.

Scotland

In Scotland children typically spend seven years in a primary school, whose years are named P1 to P7. Children enter P1 at the age of four or five (according to a combination of birth date and parental choice).

Primary 1 (aged 4–6)

Primary 2 (aged 5–7)

Primary 3 (aged 6–8)

Primary 4 (aged 7–9)

Primary 5 (aged 8–10)

Primary 6 (aged 9–11)

Primary 7 (aged 10–12)

1st year - aged 12 to 13

2nd year - aged 13 to 14

3rd year - aged 14 to 15

4th year - aged 15 to 16

5th year - aged 16 to 17

6th year - aged 17 to 18

Wales

Children in Wales spend 7 years at primary school between the ages of 4 and 11.

United States

In the United States the first stage of compulsory education is generally known as elementary education. It takes place in elementary schools which usually incorporates grades 1-5. Some schools have a kindergarten and some go up to sixth grade. Elementary schools in the US are also known as grade schools or grammar schools. In some schools, teachers utilize a "looping system" where the same teacher teaches the same group of students for two years. For example, a third-grade class may have one teacher who would teach those students for an entire year, then that teacher would teach fourth-grade the next year, and thereby teach the same class again. The teacher would then revert to the third grade the following year to start the process all over again with a different group of students.

Over the past few decades, schools in the USA have been testing various arrangements which break from the one-teacher, one-class model. Multi-age programmes, where children in different grades (e.g. Kindergarten through to second grade) share the same classroom and teachers, is one increasingly popular alternative to traditional elementary instruction. Another alternative is that children might have a main class and go to another teacher's room for one subject, such as science, while the science teacher's main class will go to the other teacher's room for another subject, such as social studies. This could be called a two-teacher, or a rotation. It is similar to the concept of teams in junior high school. Another method is to have the children have one set of classroom teachers in the first half of the year, and a different set of classroom teachers in the second half of the year.

Preschool: Ages 3–4

Pre-K: Ages 4–5

Kindergarten: Ages 5–6

1st Grade: Ages 6–7

2nd Grade: Ages 7–8

3rd Grade: Ages 8–9

4th Grade: Ages 9–10

5th Grade: Ages 10–11

6th Grade: Ages 11–12

7th Grade: Ages 12–13

8th Grade: Ages 13–14

9th Grade: Ages 14–15

10th Grade: Ages 15–16

11th Grade: Ages 16–17

12th Grade: Ages 17–18

English as a Second Language

Definition: English as a second language (ESL) by definition refers to the specialized instruction designed for students who are either limited in English proficiency or have a primary language other than English. The government often refers to EL students as Limited English Proficiency (LEP) students.

History of the English Language in the United States

During European settlement, early in the history of the United States of America a variety of languages were spoken, not to mention the language of the indigenous peoples who were the first to live in the continent. However, when the United States was forming as a country, it became clear that English would undoubtedly become the language of the country. As influential men such as Thomas Jefferson, Benjamin Franklin, and John Jay strived to establish a distinguished American society and culture, they created an American identity that reflected their own Anglo-Saxon cultural identity. English did not become the official language, but it was the language of schools, the government, and the laws.

Similarly, throughout the course of United States history, there have been massive immigration into the country that have created communities where the population speaks languages other than English.

Statistics

- 6% of all schools in the United States have English as a second language students, with certain states having large numbers of English as a second language students
    - 87% of Arizona schools have ESL students
    - 90% of California schools have ESL students
    - 96% of Hawaii schools have ESL students

Only 18% of all schools offer bilingual education programmes and 43% offer ESL programmes. However, 27% of these schools find it difficult or impossible to fill these teaching positions with qualified instructors. Therefore, many English as a second language students are inadequately served.

California

- 60% of ESL students in California high schools have not achieved written proficiency in the language, even after six years of a U.S. education

- 1/4 of all public school attendees in California are English-learners — 1.6 million, "the largest bloc of English-learners in the nation"

Unequal Access to Trained Teachers

Students that are learning English as a second language require teachers with specialized training. However, the demand for teachers with specialized training does not meet the amount of ESL students; there is a significantly low percentage of teachers well prepared to teach. Thus, English learners are more likely to be placed in classes that are taught by teachers who are not fully credentialed. According to the 2000 Class Size Reduction (CSR) teacher survey, 53% of English learners enrolled in grades 1-4, in California, during the 1999-2000 school year, were taught by a teacher with prior specialized training. EL students are less likely than their English-speaking peers to have a qualified teacher direct classroom instruction in their classes. This inevitably creates challenges for the EL students as their needs are not met.

Millennium Development Goals

The Millennium Development Goals (MDGs) are eight international development goals that were established following the Millennium Summit of the United Nations in 2000, following the adoption of the United Nations Millennium Declaration. All 189 United Nations member states and at least 23 international organizations committed to help achieve these goals by the year 2015. The goals are:

1. Eradicating extreme poverty and hunger
2. Achieving universal primary education
3. Promoting gender equality and empowering women
4. Reducing child mortality rates
5. Improving maternal health
6. Combating HIV/AIDS, malaria, and other diseases
7. Ensuring environmental sustainability
8. Developing a global partnership for development

Each goal has specific targets and dates for achieving those targets. To accelerate progress, the G8 Finance Ministers agreed in June 2005 to provide enough funds to the World Bank, the International Monetary Fund (IMF) and the African Development Bank (AfDB) to cancel $40 to $55 billion in debt owed by members of the Heavily Indebted Poor Countries (HIPC) to allow them to redirect resources to programmes for improving health and education and for alleviating poverty.

Criticisms accompanied the MDGs, focusing on lack of analysis and justification behind the chosen objectives, the difficulty or lack of measurements for some goals and uneven progress, among others. Although developed countries' aid for achieving the MDGs rose during the challenge period, more than half went for debt relief, with much of the remained going towards natural disaster relief and military aid which do not further development.

As of 2013 progress towards the goals was uneven. Some countries achieved many goals, while others were not on track to realize any. A UN conference in September 2010 reviewed progress and concluded with the adoption of a global plan to achieve the eight goals by their target date. New commitments targeted women's and children's health and new initiatives in the worldwide battle against poverty, hunger and disease.

Goal 2: Achieve Universal Primary Education

The second goal in the United Nations Millennium Development Goal is to achieve Universal Primary Education, more specifically, to "ensure that by 2015, children everywhere, boys and girls alike will be able to complete a full course of primary schooling." Currently, there are more than 75 million children around the world of primary school age who are not in school. The majority of these children are in regions of sub-Saharan Africa and South Asia and within these countries, girls are at the greatest disadvantage in receiving access to education at the primary school age. Since the Millennium Development Goals were launched, many developing countries, such as China, Chile, Cuba, Singapore and Sri Lanka, have successfully completed a campaign towards universal primary education.

There has been great progress achieved since 1999 in the achievement of the millennium development goal (MDG). UNESCO has found that:

- number of children enrolled in primary schools worldwide rose by more than 40 million between 1999 and 2007
- net primary enrollment in sub-Saharan Africa rose from 58% to 74% over the same period

- international aid commitments to basic education almost doubled from $2.1 billion in 2002 to $4.1 billion in 2007

However, despite all these important achievements, the world is currently not on course to achieve its target of universal primary education (UPE) by 2015. Currently, 120 million children could still be out of school in 2015 and girls will still lag behind boys in school enrollment and attendance. Sub-Saharan Africa is particularly affected as over a quarter of its children of primary school age were out of school in 2007. It is estimated that there is a $16.2 billion annual external financing gap between available domestic resources and what is needed to achieve the basic education goals in low income countries, with current aid levels addressing only 15% of that gap and resources are all too often not provided to those countries who need it most and the amounts pledged not fully honoured. Difficulties faced by donors in the sphere of achieving UPE, highlighted by researchers at the Overseas Development Institute, include:

- failings in aid architecture (though the Paris Declaration and FTI initiatives represent significant improvements)
- the evidence-based case for further investment in basic education has not been made strongly enough
- recipient governments are reluctant to borrow funds for the recurrent costs education entails.

Factors contributing to lack of access and poor attendance

Location (Climate): Location contributes to a child's lack of access and attendance to primary education. In certain areas of the world it is more difficult for children to get to school. For example; in high-altitude areas of India, severe weather conditions for more than 7 months of the year make school attendance erratic and force children to remain at home (Postiglione).

In these remote locations, insufficient school funds contribute to low attendance rates by creating undesirable and unsafe learning environments. In 1996, the General Accounting Office (GAO) reported that poor conditions existed in many rural areas; one out of every two rural schools had at least one inadequate structural or mechanical feature (Lawrence). In these situations where regular school attendance is rare, a low population contributes to the problem. In other locations, large numbers are often the cause of low attendance rates. Due to population growth, many urban schools have expanded their boundaries making school transportation more complicated. "For over 50 years the U.S. has been shifting away from small, neighbourhood schools to larger schools in lower density areas. Rates of children walking and biking to school have declined significantly over this period" (Schlossberg). There is evidence to prove that the distance to and from school contributes a child's attendance, or lack thereof. In a study done investigating the relation between location (distance) and school attendance in Mali, about half the villages reported that the school was too far away, causing students not to enroll (Birdsall).

There is still speculation as to whether primary schools are more accessible in rural or urban areas because situations differ depending on geographic location. In a study done examining the correlation between location and school attendance in Argentina and Panama, researchers found that urban residence was positively correlated with school attendance (De Vos), but another study in a Louisiana school district found that schools with the lowest attendance rates were in metropolitan areas (Moonie).

More research needs to be done to determine geography's specific effects on attendance, but no matter where you live, there is evidence that location will contribute to a child's access and attendance to education.

Gender

Gender contributes to a child's lack of access and attendance to education. Although it may not be as an obvious a problem today, gender equality in education has been an issue for a long time. Many investments in girls' education in the 1900s addressed the widespread lack of access to primary education in developing countries (Dowd).

There is currently a gender discrepancy in education. In 25 countries the proportion of boys enrolling in secondary school is higher than girls by 10% or more, and in five; India, Nepal, Togo, Turkey and Yemen, the gap exceeds 20%. Enrollment is low for both boys and girls in sub-Saharan Africa, with rates of just 27% and 22%. Girls trail respectively behind (Douglas). It is generally believed that girls are often discouraged from attending primary schooling, especially in less developed countries for religious and cultural reasons, but there is little evidence available to support this association. However, there is evidence to prove that the disparity of gender in education is real. Today some 78% of girls drop out of school, compared with 48% of boys (Douglas). A child's gender continues to contribute to access and attendance today.

Cost

Costs contribute to a child's lack of access and attendance to primary education. High opportunity costs are often influential in the decision to attend school. For example; an estimated 121 million children of primary-school age are being kept out of school to work in the fields or at home (UNICEF). For many families in developing countries the economic benefits of no primary schooling are enough to offset the opportunity cost of attending.

Besides the opportunity costs associated with education, school fees can be very expensive, especially for poor households. In rural China, families dedicate as much as a third of their income to school fees (Peverly). Sometimes, the cost gets too expensive and families can't support their children's education anymore, although the statistics disagree. "China has 108.6 million primary school students, with a 1 percent dropout rate, but experts doubt these figures because the dropout rates in rural areas appear much higher" (Peverly).

Although the relationship between school fees and attendance still isn't perfectly clear (Peverly), there is evidence to prove that cost is a factor that contributes to a child's access and attendance to primary education.

Language

In developing countries throughout the world the educational context is characterized not by monolingual settings, but rather multilingual situations. Often children are asked to enroll in a primary school where the Medium of Instruction (MI) is not her home language, but rather the language of the government, or another dominant society. Studies throughout the world demonstrate the importance of the MI in determining a child's educational attainment.

According to Mehrotra (1988) "In a situation where the parents are illiterate..., if the medium of instruction in school is a language that is not spoken at home the problems of learning in an environment characterized by poverty are compounded, and the chances of drop-out increase correspondingly. In this context, the experience of the high- achievers has been unequivocal: the mother tongue was used as the medium of instruction at the primary level in all cases. ... There is much research which shows that students learn to read more quickly when taught in their mother tongue. Second, students who have learned to read in their mother tongue learn to read in a second language more quickly than do those who are first taught to read in the second language. Third, in terms of academic learning skills as well, students taught to read in their mother tongue acquire such skills more quickly".

Education and Global Health

Education is a crucial factor in ending global poverty. With education, employment opportunities are broadened, income levels are increased and maternal and child health is improved.

In areas where access, attendance and quality of education have seen improvements, there has also been a slow in the spread of HIV/AIDS and an increase in the healthiness of the community in general. In fact, children of educated mothers are 50% more likely to live past the age of five. Not only does education improve individual and familial health, but it also improves the health of a community. In countries with solid education systems in place, there are lower crime rates, greater economic growth and improved social services.

School Feeding Programmes

"There are approximately 300 million chronically hungry children in the world. One hundred million of them do not attend school, and two thirds of those not attending school are girls. World Food Programme's school feeding formula is simple: food attracts hungry children to school. An education broadens their options, helping to lift them out of poverty." –World Food Programme

One successful method to ensuring that children attend school on a regular basis is through school feeding programmes. Many different organizations fund school feeding programmes, among them the World Food Programme and the World Bank. The idea of a school feeding programme is that children are provided with meals at school with the expectation that they will attend school regularly. School feeding programmes have proven a huge success because not only do the attendance rates increase, but in areas where food is scarce and malnutrition is extensive, the food that children are receiving at school can prove to be a critical source of nutrition. School meals have led to improved concentration and performance of children in school. Another aspect of school feeding programmes is take home rations. When economic reasons, the need to care for the elderly or a family member suffering from HIV, or cultural beliefs keep a parent from sending their child (especially a female child) to school, these take home rations provide incentives to sending their children to school rather than to work

Progress

According to the United Nations, in 2008, overall enrollment in primary education in developing areas reached 89 percent. This was a major increase from the 83 percent in 2000. Due to the fact that the United Nations is specifically focusing on Sub-Saharan Africa and Southern Asia, as they are both home to the vast majority of children out of school, they hypothesize that they might not be able to reach their goal by 2015. According to the September 2010 fact sheet, this is because there are still about 69 million school-age children are not in school and almost half of them are in sub-Saharan Africa and more than a quarter are in Southern Asia.

To Achieve the Goal

In order to achieve the goal by 2015, the United Nations estimates that all children at the official entry age for primary school would have had to be attending classes by 2009. This would depend on the duration of the primary level as well as how well the school schools retain students until the end of the cycle. In half of the sub-Saharan African countries, however, "at least one in four children of primary-school age were out of school in 2008." Also, not only is it important for children to be enrolled but countries will need to ensure that there are a sufficient amount of teachers and classrooms to meet the demand. As of 2010 and 2015, the number of new teachers needed in sub-Saharan Africa alone equals the current teaching force in the region.

Close Gender Gap

The gender gap in the number of students not in school has also narrowed. Between 1999 and 2008, the number of girls not in school decreased from 57 percent to 53 percent globally. In some regions, however, there is a greater percentage; for example, in Northern Africa, 66 percent of "out-of-school children" are girls.

What Has Been Done

According to the United Nations, there are many things in the regions that have been accomplished. Although enrollment in the sub-Saharan area of Africa continues to be the lowest of all regions, by 2010 "it still increased by 18 percentage points—from 58 per cent to 76 per cent—between 1999 and 2008." There was also progress in both Southern Asia and Northern Africa, where both countries witnessed an increase in enrollment. Southern Asia increased by 11 percentage points and Northern Africa by 8 percentage points over the last decade. Also, major advances have been made even in some of the poorest countries, again the majority of them in the sub-Saharan region of Africa. With the abolition of primary school fees in Burundi, there was an increase in primary-school enrollment since 1999; it reached 99 percent in 2008. The United Republic of Tanzania experienced a similar outcome. The country doubled its enrollment ratio over the same period. Other regions in Latin America such as Guatemala and Nicaragua as well as Zambia in Southern Africa "broke through the 90 percent towards greater access to primary education."

Secondary Schools

Figure: *Students working with a teacher at Albany Senior High School, New Zealand*

In most contemporary educational systems of the world, secondary education comprises the formal education that occurs during adolescence. It is characterized by transition from the typically compulsory, comprehensive primary education for minors, to the optional, selective tertiary, "post-secondary", or "higher" education (e.g. university, vocational school) for adults. Depending on the system, schools for this period, or a part of it, may be called secondary or high schools, gymnasiums, lyceums, middle schools, colleges, or vocational schools. The exact meaning of any of these terms varies from one system to another. The exact boundary between primary and secondary education also varies from country to country and even within them, but is generally around the seventh to the tenth year of schooling. Secondary education occurs mainly during the teenage years. In the United States, Canada and Australia primary and secondary education together are sometimes referred to as K-12 education, and in New Zealand Year 1–13 is used. The purpose of secondary education can be to give common knowledge, to prepare for higher education or to train directly in a profession.

***Figure:** Students in a classroom at Samdach Euv High School, Cambodia*

The emergence of secondary education in the United States did not happen until 1910, caused by the rise in big businesses and technological advances in factories (for instance, the emergence of electrification), that required skilled workers.

In order to meet this new job demand, high schools were created, with a curriculum focused on practical job skills that would better prepare students for white collar or skilled blue collar work. This proved to be beneficial for both employers and employees, for the improvement in human capital caused employees to become more efficient, which lowered costs for the employer, and skilled employees received a higher wage than employees with just primary educational attainment.

In Europe, grammar schools or academies date from as early as the 16th century, in the form of public schools, fee-paying schools, or charitable educational foundations, which themselves have an even longer history.

Secondary Education

Secondary education takes place in secondary schools and is the stage of education following primary education. In some countries, only primary or basic education is compulsory, but secondary education is included in compulsory education in most countries. If students go on to another stage of education, this is post-secondary or tertiary education and consists of higher education (college or university), or further education / continuing education. Depending on the country, secondary schools may be called *high schools*, *gymnasia*, *lyceums*, *middle schools*, *sixth-form*, *sixth-form colleges*, *vocational schools*, or *preparatory schools*, and the exact meaning of any of these varies between the countries.

Secondary Education in the EU

Secondary education is a stage of education following primary school. Except in a few countries where only primary or basic education is compulsory, secondary education includes the final stage of compulsory education. However, secondary education in some countries includes a period of compulsory and a period of non-compulsory education. After secondary education, the next stage of education is usually college or university. Secondary education is characterized by transition from primary education for minors to tertiary, "post-secondary", or "higher" education (e.g., university, vocational school) for adults. Depending on the system, schools for this period or a part of it may be called *secondary schools*, *high schools*, *gymnasia*, *lyceums*, *middle schools*, *colleges*, *vocational schools* and *preparatory schools*, and the exact meaning of any of these varies between the systems.

Belgium

The Belgian school has a three-tier education system, each stage being divided into various levels:

- Basic education (F enseignement fondamental D basisonderwijs)
  - o Nursery school (F enseignement maternel D kleuteronderwijs): for children aged 3 to 6 – is not compulsory
  - o Primary school (F : enseignement primaire D lager onderwijs): for children aged 6 to 12 – is compulsory
- Secondary education: there are three cycles (F degrés D graden)
- Post secondary education: organised by universities or schools of higher education, but also by adult education institutions

   - o 3-year further education (enseignement supérieur de type court) at bachelor level
   - o 5-year further education (enseignement de type long) at master's level (one or two more years for doctoral training)

Cyprus

1.1 General overview of education stages Cyprus has a three-tier educational system, each stage being divided into specific levels:

- Basic education
  - o Nursery (Ages 3–5) Not obligatory
  - o Pre-primary school (Ages 5–6) At the age of five, children normally attend the pre primary class, which prepares them to join Primary school
- Primary school (Ages 6–12) Primary school has six grades.
- Secondary education
  - o Gymnasium (Ages 12–15) After primary school, students attend the lower secondary school (GYMNASIUM) which has three grades.
  - o Eniaio Lykeio or Unified Lyceum (Ages 15–18)
- Post secondary education Public Tertiary Institutions or Universities

Czech Republic

The Czech school system is, due to historic reasons, almost the same as the German school system. The school system is free and mandatory to age 15. After the *Základní škola* (Elementary School) in age of 15, students are directed to three different optional secondary education schools:

- Støední odborné uèilištì (SOU) - designed for students going into a trade (e.g., carpentry, masonry, auto-mechanic etc.) Education is 3 years long and entrance exam free, combined with practice (one week study in school/one week practice in factory, bakery, building site... etc.), finished with a certificate.
- Støední odborná škola (SOŠ) - designed for students going into a profession (accountant, technician, kindergarten teacher..) and finishes with *maturita* as exit exam. The leaving exam consist of 2 compulsory and 2 optional subjects. Compulsory subjects are *Czech language and World Literature* and *one other language*. Optional ones depend on the type of school

(mathematics, physics, accounting, etc.) The study is 4 years long and you need to pass an entrance exam (Czech Language and Mathematics or Physics, varies with the type of school)

- Gymnázium - designed for students going to university/college and finishes with a *maturita* exam. Also with two mandatory subjects *Czech language and World Literature* and *one other language*. Optional subjects vary, usually between humanistic and science. The study is 4, 6 or 8 years long. In case of 6 (8) years one, the pupils finish elementary school two (four) years earlier and this two (four) years has harder studying programme on Gymnasium. There are also entry exams to all these programmes.

The *maturita* is required for study in University. The Abitur from Gymnasium is better for Humanistic pointed University and SOŠ Abitur is better for Technical pointed university.

Croatia

Secondary education is now compulsory.

Secondary schools in Croatia are subdivided into:

- gymnasiums with four available educational tracks; *prirod-oslovno-matematièka gimnazija* (specializing in math, informatics and science), *jezièna gimnazija* (with at least three foreign languages required), *klasièna gimnazija* (with a curriculum centred around classics, namely Latin and Ancient Greek) and *opœa gimnazija* (which covers a general education and is not as specific).
- vocational schools.

Gymnasiums, schools of economics and schools of engineering take four years. There are also some vocational schools that last only three years. Secondary schools supply students with primary subjects needed for the necessary work environment in Croatia. People who completed secondary school are classified as "medium expertise" (*srednja struèna sprema* or SSS). There are currently around 90 gymnasiums and some 300 vocational schools in Croatia. The public secondary schools are under the jurisdiction of regional government, the counties.

Denmark

In Denmark it is mandatory to receive education answering to the basic school syllabus until the 10th year of school education. Since 2009 it has been compulsory to also attend pre-school. Furthermore, pupils can choose an 11th year of school.

Figure: *Krabbesholm Højskole*

After the basic school the majority of pupils between ages 15–19 usually choose to go through the 3-year "Gymnasium", which is University-preparatory. Youngsters not attending Gymnasium most commonly attend vocational training. There are over 100 different vocational courses in Denmark.

Finland

Figure: *Helsingin normaalilyseo*

The Finnish education system is a comparatively egalitarian Nordic system. This means for example no tuition fees for full-time students and free meals are served to pupils. There are private schools but they are made unattractive by legislation.

The second level education is not compulsory, but an overwhelming majority attends. There is a choice between upper secondary school (*lukio, gymnasium*) and vocational school (*ammatillinen oppilaitos, yrkesinstitut*). Graduates of both upper secondary school and vocational school can apply to study in further education (University and Polytechnics).

Upper secondary school, unlike vocational school, concludes with a nationally graded matriculation examination (*ylioppilastutkinto, studentexamen*). Passing the test is a *de facto* prerequisite for further education. The system is designed so that approximately the lowest scoring 5% fails and also 5% get the best grade. The exam allows for a limited degree of specialization in either natural sciences or social sciences. The graduation is an important and formal family event, like christening, wedding, and funeral.

In the OECD's international assessment of student performance, PISA, Finland has consistently been among the highest scorers worldwide; in 2003, Finnish 15-year-olds came first in reading literacy, science, and mathematics; and second in problem solving, worldwide. The World Economic Forum ranks Finland's tertiary education #1 in the world."The Global Competitiveness Report 2006–2007: Country Highlights". *World Economic Forum*. Retrieved 2007-01-22.

Germany

The German school system is free and compulsory until 9th grade. After the *Grundschule* (primary/elementary school lasting four to six years), teachers recommend each pupil for one of three different types of secondary education. Parents have the final say about which school their child will attend.

- Hauptschule - designed for students going into trades such as construction; complete after 9th or 10th grade (ages 14 to 16). During apprenticeships, pupils then attend Berufsschule, a dual-education vocational high school. The Hauptschule has been subject to significant criticism, as it tends to segregate the children of immigrants with schoolmates whose German is also poor, leading to a cycle of poverty.
- Realschule - designed for students who want to apprentice for white-collar jobs not requiring university studies, such as banking; complete after 10th grade (age 15 to 16). Those who change their minds and decide to attend university can proceed after testing to:

- Gymnasium - academic preparatory school for pupils planning to attend universities or polytechnics. Some offer a classical education (Latin, Greek), while others concentrate on economics and the like. The curriculum leading to the Abitur degree were recently reduced from 13th grade to 12th grade (ages 17 to 18 - "G8," eight years of Gymnasium).
- The Gesamtschule, a mixed ability school, puts all pupils in a single building, combining the three main types; these are still quite rare.

Students with special needs are assigned to Förderschule.

Ireland

Figure: *St. Enda's School*

In Ireland secondary school starts at the age of 12, and lasts three or optionally five or six years. The main types of secondary school are: community schools, comprehensive schools, *colleges* (though this term is more usually applied to third-level institutions like universities), vocational schools, voluntary secondary schools and meánscoileanna (secondary schools that teach all subjects through Irish). After three years (age 14-16), every student takes a compulsory state exam known as the Junior Certificate. Typically a student will sit exams in 9 to 11 subjects; English (L1), Irish (L2) and Mathematics are compulsory. After completing the Junior Certificate, a student may continue for two years to take a second state exam, the Leaving Certificate, around age 17-18. Students typically take 6-8 subjects. Except in exceptional circumstances, subjects taken must include Irish (L1), English (L2), a foreign language (L3) and Mathematics. Leaving Certificate results directly determine admission to university via a ranking system managed by the CAO. More than 80% of students who complete the Junior Certificate continue to the Leaving Certificate.

There is an optional year in many secondary schools in Ireland known as Transition Year, which some students choose to take after completing the Junior Certificate, and before starting the Leaving Certificate. Focusing on broadening horizons, the year is often structured around student projects such as producing a magazine, charity work, running a small business, etc.

Regular classes may be mixed with classes on music, drama, public speaking, etc. Transition Year is not formally examined but student progress is monitored by teachers on a continuous basis. Programmes vary from school to school. This year also focuses on giving the children an insight into the working world through work experience placements.

In addition to the main school system, Ireland has a parallel system of vocational schools, which place less focus on academic subjects and more on vocational and technical skills - around 25% of students attend these. Many vocational schools also offer night classes to adults. There is also a prominent movement known as Gaelscoileanna where every subject is taught through the Irish Language, and these are growing fast in number.

Italy

Secondary school (*Scuola secondaria*) starts at age 11, after 5 years of Primary school, and lasts 8 years.

Secondary school is divided in 3 + 5 years, according to the following scheme:

- Scuola secondaria di I grado (*first grade secondary school*, previously scuola media, *middle school*, by which it is still called): it is mandatory and lasts 3 years and is the first stage in which different specialized professors teach different subjects. It has a common programme for all pupils, and covers all the classical subjects (Italian language and literature, History, Geography, Mathematics, Natural sciences, English language, a second Foreign Language - usually French, German or Spanish, Technology, Arts, Music, and Physical Education).

It ends with a final exam, which awards a diploma, which includes:

- o 4 written tests prepared by each examining board: Italian, Mathematics, and the two foreign languages
- o an experimental nationally assessed test for tracking progresses in reading comprehension, language knowledge, reasoning skills and basic mathematical skills
- o an overall oral examination on all subjects.

The final grade is a number from 6 to 10 (the best).

- Scuola secondaria di II grado (*second grade secondary school*): it lasts 5 years and many different paths exist, which can freely be chosen by the pupil and his/her family; the first 2 years are madatory, the other 3 are not.
  - o Liceo: it is the general purpose kind of school, traditionally chosen by those wanting to pursue higher education (university or arts academy). Depending on the area of interest of the pupils, different subkinds exist whose programmes are mostly decided at national level, but all offer at least basic teachings in Italian language and Literature, History, Geography, Philosophy, Mathematics, Physics, Biology, Chemistry, a foreign language (usually English, but also French, German or Spanish), History of Arts and Physical Education:
  - – Liceo Classico which focuses on Literature and Classical Studies (Latin and ancient Greek)
  - – Liceo Scientifico which focuses on Mathematics and Sciences
  - – Liceo Linguistico which focuses on Modern languages
  - – Liceo delle Scienze Umane which focuses either on Psychology and Sociology or Law and Economics
  - – Liceo Artistico which focuses on different arts (graphical, sculpture, etc...)
  - – Liceo Musicale e Coreutico which focuses on music or dance
- o Istituto Tecnico: it is a technical school originally reserved for those who sought a highly qualified work, but today more and more used as a different route to access university. Different paths exist whose programmes are mostly decided at national level, but a general basic education is provided to every pupil, similarly to the *liceo*, but less focused on the Humanities (no philosophy or arts, but more mathematics than in the non-scientific *liceo*); the main ones are:

- Economico which focuses on how to run all aspects of running the economical and managing part of a business
- Meccanico which focuses on the processes of design and production of machinery and vehicles
- Elettronico which focuses on the process of production of electrical and electronic devices
- Informatico which focuses on managing computers and communication devices
- Chimico focusing on chemical processes for the industry
- Agrario focusing on agronomy and farming
- Costruzioni focusing on the processes linked to the civil engineering and building industry
    - o Istituto Professionale: it is a manly vocational school which offers a very specialized formation on a specific field for those looking into entering work; it is generally organized at local level according to the local economy and industry and based on broad national guidelines; it offers periods of stage in the local firms as a part of their courses. A general basic education is given to all pupils.

All kind of secondary schools end with an examination (Esame di Stato, *state exam*, but usually still called with the traditional name Esame di Maturità, *Maturity exam*) whose score is on a 100 point scale:

- up to 25 points for the general marks obtained through the last 3 years (students barely passing each year are awarded 10 points total)
- up to 45 points (15 each) on three (or four for some special cases) different written tests (each test judged sufficient is awarded at least 10 points):
    - o Italian Language and Literature, decided at national level and the same for all examinees: either a text comprehension and critique, or the writing of an essay
    - o a subject dependent on the kind of school followed, decided at national level for each different path
    - o a third test prepared by each examining board based on the programmes of all the subjects of the last year of study
- up to 30 points on an overall oral exam regarding all the subjects of the last year (an oral exam judged sufficient is awarded at least 20 points)

- up to 5 points (to a maximum of 100) in cases the examining board judges appropriate to meriting students.

The exam is passed with a score of 60 or more, and any secondary school diploma is valid for access to any university course.

Netherlands

In The Netherlands, high school is called *middelbare school* (literally: "middle-level school") and starts right after the 6th grade of primary school (group 8). The pupils who attend high school are around the age of 12. Because education in the Netherlands is compulsory between the ages of 4 and 16 (and partially compulsory between the ages of 16 and 18), all pupils must attend high school.

The high schools are part of the *voortgezet onderwijs* (literally: "continued education"). The *voortgezet onderwijs* consists of 3 main streams: vmbo, which has 4 grades and is subdivided over several levels; havo, which has 5 grades, and vwo, which has 6 grades. The choice for a particular stream is made based on the scores of an aptitude test (most commonly the CITO test), the advice of the grade 6 teacher, and the opinion of the pupil's parents or caretakers. It is possible to switch between streams. After completing a particular stream, a pupil can continue in the penultimate year of the next stream, from vmbo to havo, and from havo to vwo.

Successfully completing a particular stream grants access to different levels of tertiary education. After vmbo, a pupil can continue training at the mbo ("middle-level applied education"). A havo diploma allows for admission to the hbo ("higher professional education"), which are universities of professional education. Only with vwo can a pupil enter into a research university.

Portugal

Slovenia: In Slovenia, a variety of high-school institutions for secondary education exists one can choose in accordance with his or her interests, abilities and beliefs. The majority of them are public and government-funded, although there are some diocesan upper secondary schools and a Waldorf upper secondary school, which are private and require tuition to be paid.

Upper secondary schools (Sln. *gimnazije*) are the most elite and the most difficult high-school programmes, intended for the best students that wish to pursue university education in the future. They are further divided into general upper secondary schools, classical upper secondary schools, technical upper secondary schools, upper secondary schools for arts, and upper secondary schools for business. They all last for four years and conclude with a compulsory leaving examination (Sln. *matura*) that is a prerequsite for studying at universities. Their curricula include a wide range of subjects that should deliver a broad general knowledge.

Technical high schools last for four years and cover a wide range of disciplines. They end with a vocational leaving examination and allow pupils to study at vocational or professional colleges.

Vocational High Schools Come in Two Varieties: the dual and in school-based programme. For the former, the apprenticeship is provided by employers, while the practical training for the latter is offered in school. Both of them complete with a final examination. Students may continue their education in the two-year vocational-technical programme (colloquially known as 3+2 programme), which prepares them for vocational leaving exam if they want to pursue higher education.

The leaving exam course is a one-year programme, intended for vocational leaving exam graduates. After completing leaving exam course, they take the leaving examination, which makes the eligible for university education.

The Vocational course is a one-year programme provided to upper secondary school students who, for various reasons, do not want to continue their education. It concludes with a final examinations, qualifying the applicants for a selected occupation.

Spain

Secondary education in Spain is called *Educación Secundaria Obligatoria* (*Compulsory Secondary Education*), usually known as E.S.O., and lasts for 4 years (12 to 16). As its name indicates, every Spanish citizen must, by law, attend secondary education when they arrive at the defined age. The State is also committed to guaranteeing every student the possibility of attending it, and also at a state run school (hence no tuition fees) if so demanded.

United Kingdom

In the United Kingdom secondary schools offer secondary education covering the later years of schooling. State secondary schools in England and Wales are classed as either (selective) grammar schools, (non-selective) comprehensive schools, city technology colleges or academies.

Within Scotland, there are only two types of state-run schools, Roman Catholic or non-denominational. Most secondary schools in England and Wales are comprehensive schools. Grammar schools have been retained in some counties in England. Academies (previously known as city academies) are a new type of school introduced in 2000 by the New Labour government of Tony Blair. Independent secondary schools generally take pupils at 13.

Figure: *The table below lists the equivalent secondary school year systems used in the United Kingdom:*

Scotland	*England, Wales*	*Northern Ireland*	*Equivalent Ages*
Primary 7	Year 7 (First Form)	Year 8 (First Form)	11-12
First Year (Secondary 1)	Year 8 (Second Form)	Year 9 (Second Form)	12-13
Second Year (Secondary 2)	Year 9 (Third Form)	Year 10 (Third Form)	13-14
Third Year (Secondary 3)	Year 10 (Fourth Form)	Year 11 (Fourth Form)	14-15
Fourth Year (Secondary 4)	Year 11 (Fifth Form)	Year 12 (Fifth Form)	15-16
Fifth Year (Secondary 5)	Year 12Lower Sixth AS First Year College	Year 13 [Post 16] Lower Sixth	16-17
Sixth Year (Secondary 6)	Year 13Upper Sixth A2 Second Year College	Year 14 [Post 16] Upper Sixth	17-18

Private schools in England and Wales generally still refer to years 7-11 as 1st-5th Form, or alternatively privates schools refer to Year 7 as IIIrds (Thirds), Y8 as LIV (Lower Four), Y9 as UIV (Upper Four), Y10 as LV (Lower Fifth), Y11 as UV (Upper Fifth) and then Sixth-Form.

England, Wales and Northern Ireland

Education in England, Wales, Northern Ireland: In England, Wales and Northern Ireland, students usually transfer from primary school straight to secondary school at age 11. In a few parts of the UK there are middle schools for ages 9 to 13 (similar to American middle schools), and upper schools for ages 13–18. A handful of 8-12 middle schools, an 12-16 or 18 secondary schools still exist. These schools were first introduced in September 1968, and the number rose dramatically during the 1970s, but the number of such schools has declined since the mid-1980s.

It is uncommon, but sometimes secondary schools (particularly in South West Wales) can also be split into 'Upper' (ages 13–16) and 'Lower' secondary schools (ages 11–13). Education is compulsory up until the end of year 11 (the last Friday in June in the academic year a person turns 16), and schooling can continue for a further two years after that. Traditionally the five years of compulsory secondary schooling from ages 11 to 16 were known as "first year" through to "fifth year," (and still are in the private sector) but from September 1990 these years were renumbered Year 7 through to Year 11 (Year 8 to Year 12 in Northern Ireland) with the coming of the National Curriculum. After Year 11 a student can opt to remain at school, transfer to a college, or to leave education and seek work or to start an apprenticeship. Those who stay at school enter Years 12 and 13 (Years 13 and 14 in Northern Ireland). These years are traditionally known as the Sixth Form ("Lower Sixth" and "Upper Sixth"), and require students to specialise in three to five subjects for their A Levels. In ever-increasing numbers since the 1990s some students also undertake more vocational courses at college such as a BTEC or other such qualification.

This is an unusually specialised curriculum for this age group by international standards, and recently some moves have been made to increase the number of subjects studied. After attaining the relevant A Level qualifications the student can enter university.

Scotland

Figure: *Balwearie High School*

In Scotland, students usually transfer from primary to secondary education at 12 years old."A Guide to Education and Training in Scotland". *A World of opportunity*. Edinburgh: Scottish Government. Retrieved 17 October 2012. The first and second years of secondary school (abbreviated to S1 and S2) is a continuation of the 5-14 curriculum started in primary school. After which students choose which subjects they wish to study with certain compulsory subjects such as English and Mathematics for S3 and S4. These are called Standard Grades, but some schools use Intermediates which take two years to complete with an exam at the end of S4. After Standard Grades/Intermediates, some students leave to gain employment or attend further education colleges, however nowadays most students study for Highers, of which five are usually studied. These take a year to complete. After which some students decide to apply for university or stay on for 6th year, where other Highers are gained, or Advanced Highers are studied. Due to the nature of schooling in Scotland, undergraduate honours degree programmes are four years long as matriculation is normally at the completion of highers in S5 (age 16-17), which compares with three years for the rest of the UK. As well as instruction through the English language education Gaelic medium education is also available throughout Scotland.

Secondary education in other countries

Argentina: The school system is free and mandatory.

Australia:

Figure: *Sydney Boys High School*

School is compulsory in Australia between the ages of five/six-fifteen/sixteen or seventeen, depending on the state, with, in recent years, over three-quarters of people staying on until their thirteenth year in school. Government schools educate about two-thirds of Australian students, with the other third in independent schools.

Government schools are free although most schools charge what are known as "voluntary contributions" or "Tax Levies", while independent schools, both religious and secular, charge fees as well as levies. Regardless of what whether a school is government or independent, it is required to adhere to the same curriculum frameworks. Most school students, be they in government or independent school, usually wear uniforms, although there are varying expectations and a few school exceptions.

Each State and Territories has its own format of Year 12 Matriculation:

- Australian Capital Territory: ACT Year 12 Certificate
- South Australia: South Australian Certificate of Education (SACE)
- Northern Territory: Senior Secondary Studies Certificate / Northern Territory Certificate of Education (NTCE)
- Queensland: Queensland Certificate of Education (QCE)
- New South Wales: Higher School Certificate (HSC)
- Tasmania: Tasmanian Certificate of Education (TCE)
- Victoria: Victorian Certificate of Education (VCE) or Victorian Certificate of Applied Learning (VCAL)
- Western Australia: Western Australian Certificate of Education (WACE)

Malaysia

The national secondary education in Malaysia, modelled after the (historical) English system, consists of 5 school years referred to as "forms" (*tingkatan* in Malay). Students begin attending secondary schools in the year they turn 13, after sitting for the UPSR (Ujian Pencapaian Sekolah Rendah or Primary School Assessment Examination) at the end of primary school. Students failing the academic requirement in UPSR are required to read an additional year called the Remove (*Peralihan*) year before they are allowed to proceed to Form 1. Automatic promotion up to Form 5 has been in place since 1996. Some secondary schools offer an additional two years known as *sixth form*, divided into *lower sixth* and *upper sixth*.

Forms 1 to 3 are known as Lower Secondary (*Menengah Rendah*), while Forms 4 and 5 are known as Upper Secondary (*Menengah Tinggi*). Streaming into Art, Science or Commerce streams is done at the beginning of the Upper Secondary stage. Students sit for a standardised test at the end of both stages; Penilaian Menengah Rendah (PMR) for Lower Secondary, and Sijil Pelajaran Malaysia (SPM, equivalent to the O-Level examination) for Upper Secondary. At the end of the sixth form, students sit for the Sijil Tinggi Pelajaran Malaysia or the Malaysian Higher School Certificate (equivalent to the A levels). The language of instruction in national secondary schools is Malay except for language, science and mathematics subjects. Science and mathematics subjects are taught in English since 2003, but Malay will be reintroduced in stages from 2012.

Brazil

In Brazil, since 1996 high school is officially called *Ensino Médio* (formerly *Segundo Grau*). Until the year 1971, *ensino médio* had three different names: *curso científico*, *curso normal* and *curso clássico* (which means *classic*). As a result, the course was changed after and called *colegial*, also divided, with the first three years were the same for everyone and anyone who would subsequently make the old *normal* and *clássico*, had to do another year.

Historically, in Brazil, is called the secondary what is now the second part of the school (from the sixth year of primary school, 11 years) together with the high school.

It is the last phase to basic education, Brazilian high school lasts 3 years, attempting to deepen what students have learned in the *Ensino Fundamental*. Brazilian high school students are referenced by their year – 1st, 2nd and 3rd years.

Unlike other countries, Brazilian students don't have a final test to conclude studies. Their approval depends only on their final grade on each subject. Each university elaborates its own test to select new students – this test, the *vestibular*, generally happens once a year. Enem, a non-mandatory national exam, evaluates high school students in Brazil and is used to rank both private and public schools.

The best scores in vestibular and in Enem Do G1, em São Paulo. "G1 > Vestibular e Educação - NOTÍCIAS - Veja as 20 melhores escolas do país no Enem 2007". G1.globo.com. Retrieved 2011-09-25. and the best universities are concentrated on the Southern and Southeastern regions of the country, mainly in the states of São Paulo, Rio de Janeiro, Minas Gerais, Espírito Santo, Rio Grande do Sul, Santa Catarina and Paraná, and in the Federal District. The lack of funds and historical and social problems contribute to poor attendance from the students, especially those in public schools.

Private establishments, on the other hand, may be recognized as academically excellent or merely as investments in social networking. Schedules vary from school to school. The subjects taught, however, are conceived by the *Ministério da Educação* (Ministry of Education) which emphasises the hard sciences. The educational year begins in February and finishes in December; institutions are permitted to define their own actual start and end dates. They must, however, provide at least 200 days of classes per year.

Universities are also divided into public and private. At this level, public ones are considered excellent and their vestibular exam is highly competitive (the exam for med school in UNICAMP may hit 300 candidates per place). For better preparation, therefore, many students take a *curso pré-vestibular* (university preparation course), which is offered by large private high schools.

Hong Kong

Secondary education in Hong Kong is largely based on the British education system. Secondary school starts in the seventh year, or Form One, of formal education, after Primary Six. Students normally spend five years in secondary schools, of which the first three years (Forms One to Three) are compulsory like primary education. Forms Four and Five students prepare for the Hong Kong Certificate of Education Examination (HKCEE), which takes place after Form Five. Students obtaining a satisfactory grade will be promoted to Form Six. They then prepare for the Hong Kong Advanced Level Examination (HKALE) (colloquially *the A-levels*), which is to be taken after Form Seven. The HKALE and HKCEE results will be considered by universities for admission. Some secondary schools in Hong Kong are called 'colleges'. In some schools, Form Six and Form Seven are also called Lower Six and Upper Six respectively.

The HKCEE is equivalent to the British GCSE and HKALE is equivalent to the British A-level. As of October 2004, there has been heated discussion on proposed changes in the education system, which includes (amongst others) reduction of the duration of secondary education from seven years to six years, and merging the two exams HKCEE and HKALE into one exam, Hong Kong Diploma of Secondary Education (HKDSE). The proposed changes will take effect in 2009.

The secondary education system of Hong Kong, just as other East Asian countries, is examination-oriented. This does the strong but controversial post-school tutorial education industrya favour.

India

Singapore: Children attend Primary school for the first 6 levels, then secondary schools for the next 4/5 levels, which is followed by either *junior college* for 2-year courses or *centralised institutes* for 3-year courses.

Based on results of the Primary School Leaving Examination (PSLE), Singapore's students undergo secondary education in either the Special (Abolished in 2008), Express, Normal streams or the Integrated Programme (implemented in 2004). Both the Special and Express are 4-year courses leading up to a Singapore-Cambridge General Certificate of Education (GCE) 'Ordinary' - 'O' level examination. The difference between Special and Express is that the former takes higher Mother Tongue, which can be used as a first language in exams instead of the subject "mother tongue" that Express students take. However if some Express students can cope with higher Mother Tongue, they are allowed to used it as a first language in exams too.

The Normal stream is a four-year course leading up to a Singapore-Cambridge GCE "Normal" - "N" level examination, with the possibility of a 5th year followed by a Singapore-Cambridge GCE "Ordinary" - "O" level examination. It is split into "Normal (Academic)" and "Normal (Technical)" where in the latter students take subjects that are technical in nature, such as Design and Technology.

The Integrated Programme (IP) is a 6-year programme offered to the top 10 percent of the cohort to pass through the O level exams, and go straight to the affiliated JC.

After the second year of a secondary school course, students are typically streamed into a wide range of course combinations, making the total number of subject they have to sit for in "O" level six to ten subjects. This includes science (Physics, Biology and Chemistry), humanities (Elective Geography/History, Pure Geography/History, Social Studies, Literature, etc.) and additional mathematics subject at a higher level, or "combined" subject modules.

Some schools have done away with the O level examination, and pupils only sit for the A level examination or the International Baccalaureate at the end of their sixth year (known as Year 6 or Junior College 2).

Co-curricular activities have become compulsory at the Secondary level, where all pupils must participate in at least one core CCA, and participation is graded together with other things like Leadership throughout the four years of Secondary education, in a scoring system. Competitions are organised so that students can have an objective towards to work, and in the case of musical groups, showcase talents. "Co-Curricular Activities". Archived from the original on 2007-08-29. Retrieved 2007-09-07.

Turkey

Figure: *Robert College in Istanbul*

Figure: *Istanbul Lisesi*

Secondary education includes all of the general, vocational and technical education institutions that provide at least three years of education after primary school. The system for being accepted to a high school changes almost every year. Sometimes private schools have different exams, sometimes there are 3 exams for 3 years, sometimes there's only one exam but it is calculated differently, sometimes they only look at your school grades. Secondary education aims to give students a good level of common knowledge, and to prepare them for higher education, for a vocation, for life and for business in line with their interests, skills and abilities. In the academic year 2001-2002 2.3 million students were being educated and 134,800 teachers were employed in 6,000 education institutions. General secondary education covers the education of children between 15-17 for at least three years after primary education.

General secondary education includes high schools, foreign language teaching high schools, Anatolian High Schools, high schools of science, Anatolia teacher training high schools, and Anatolia fine arts high schools.

Vocational and technical secondary education involves the institutions that both raise students as manpower in business and other professional areas, prepare them for higher education and meet the objectives of general secondary education. Vocational and technical secondary education includes technical education schools for boys, technical education schools for girls, trade and tourism schools, religious education schools, multi-programme high schools, special education schools, private education schools and health education schools. Secondary education is often referred as high school education, since the schools are called lyceum (tr: lise).

Ukraine

United States:

Figure: West Orange-Stark High School

As part of education in the United States, secondary education comprises grades 5, 6, 7, 8, and 9 through 12. This varies among school districts. Grades 9 through 12 is the most common grade structure for high school.

Vietnam

High school in Vietnam is called *Trung hÍc phÕ thông*, which means "Popular Middle School", for children from grade ten to grade twelve (age of 16 to 18). In high school, students have 12 subjects to learn, and all the 12 subjects are compulsory. For each main subject (Literature, Mathematics, Chemistry, Physics, Biology, History, Geography and Foreign language), there are two levels of study: Basic and Advanced. Subjects in advanced level will receive more time and intensiveness than the basic ones do. Students are divided into five groups:

- Basic group: All subjects are in basic level.
- Group A: Mathematics, Physics and Chemistry are in advanced level.
- Group B: Mathematics, Chemistry and Biology are in advanced level.
- Group C: Literature, History and Geography are in advanced level.
- Group D: Mathematics, Literature and Foreign language are in advanced level.

Students will graduate from high school if they have passed Graduation Tests of 6 subjects. If not, they must wait for the next year's tests. Students must graduate from high school to attend a university.

Egypt

The secondary school, or publicly known as Thanawya Amma. It is a three years programme after which the student, according to his score in the final 2 years, can join a higher level of education in a university or, when the score is less, an institution of education that issues a degree not equal with the university one.

3

Alternative Education

Alternative education, also known as *non-traditional education* or *educational alternative*, is a broad term that may be used to refer to all forms of education outside of traditional education (for all age groups and levels of education). This may include not only forms of education designed for students with special needs (ranging from teenage pregnancy to intellectual disability), but also forms of education designed for a general audience and employing alternative educational philosophies and methods.

Alternatives of the latter type are often the result of education reform and are rooted in various philosophies that are commonly fundamentally different from those of traditional compulsory education. While some have strong political, scholarly, or philosophical orientations, others are more informal associations of teachers and students dissatisfied with certain aspects of traditional education. These alternatives, which include charter schools, alternative schools, independent schools, homeschooling and autodidacticism vary, but often emphasize the value of small class size, close relationships between students and teachers, and a sense of community.

Alternative education may also allow for independent learning and engaging class activities.

Origins

"Alternative education" presupposes a kind of tradition to which the "alternative" is opposed. In general, this limits the term to the last two or three centuries, with the rise of standardized and, later, compulsory education at the primary and secondary levels. Many critics during this period suggested that the education of young people should be undertaken in radically different ways than the one in practice. In the 19th century, the Swiss humanitarian Johann Heinrich Pestalozzi; the American transcendentalists Amos Bronson Alcott, Ralph Waldo Emerson, and Henry David Thoreau; the founders of progressive education, John Dewey and Francis Parker; and educational pioneers, such as Friedrich Fröbel, Maria Montessori and Rudolf Steiner (founder of the Waldorf schools); among others, all insisted that education should be understood as the art of cultivating the moral, emotional, physical, psychological, and spiritual aspects of the developing child. Anarchists such as Leo Tolstoy and Francisco Ferrer Guardia emphasized education as a force for political liberation, secularism, and elimination of class distinctions. After World War II alternative approaches to early childhood education were developed in Reggio Emilia, Italy; this is known as the Reggio Emilia approach.It was started by Loris Malaguzzi.

More recently, social critics such as John Caldwell Holt, Paul Goodman, Frederick Mayer, George Dennison and Ivan Illich have examined education from more individualist, anarchist, and libertarian perspectives, that is, critiques of the ways that they feel conventional education subverts democracy by molding young people's understandings. Other writers, from the revolutionary Paulo Freire to American educators like Herbert Kohl and Jonathan Kozol, have criticized mainstream Western education from the viewpoint of their varied left-liberal and radical politics. The argument for an approach that caters more to the personal interest and learning style of each individual is supported by recent research that suggest that learner-responsible models prove to be more effective than the traditional teacher-responsible models. Ron Miller has identified five core elements common to many contemporary educational alternatives:

1. Respect for every person
2. Balance
3. Decentralization of authority
4. Noninterference between political, economic, and cultural spheres of society
5. A holistic worldview

Modern Forms

A wide variety of educational alternatives exist at the elementary, secondary, and tertiary levels of education. These generally fall into four major categories: school choice, alternative school, independent school, and home-based education. These general categories can be further broken down into more specific practices and methodologies.

School Choice

School choice is a term or label given to a wide array of programmes offering students and their families alternatives to publicly provided schools, to which students are generally assigned by the location of their family residence. In the United States, the most common option offered by 'school choice' programmes are educational voucher programmes. These programmes offer a given student and their family the option to take a subsidy from public educational funds and put that money towards tuition in private schools. This subsidy may also be accomplished through tax-credit programmes. Other 'school choice' options include open enrollment laws that allow students to attend other public schools and charter schools, and homeschooling.

Forms

Open Enrollment: Open enrollment refers to educational policies which allow residents of a state to enroll their children in any public school, provided the school has not reached its maximum capacity number for students, regardless of the school district in which a family resides. Open enrollment can be either intra-district or inter-district. Intra-district choice allows parents to send their children to any school within their designated district. Parents can enroll their children in schools outside of their catchment area. Inter-district school choice allows parents to select public schools outside of their resident district.

Inequality of Open Enrollment

An open enrollment policy allows parents to choose the school they want their children to attend from any of the schools in their area, provided there is space for them. This definition gives the impression that everyone has an equal opportunity to choose a school, but the reality of such equality has been called into question. For example, in rural areas the option of taking advantage of open enrollment is greatly diminished because of limited access to alternate schools.

A family's socio-economic status also plays a role in its ability to take advantage of an open enrollment policy. Choosing a school for a child often requires financial resources and knowledge of the available options and appropriate criteria on which to base selections, which are shaped by parental income and education. Neighbourhoods of higher poverty rates also often have the reputation of being inferior or academically less successful than other schools, and because of this there is often a higher turnover rate of teachers. Parents also have a tendency to believe this stereotype without looking further into the school's quality.

To test the relationship between a neighbourhood's contextual factors and school performance Geographic Information Systems (GIS) are used. In one study complete in South Carolina using a GIS, it was found that a neighbourhood's socio-economic status played an important role in elementary school achievements.

Another criticism of open enrollment policies is that school choice in Western industrialized countries benefits middle-class families more than lower-class families. While upper-class families tend to take advantage of private schools, middle-class families are more likely to take advantage of inter-district and intra-district open enrollment. More specifically, in Westernised countries white middle-class families benefit more from school choice than minority or lower-class families.

Vouchers

When the government pays tuition to a private school on behalf of the parents, this is usually referred to as a voucher. A voucher is given to the family for them to spend at any school of their choice for their child's study. The two most common voucher designs are universal vouchers and means-tested vouchers. Means-tested vouchers are directed towards low-income families and constitute the bulk of voucher plans in the United States.

Tuition Tax Credits

A tuition tax credit is similar to most other familiar tax credits. Certain states allow individuals and/or businesses to deduct a certain amount of their income taxes to donate to education. Depending on the programme, these donations can either go to a public school or to a School Tuition Organization (STO), or both. The donations that go to public schools are often used to help pay for after-school programmes, schools trips, or school supplies. The donations that go to School Tuition Organizations are used by the STO to create scholarships that are then given to students. These programmes currently exist in Arizona, Florida, Illinois, Iowa, Minnesota, Pennsylvania and Rhode Island in the United States.

Charter Schools

Charter schools are public schools with more relaxed rules and regulations. These relaxed rules tend to deal with things like Teacher Union contracts and state curriculum. The majority of states (and the District of Columbia) have charter school laws. Minnesota was the first state to have a charter school law and the first charter school in the United States, City Academy High School, opened in St. Paul, Minnesota in 1992. Dayton, Ohio has between 22–26% of all children in charter schools. This is the highest percentage in the nation. Other hotbeds for charter schools are Kansas City (24%), Washington, D.C. (20-24%) and Arizona. Almost 1 in 4 public schools in Arizona are charter schools, comprising about 8% of total enrollment. Charter schools can also come in the form of Cyber Charters. Cyber charter schools deliver the majority of their instruction over the internet instead of in a school building. And, like charter schools, they are public schools, but free of many of the rules and regulations that public schools must follow.

Magnet Schools

Magnet schools are public schools that often have a specialized function like science, technology or art. These magnet schools, unlike charter schools, are not open to all children. Much like many private schools, there are some (but not all) magnet schools that require a test to get in.

Home Schooling

"Home education" or "home schooling" is instruction in a child's home, or provided primarily by a parent, or under direct parental control. Informal home education has always taken place, and formal instruction in the home has at times also been very popular. As public education grew in popularity during the 1900s, however, the number of people educated at home using a planned curriculum dropped. In the last 20 years, in contrast, the number of children being formally educated at home has grown tremendously, in particular in the United States. The laws relevant to home education differ throughout the country. In some states the parent simply needs to notify the state that the child will be educated at home. In other states the parents are not free to educate at home unless at least one parent is a certified teacher and yearly progress reports are reviewed by the state. Such laws are not always enforced however. According to the federal government, about 1.1 million children were home educated in 2003.

Support

The goal of school choice programmes is to give parents more control over their child's education, and to allow parents to pursue the most appropriate learning environments for children. For example school choice may enable parents to choose a school that provides religious instruction for their children; stronger discipline; better foundational skills including reading, writing, mathematics, and science; everyday skills from handling money to farming, or other desirable foci.

Supporters of voucher models school choice argue that choice creates competition between schools for students. Schools that fail to attract students can be closed. Advocates of school choice argue that this competition for students (and the education dollars that come with them) create a catalyst for schools to create innovative programmes, become more responsive to parental demands, and to increase student achievement. Caroline Hoxby suggests that this competition increases the productivity of a school. Hoxby describes a productive school as being one that produces high achievements in its student for each dollar that is spends. Others suggest that this competition gives parents more power to influence their child's school in the school marketplace. Parents and students become the consumers and schools must work to attract new students with new programmes. Parents also have the ability to punish schools that they judge to be inferior by leaving the 'bad' school for a better, more highly ranked school. Parents look for schools that will advocate for the needs of their child and if the school does not meet the needs required for that child, parents have the choice to find a school that will be more suitable

Another argument in favour of school choice is based on cost-effectiveness. Studies undertaken by the Cato Institute and other libertarian and conservative thinktanks conclude that privately run education usually costs between one quarter and one half of publicly run education while giving superior outcomes.

Others argue that since children from impoverished families almost exclusively attend public schools, school choice programmes would allow these students to opt out of bad schools and acquire a better education, thereby granting the decision-making power to students and their parents, not school administrators. Supporters say this would level the playing field by broadening opportunities for low-income students to attend as good of schools as the middle classes instead of the current two-tiered system which educates the middle and upper classes, but not the lower classes, particularly minorities. The Organisation Internationale pour le Droit à l'Education et la Liberté d'Enseignement (OIDEL), an international non-profit organization for the development of freedom of education, maintains that the right to education is a fundamental human right which cannot exist without the presence of State benefits and the protection of individual liberties. According to the organization, freedom of education notably implies the freedom for parents to choose a school for their children without discrimination on the basis of finances. To advance freedom of education, OIDEL promotes a greater parity between public and private schooling systems.

Criticisms

Many opponents of school choice such as Martin Carnoy argue that public schools perform similarly to private schools when teaching similar groups of students, and that the conception of public schools as "failing" in comparison to private schools is more due to the demographic differences between public and private schools than to actual differences in the quality of the education the schools offer. "School choice" as it entails a switch from public to private schooling would therefore do little to solve the problems facing the educational system, since a private school would perform no better than a public school when faced with exactly the same student body.

Opponents of school choice often object to the use of the term itself, viewing it as loaded political vocabulary.

Opponents also argue that school choice in the form of vouchers could result in nothing more than a cash-handout for many middle-class and wealthy families already sending their kids to private schools, with disadvantaged families either unable to secure enrollment or unable to cover costs in addition to the vouchers. Under voucher programmes, private schools may be able to reject students who are expensive to educate due to special needs or students who they feel would disrupt the learning environment, and opponents of voucher programmes argue that this would leave such students under a system of de facto segregation. School choice opponents also charge that students who are unable, because of their parents' educational level or the lack of reliable transportation, to leave their local schools may be hurt as additional funding is cut from their schools. Research indicates that adoption of current public school reform proposals, particularly the idea of providing parents with education vouchers, is likely to lead to an increase in private school enrollment or at least an increase in enrollment at schools traditionally defined as private with a blurring of the distinction between public and private schools due to the public source of the voucher financing.

Although school choice does give parents the option to move their children to a better school, opponents of school choice draw attention to the effects this choice has on the 'bad' schools left behind. They argue that the movement from bad schools leaves behind an increased ethnic segregation. Although the neighbourhoods around a school may be ethnically diverse, because of the option for intra-district choice, there has been an increasing amount of segregation within some schools. Schools that are failing to attract students often are found to have larger students poverty rates as well as higher proportions of minority students.

Within countries with high immigration rates, such as Canada, parents within the dominate group leave behind schools that have high levels of immigrant students in order to attend schools that have a higher majority of students that are fluent in the national language. Parents move their children away from these schools in order to protect them from ethno-linguistic neediness that may cause their children to receive less attention or get behind academically because of new immigrant students.

It has also been found in countries with large proportions of immigrants, that although school choice is an option for all parents, parents who do not fluently speak the official language have a much harder time accessing information related to ratings of schools and school activities that would give them the necessary knowledge to make the appropriate school selection.

School Choice is also criticized as being beneficial to urban and suburban families, but not to families living in remote rural areas. School Choice is not practical for rural families who live in areas with limited accessibility to different choices of schools within reasonable distances. While urban schools provide more options to move away from schools that are failing, rural families do not have the options available to provide an 'escape' from bad schools, making the use of school choice as competition for schools to create innovative programmes, unproductive in rural areas. Families in rural areas are therefore only able to make improvements in academic quality is to actively work toward these changes instead of creating competition to encourage the school to make changes on its own.

International Overview and Major Institutional Options

France: The French government subsidizes most private primary and secondary schools, including those affiliated with religious denominations, under contracts stipulating that education must follow the same curriculum as public schools and that schools cannot discriminate on grounds of religion or force pupils to attend religion classes.

This system of *école libre* (Free Schooling) is mostly used not for religious reasons, but for practical reasons (private schools may offer more services, such as after-class tutoring) as well as the desire of parents living in disenfranchised areas to send their children away from the local schools, where they perceive that the youth are too prone to delinquency or have too many difficulties keeping up with schooling requirements that the educational content is bound to suffer. The threatened repealing of that status in the 1980s triggered mass street demonstrations in favour of the status.

Sweden

Sweden reformed its school system in 1992. Its system of school choice is one of the freest in the world, allowing students to use public funds for the publicly or privately run school of their choice, including religious and for-profit schools. Fifteen years after the reform, private school enrolment had increased from 1% to 10% of the student population.

Canada

Ontario is the only large province in Canada with limited school choice funding, Catholic, Secular and one Protestant school receive funding and are open to all students. In 2003, following an international human rights ruling, the provincial Conservative government gradually introduced a tax credit over 5 years, (when it would have been fully implemented it would have been worth up to 50% of tuition to a maximum of $3,500 at any independent school in Ontario) in order to meet the human rights norms and expand funded choice to all interested parents. However, the tax credit was retroactively canceled by the subsequent Liberal government when it had been only been in place for two years to the $1,000 point. Currently there are over 900 independent schools in Ontario. The only school choice programme available to non-rich parents who wish to send their children to an independent school is a privately funded programme called Children First, a programme of The Fraser Institute.

Chile

In Chile, there is an extensive voucher system in which the state pays private and municipal schools directly, based on average attendance (90% of the country students utilize such a system). The result has been a steady increase in the number and recruitment of private schools that show consistently better results in standardized testing than municipal schools. The reduction of students in municipal schools has gone from 78% of all students in 1981, to 57% in 1990, and to less than 50% in 2005.

Regarding vouchers in Chile, researchers have found that when controls for the student's background (parental income and education) are introduced, the difference in performance between public and private subsectors is not significant. There is also greater variation within each subsector than between the two systems.

United States

A variety of forms of school choice exist in the United States.

Vouchers

Vouchers currently exist in Wisconsin, Ohio, Florida, and, most recently, the District of Columbia and Georgia. The largest and oldest Voucher programme is in Milwaukee. Started in 1990, and expanded in 1995, it currently allows no more than 15% of the district's public school enrollment to use vouchers. As of 2005 over 14,000 students use vouchers and they are nearing the 15% cap.

School vouchers are legally controversial in some states; in 2005 the Florida Supreme Court found that school vouchers were unconstitutional under the Florida Constitution.

In the U.S., the legal and moral precedents for vouchers may have been set by the G.I. bill, which includes a voucher programme for university-level education of veterans. The G.I. bill permits veterans to take their educational benefits at religious schools, an extremely divisive issue when applied to primary and secondary schools.

In *Zelman v. Simmons-Harris*, 536 U.S. 639 (2002), the Supreme Court of the United States held that school vouchers could be used to pay for education in sectarian schools without violating the Establishment Clause of the First Amendment. As a result, states are basically free to enact voucher programmes that provide funding for any school of the parent's choosing.

The Supreme Court has not decided, however, whether states can provide vouchers for secular schools only, excluding sectarian schools. Proponents of funding for parochial schools argue that such an exclusion would violate the free exercise clause. However, in *Locke v. Davey*, 540 U.S. 712 (2004), the Court held that states could exclude majors in "devotional theology" from an otherwise generally available college scholarship. The Court has not indicated, however, whether this holding extends to the public school context, and it may well be limited to the context of individuals training to enter the ministry.

Tuition Tax Credits

Tuition tax credit programmes currently exist in Arizona, Florida, Illinois, Iowa, Minnesota, Pennsylvania, Rhode Island and recently Georgia. Arizona has probably the most well known and fastest growing tax credit programme. In the Arizona School Tuition Organization Tax Credit programme individuals can deduct up to $500 and couples filing joint returns can deduct up to $1000. About 20,000 children received scholarships in the 2003-2004 school year. And, since the programme has started in 1998, over 77,000 scholarships have been granted. The Arizona programme was challenged in court by a group of state taxpayers on the grounds that the tax credit violated the First Amendment because the tuition grants could go to students who attend private schools including schools with religious affiliations. Typically, taxpayers are not allowed to bring suit against the government regarding how taxes are spent because injury would be purely speculative. The Court ruled 5-4 to let the tax credit programme stand In April 2011, a Fairleigh Dickinson University PublicMind poll found that a majority of American voters (60%) felt that the tax credits support school choice for parents whereas 26% felt as it the tax credits support religion.

In Iowa, the Educational Opportunities Act was signed into law in 2006, creating a pool of tax credits for eligible donors to student tuition organizations (STOs). At first, these tax caps were $5 million but in 2007, Governor Chet Culver increased the total amount to $7.5 million. The Iowa Alliance for Choice in Education (Iowa ACE) oversees the STOs and advocates for school choice in Iowa.

Greater Opportunities for Access to Learning (GOAL) is the Georgia programme which offers a state income tax credit to donors of scholarships to private schools. Representative David Casas was responsible for passing the Georgia version of the school choice legislation.

Charter Schools

The majority of states (and the District of Columbia) have charter school laws. Minnesota was the first state to have a charter school law and the first charter school in the United States, City Academy, opened in St. Paul, Minnesota in 1992. Dayton, Ohio has between 22–26% of all children in charter schools. This is the highest percentage in the nation. Other hotbeds for charter schools are Kansas City (24%), Washington, D.C. (20-24%) and the State of Arizona. Almost 1 in 4 public schools in Arizona are charter schools, comprising about 8% of total enrollment. Charter schools can also come in the form of Cyber Charters. Cyber charter schools deliver the majority of their instruction over the internet instead of in a school building. And, like charter schools, they are public schools, but free of many of the rules and regulations that public schools must follow.

Magnet Schools

Magnet schools are public schools that often have a specialized function like science, technology or art. These magnet schools, unlike charter schools, are not open to all children. Much like many private schools, the students must test into the school.

Home Schooling

The laws relevant to homeschooling differ between US states. In some states the parent simply needs to notify the state that the child will be educated at home. In other states the parents are not free to educate at home unless at least one parent is a certified teacher and yearly progress reports are reviewed by the state. Such laws are not always enforced however. According to the Federal Government, about 1.1 million children were Home Educated in 2003.

College

The United States has school choice at the university level. College students can get subsidized tuition by attending *any* public college or university within their state of residence. Furthermore, the U.S. federal government provides tuition assistance for both public and private colleges via the G.I. Bill and federally guaranteed student loans.

Alternative School

The term alternative school is used to describe a wide variety of educational approaches employing nontraditional philosophies, curricula and/or methods. Some alternative schools have strong philosophical, political, or practical orientations, while others are more *ad-hoc* assemblies of teachers and students seeking to explore possibilities not available within mainstream or traditional education.

Alternative Education of At-Risk Students and Drop-out Prevention

Advocates of programmes designed to prevent, or discourage, students from dropping out before they graduate (usually from high school) believe that leaving school without a diploma negatively impacts an individual's professional and personal life. Collectively, this negatively impacts society.

Drop Out Prevention Methods

Individual schools in the U.S. have tried to tackle the problem through their own programme initiatives. Three that have been used and studied for success are: the Check & Connect programme; the Career Academies initiative; and the Talent Development High School model. These programmes are designed to work with high risk students before they drop out of school. The Check & Connect Programme This alternative is a dropout prevention model that was developed in Minnesota through a partnership with the University of Minnesota, the local public schools and community service organizations. It was used in the Minneapolis public schools, specifically focusing in on students with learning, emotional and behavioural disabilities. The "Check" portion pairs each student with a mentor, deemed a "monitor". This mentor figure assesses attendance, academics and overall performance with regular discussions about twice a month. The "Connect" aspect utilizes this individualized attention to connect this student with school personnel, family and community service providers that can intervene to keep the student on track.

Effectiveness: A 1998 study conducted by Sinclair and colleagues shows overall positive effects on 94 high school students from Minneapolis public schools in the Check & Connect programme. The study found that students enrolled in the programme were significantly less likely to have dropped out of school after the end of freshman year (9% compared with 30%). This positive outcome remained after the final check-up at the end of senior year—39% of students enrolled dropped out of high school compared to 58% of those not enrolled. In addition to actually staying in school, the study also found the students' progress in school to be positive as well; Check & Connect students earned more course credits in their night-grade year than non-intervention students.

Cost Efficiency: According to the Dakota County schools in Minnesota, the cost of implementing the Check & Connect programme is around $1,400 per student in 2001-2002. This model is very cost-inefficient, and now in 2011, the total may even be costlier.

The Career Academies Initiative

This alternative intervenes to target the most at-risk students. The Career Academies is a school-within-a-school model with a career-themed approach to learning. Developed 35 years ago, this alternative has evolved and around 2,500 academies are operated nationwide. It tends to be found in larger high schools and helps create a smaller community by keeping students with the same teachers for three or fours years of high school. The programme requires students to take the career-related courses with the "Academy" in subjects such as finance or technology and even partners with local employers to offer internship opportunities.

Effectiveness: A 2000 study conducted by Kemple and Snipes shows overall positive effects for 1,700 high school students in nine different Career Academies. The study found that the most at-risk students participating in the programme produced significantly fewer dropouts (21% compared with 32%). When assessing progress in school, the high-risk students earned more credits by their senior year and 40% had earned enough credits to graduate, as opposed to only 25% of non-intervention students, posting positive results for the programme.

Cost Efficiency: According to the California Partnership Academies, average cost estimates for the Career Academies intervention are $600 more per pupil than the average cost for a non-Academy student in 2004. This figure does not include additional costs of intensive services for high-risk students.

The Talent Development High School Model

This alternative was developed in 1994 by The Centre for Research on the Education of Students Placed at Risk and initiated at Patterson High School in Baltimore, Maryland. The Talent Development High School (TDHS) approach is an entire reform intervention, with dropout prevention as one component. It includes breaking the larger high school into smaller learning communities, like Career Academies, but is more extensive. There is a separate ninth grade academy, a career academy for the upper grades and an additional "Twilight School" after school programme for those with chronic discipline and attendance issues. This model homes in on reforming students' low expectations and schools' poor academic preparation through a college-preparatory sequence in ninth and tenth grade as well as increased focus on English and Math courses.

Effectiveness: A 2005 study conducted by Kemple, Herlihy, and Smith, which followed 30 cohorts of participants for four years in Philadelphia, Pennsylvania, shows positive effects of the Talent Development High School (TDHS) model, primarily on academic progress. The study found that students using this model earned more course credits over the first two years of high school than those not in the programme (9.5 credits compared with 8.6 credits). These students were also more likely to move onto the tenth grade (68% compared with 60%).

Cost Efficiency: According to Johns Hopkins University 's Centre for the Social Organization of Schools (CSOS), the developer of the initiative, average costs for a student participating in the Talent Development High School model run an additional $350 a year per student. This estimate includes the cost of materials and ongoing technical assistance. These are just three of many possible alternative education models to help at-risk students.

The matter has also gained national attention. On March 1, 2010, President Barack Obama called on states to identify and focus on schools with graduation rates below 60 percent. Those districts could be eligible for federal aid as his budget proposal includes $900 million in "school turnaround grants" on top of $3.5 billion in federal dollars the administration has committed to persistently low-performing schools. With respect to keeping students engaged and on-track to graduation specifically, he committed $50 million to the Graduation Promise Fund.

Popular Education

Popular education was related in the 19th century to the workers' movement. Such experiences have been continued throughout the 20th century, such as the folk high schools in Scandinavian countries, or the "popular universities" in France.

Popular education is a concept grounded in notions of class, political struggle, and social transformation. The term is a translation from the Spanish educación popular or the Portuguese educação popular and rather than the English usage as when describing a 'popular television programme,' popular here means 'of the people.' More specifically 'popular' refers to the 'popular classes,' which include peasants, the unemployed, the working class and sometimes the lower middle class. The designation of 'popular' is meant most of all to exclude the upper class and upper middle class.

Popular education is used to classify a wide array of educational endeavours and has been a strong tradition in Latin America since the end of the first half of the 20th-century. These endeavours are either composed of or carried out in the interests of the popular classes. The diversity of projects and endeavours claiming or receiving the label of popular education makes the term difficult to precisely define. Generally, one can say that popular education is class-based in nature and rejects the notion of education as transmission or 'banking education.' It stresses a dialectic or dialogical model between educator and educand. This model is explored in great detail in the works of one of the foremost popular educators Paulo Freire.

Though sharing many similarities with other forms of alternative education, popular education is a distinct form in its own right. In the words of Liam Kane: "What distinguishes popular education from 'adult, ' 'non-formal,' 'distance, ' or 'permanent education, for example, is that in the context of social injustice, education can never be politically neutral: if it does not side with the poorest and marginalised sectors- the 'oppressed' – in an attempt to transform society, then it necessarily sides with the 'oppressors' in maintaining the existing structures of oppression, even if by default."

Europe

Popular education began at the crossroads between politics and pedagogy, and strongly relies on the democratic ideal of the Enlightenment, which considered public education as a main tool of individual and collective emancipation, and thus the necessary conditions of autonomy, in accordance to Immanuel Kant's *Was Ist Aufklärung?* (What is Enlightenment?), published five years before the 1789 French Revolution, during which the Condorcet report established public instruction in France.

Jean-Jacques Rousseau's *L'Emile: Or, On Education* (1762) was another obvious theoretical influence, as well as the works of Nikolaj Frederik Severin Grundtvig (1783–1872), at the origins of the Nordic movement of folk high schools. During the 19th century, popular education movements were involved, in particular in France, in the Republican and Socialist movement. A main component of the workers' movement, popular education was also strongly influenced by positivist, materialist and laïcité, if not anti-clerical, ideas. Popular education may be defined as an educational technique designed to raise the consciousness of its participants and allow them to become more aware of how an individual's personal experiences are connected to larger societal problems. Participants are empowered to act to effect change on the problems that affect them.

19th Century

One of the roots of popular education was the Condorcet report during the 1789 French Revolution. These ideas became an important component of the Republican and Socialist movement. Following the split of the First International at the 1872 Hague Congress between the "anti-authoritarian socialists" (anarchists) and the Marxists, popular education remained an important part of the workers' movement, in particular in the anarcho-syndicalist movement, strong in France, Spain and Italy. It was one of the important theme treated during the 1907 International Anarchist Congress of Amsterdam.

In France

During the Second Empire, Jean Macé founded the *Ligue de l'enseignement* (Teaching League) in 1866; during the Lille Congress in 1885, Macé reaffirmed the masonic inspiration of this league devoted to popular instruction. Following the 1872 Hague Congress and the split between Marxists and anarchists, Fernand Pelloutier set up in France various *Bourses du travail* centres, where workers gathered and discussed politics and sciences.

The Jules Ferry laws in the 1880s, establishing free, laic, mandatory and public education, were one of the founding stones of the Third Republic (1871–1940), set up in the aftermaths of the 1870 Franco-Prussian War and the Paris Commune.

Furthermore, most of the teachers, who were throughout one of the main support of the Third Republic, so much that it has been called the *République des instituteurs* ("Republic of Teachers"), while the teachers themselves were called, because of their Republican anti-clericalism, the *hussards noirs de la République*, supported Alfred Dreyfus against the conservatives during the Dreyfus Affair. One of its consequences was for them to set up free educational lectures of humanist topics for adults in order to struggle against the spread of anti-semitism, which was not limited to the far-right but also affected the workers' movement.

Paul Robin's work at the orphanage in Cempuis was the model for Francisco Ferrer's Modern School in Spain. Robin taught atheism and internationalism, and broke new ground with co-ed schooling, and teaching orphans with the same respect given to other children. He taught that the individual should develop in harmony with the world, on the physical, moral, and intellectual planes.

Scandinavia

In Denmark, the concept of *folk high school* was pioneered in 1844 by Nikolaj Frederik Severin Grundtvig. By 1870, Denmark had 50 of these institutions. The first in Sweden, *Folkhögskolan Hvilan,* was established in 1868 outside of Lund.

In 1882, liberal and socialist students at Uppsala University in Sweden founded the association *Verdandi* for popular education. Between 1888 and 1954 it published 531 educational booklets on various topics (*Verdandis småskrifter*). Some Swedish proponents of *folkbildning* have adopted an anglicisation of *folkbuilding*

A Swedish bibliography on popular education with 25,000 references to books and articles between 1850 and 1950 is integrated in the Libris catalogue of the Royal Library.

20th Century

Popular education continued to be an important field of socialist politics, reemerging in particular during the Popular Front in 1936–38, while *autogestion* (self-management), a main tenet of the anarcho-syndicalist movement, became a popular slogan following the May '68 revolt.

The Escuela Moderna *(1901–1907)*

The *Escuela Moderna* (Modern School) was founded in 1901 in Barcelona by free-thinker Francesc Ferrer i Guàrdia, and became a leading inspiration of many various movements. Opposed to the "dogmas of conventional education Ferrer set a system based on reason, science, and observation." The school's stated goal was to "educate the working class in a rational, secular and non-coercive setting". In practice, high tuition fees restricted attendance at the school to wealthier middle class students. It was privately hoped that when the time was ripe for revolutionary action, these students would be motivated to lead the working classes. It closed in 1906. The *Escuela Moderna*, and Ferrer's ideas generally, formed the inspiration for a series of *Modern Schools* in the United States, Cuba, South

America and London. The first of these was started in New York City in 1911. It also inspired the Italian newspaper *Università popolare*, founded in 1901.

France

Following the 1981 presidential election which brought to power the Socialist Party (PS)'s candidate, François Mitterrand, his Minister of Education, Alain Savary, supported Jean Lévi's initiative to create a public high school, delivering the baccalauréat, but organized on the principles of *autogestion* (or self-management): this high school took the name of *Lycée autogéré de Paris* (LAP). The LAP explicitly inspired itself by the Oslo Experimental High School, opened in 1967 in Norway, as well as the Saint-Nazaire Experimental High School, opened six months before the LAP. Furthermore, the secondary school Vitruve was another source of inspiration (it opened in 1962 in the 20th arrondissement of Paris, and is still active). Theoretical references include Célestin Freinet and his comrades from the I.C.E.M., as well as Raymond Fonvieille, Fernand Oury, and others theoreticians of "institutional pedagogy", as well as those coming from the institutional analysis movement, in particular René Lourau, as well as members of the institutional psychotherapeutic movement, which were a main component in the 1970s of the anti-psychiatric movement (of which Félix Guattari was an important member). Since 2005, the LAP has created contact with others self-managed firms, in the REPAS network (*Réseau d'échanges et de pratiques alternatives et solidaires*, Network of Exchange of Solidarity and Alternative Practices").

A *second generation* for such *folk high school* meant to educate the people and the masses spread in the society (mainly for workers) just before the *French Front populaire* experience, as a reaction among teachers and intellectuals following the February 6, 1934 riots organized by far-right leagues. Issues devoted to *free-thinking* such as workers' self-management were thought and taught during that time, since the majority of attendants were proletarians interested in politics. Hence, some received the name of *Université prolétarienne* (Proletarian University) instead of *Université populaire* (Popular University) in some cities around the country. The reactionary Vichy regime put an end to such tentatives during World War II. That tendency continued in the post-war period, yet topical lectures turned to be more practical and focused on daily life matters. Nowadays, the largest remnant is located in Bas-Rhin and Haut-Rhin *départements*.

Following World War II, popular teaching attempts were initiated mainly by the anarchist movement. Already in 1943, Joffre Dumazedier, Bénigno Cacérès, Paul Lengrand, Joseph Rovan and others founded the *Peuple et Culture* (People and Culture) network, aimed at democratization of culture. Joffre Dumazedier conceptualized, at the Liberation, the concept of "cultural development" to oppose the concept of "economic development", thus foreshading the current Human Development Index. Historian Jean Maitron, for example, was director of the Apremont school in Vendée from 1950 to 1955.

Such popular educations were also a major feature of May '68 and of the following decenie, leading in particular to the establishment of the University of Paris VIII – Vincennes in Paris, in 1969. The Vincennes University (today located in Saint-Denis) was first a "Experimental University Centre," with an interest in reshaping relations between students and teachers (so-called "*mandarins*", in reference to the bureaucrats of Imperial China, for their authority and classic, Third Republic pedagogy) as well as between the University itself and society. Thus, Vincennes was largely opened to those who did not have their *baccalauréat* diploma, as well as to foreigners. Its courses were focused on Freudo-Marxism, psychoanalysis, Marxist theory, cinema, theater, urbanism or artificial intelligence. Famous intellectuals such as Gilles Deleuze, Michel Foucault, Jacques Lacan and others held seminars there, in full classrooms where no seats could be found.

The assistance was very heterogeneous. For instance, musicians such as Richard Pinhas assisted at Deleuze's courses, and after having written the *Anti-Oedipus* (1972) with Félix Guattari, Deleuze used to say that non-specialists had best understood their work. Furthermore, Vincennes had no amphitheatres, representatives of the *mandarin* teacher facing and dominating by his position several hundreds students silenciously taking notes. It also enforced a strict equality between professors and teaching assistants. The Student Revolt continued throughout the 1970s in both Vincennes and the University of Paris X: Nanterre, created in 1964. In 1980, the Minister of Education Alice Saunier-Seité imposed the transfer of Vincennes' University to Saint-Denis. Although education has been normalized in the 1980s, during the Mitterrand era, in both Saint-Denis and Vincennes, these universities have retained a less traditional outlook than the classic Sorbonne, where courses tend to be more conservative and sociological composition more middle-upper class.

Another attempt in popular education, specifically targeted towards the question of philosophy (France being one of the rare country where this discipline is taught in *terminale*, the last year of high school which culminate in the *baccalauréat* degree) was the creation, in 1983, of the open university named *Collège international de philosophie* (International Philosophy College, or Ciph), by Jacques Derrida, François Châtelet, Jean-Pierre Faye and Dominique Lecourt, in an attempt to re-think the teaching of philosophy in France, and to liberate it from any institutional authority (most of all from the University). As the ancient *Collège de France*, created by Francis I, it is free and open to everyone. The Ciph was first directed by Derrida, then by Philippe Lacoue-Labarthe, and has had as teaching members Giorgio Agamben, Alain Badiou, Sidi Mohamed Barkat, Geoffrey Bennington, François Châtelet, José Gil, Olivier LeCour Grandmaison, Antonio Negri, etc. The Ciph is still active.

In 2002 philosopher Michel Onfray initiated Université populaire de Caen in his hometown and starting a long seminar dealing with *hedonistic philosophy* from ancient times to May'68 events in French society, for at least ten years, currently year 8 will start. His very topical subject in this seminar keeps going with a *free-thinking* spirit, since people are invited on the whole to rethink History of ideas to get rid of any Christian influence. Despite the same name of *Université populaire*, it is not linked to the European federation of associations inherited from the second generation. In 2004, Michel Onfray expanded the experience to other cities such as Arras, Lyon, Narbonne, Avignon, and Mons (in Belgium) ; each with various lectures and teachers joining his idea. Last but not least of those *Universités populaires* is the one that opened in Argentan : Its focus is meant to deliver a culture of culinary tastes to nonworking people, through lectures and practises of famous *chefs*.

Latin America

Popular education is most commonly understood as an approach to education that emerged in Latin America during the 1930s. Closely linked with Marxism and particularly Liberation theology. Best known amongst popular educators is the Brazilian Paulo Freire. Freire, and consequently the popular education movement in Latin America, draws heavily upon the work of John Dewey and Antonio Gramsci. One of the features of popular education in Latin America has been participatory action research (PAR).

United States & Canada

In the United States & Canada popular education influenced social justice education and critical pedagogy, though there are differences. At the same time, however, there are examples of popular education in the U.S. & Canada that grew up alongside and independently of popular education in Latin America.

United States

Scholar and community-worker Myles Horton and his Highlander Folk School (now Highlander Research and Education Centre) and his work in Tennessee can be classified as popular education. Horton's studies at Union Theological Seminary in New York under Reinhold Niebuhr in the 1920s parallels the emergence of liberation theology in Latin America and both are heavily influenced by socialism and a focus on the practical relationships between Christianity and everyday life. Niebuhr, however, was a staunch anti-communist while liberation theology has a much closer relationship to the work of Karl Marx. Additionally, popular education has been linked to populism and land-grant universities with their cooperative extension programmes.

The connection between popular education and Marxism, unfortunately, undermined a great deal of its influence as a result of McCarthyism and the red scare during the Cold War. Nevertheless, Highlander Folk School, for example, played a significant role in the civil rights movement providing a space for leaders to consult and plan.

Independent School

Independent, or private, schools have more flexibility in staff selection and educational approach. The most plentiful of these are Montessori schools, Waldorf schools (the latter are also called Steiner schools after their founder), and Friends schools. Other independent schools include democratic, or free schools such as Sands School, Summerhill School and Sudbury Valley School, Krishnamurti schools, open classroom schools, those based on experiential education, as well as schools which teach using international curriculum such as the International Baccalaureate and Round Square schools. An increasing number of traditionally independent school forms now also exist within state-run, public education; this is especially true of the Waldorf and Montessori schools. The majority of independent schools offer at least partial scholarships.

Homeschooling

Families who seek alternatives based on educational, philosophical, or religious reasons, or if there appears to be no nearby educational alternative can decide to have home-based education. One branch is termed unschooling, an approach based on interest rather than a set curriculum. Others enroll in umbrella schools which provide a curriculum to follow. Many choose this alternative for religious-based reasons, but practitioners of home-based education are of all backgrounds and philosophies.

Higher Education

Alternative teaching methodologies in the realm of higher education may include various forms of on-line and computer-based education, various forms of classroom education other than the traditional lecture or discussion format, or alternative curricula (such as interdisciplinarity). Alternative forms of higher education are often employed by more traditional institutions alongside their regular curriculum, as the primary focus of an alternative educational institution, or as a means of self-education.

Self-education

Self-directed enquiry as an educational process is recognized at all levels of education, from the unschooling of young children to the autodidacticism of adults, and may occur either separately from or concurrently with more traditional forms of education.

Other

There are also some interesting grey areas with defining alternative education. For instance, home-educators have combined to create resource centres where they meet as often as five or more days a week, but their members all consider themselves home-educated. In some states publicly run school districts have set up programmes for homeschoolers whereby they are considered enrolled, and have access to school resources and facilities. Also, many traditional schools have incorporated methods originally found only in alternative education into their general approach, so the line between alternative and mainstream education is continually becoming more blurred.

Autodidacticism

Autodidacticism (also autodidactism) or self-education is self-directed learning that is related to but different from informal learning.

In a sense, autodidacticism is "learning on your own" or "by yourself", and an autodidact is a self-teacher. Autodidacticism is a contemplative, absorptive procession. Some autodidacts spend a great deal of time reviewing the resources of libraries and educational websites. One may become an autodidact at nearly any point in one's life. While some may have been informed in a conventional manner in a particular field, they may choose to inform themselves in other, often unrelated areas. Many notable contributions have been made by autodidacts.

Autodidactism is only one facet of learning, and is usually, but not necessarily, complemented by learning in formal and informal spaces: from classrooms to other social settings. Many autodidacts seek instruction and guidance from experts, friends, teachers, parents, siblings, and community. Enquiry into autodidacticism has implications for learning theory, educational research, educational philosophy and educational psychology.

Modern Education and Autodidacticism

Autodidacticism is always a complement of modern education. Armstrong (2012) claimed that in higher education students should be given more materials suitable for self-study. Students should be encouraged to do more independent work. While Leonardo da Vinci was a privileged autodidact, the Industrial Revolution created a new situation. The creation of secular societies allowed many to pursue scientific interests and to develop scientific knowledge through academic or autodidactic learning.

Before the 20th century only a small minority of people received an advanced academic education. As stated by Joseph Whitworth in his influential report on industry dated from 1853, literacy rates were higher in the United States. However, even in the United States, most children were not completing high school. High school education was necessary to become a teacher. A large percentage of those completing high school also attended college, usually to pursue a professional degree, such as law or medicine, or a divinity degree.

Collegiate teaching was based on the classics (Latin, philosophy, ancient history, theology) until the early 19th century. There were few if any institutions of higher learning offering studies in engineering or science before 1800. Institutions such as the Royal Society did much to promote scientific learning, including public lectures. In England there were also itinerant lecturers offering their service, typically for a fee.

Prior to the 19th century, there were many important inventors working as millwrights or mechanics who had typically received an elementary education and served an apprenticeship. Mechanics, instrument makers and surveyors had various mathematics training. James Watt was a surveyor and instrument maker and is described as being "largely self-educated". Watt, like some other autodidacts of the time, became a Fellow of the Royal Society and a member of the Lunar Society. In the 18th century these societies often gave public lectures and were instrumental in teaching chemistry and other sciences with industrial applications, which were neglected by traditional universities. Academies also arose to provide scientific and technical training.

Years of schooling in the United States began to increase sharply in the early 20th century. This phenomenon was seemingly related to increasing mechanization displacing child labour. The automated glass bottle making machine is said to have done more for education than child labour laws, because boys were no longer needed to assist. However, the number of boys employed in this particular industry was not that large; it was mechanization in several sectors of the industry that displaced child labour toward education. For males in the U.S. born 1886-90, years of school averaged 7.86, while for those born from 1926–30, years of school averaged 11.46.

One of the most recent trends in education is that the classroom environment should cater towards students' individual needs, goals and interests. This model adopts the idea of enquiry-based learning where students are presented with scenarios to identify their own research, questions and knowledge regarding the area. As a form of discovery learning, students in today's classrooms are being provided with more opportunity to "experience and interact" with knowledge, which has its roots in autodidacticism.

For autodidacts to be successful in their self-teaching, they must possess self-discipline and reflective capability. Some research suggests that being able to regulate one's own learning is something which must be modelled to students, for it is not a natural human tendency for the population at large. In order to interact with the environment, a framework has been identified to determine the components of any learning system: a reward function, incremental action value functions and action selection methods. Rewards work best in motivating learning when they are specifically chosen on an individual student basis. New knowledge must be incorporated into previously existing information as its value is to be assessed. Ultimately, these scaffolding techniques, as described by Vygotsky (1978) and problem solving methods are a result of dynamic decision making.

The secular and modern societies gave foundations for a new system of education and a new kind of autodidacts. While the number of schools and students raised from one century to the other, so did the number of autodidacts. The industrial revolution produced new educational tools used in schools, universities and outside academic circles to create a post-modern era that gave birth to the World Wide Web and encyclopaedic data banks such as Wikipedia. As this concept becomes more widespread and popular, web locations like Udacity and Khan Academy are developed to be learning centres for many people to actively and freely learn together.

Autodidacticism in History, Philosophy and Literature

The first philosophical claim supporting an autodidactic programme to the study of nature and God was in the philosophical novel Hayy Ibn-Yaqzan (Alive Son of the Vigilant), who is considered as the quintessential autodidact. The story is a medieval autodidactic utopia, a philosophical treatise in a literary form, which was written by the Andalusian philosopher Abu Baker Ibn-Tufayl in the 1160s, Marrakesh. It is a story about a wild-boy, an autodidact prodigy that takes control over nature with instruments, discovers laws of nature by practical exploration and experiments, and gained an ultimate felicity through a mystical mediation and communion with God. The story relates to human knowledge, as it rises from a blank slate to a mystical or direct experience of God after passing through the necessary natural experiences.

The focal point of the story is that human reason, unaided by society and its conventions or by religion, can self-achieve scientific knowledge, preparing the way to the mystical or highest form of human knowledge. Commonly translated as "The Self-Taught Philosopher" or "The Improvement of Human Reason," Ibn-Tufayl's story Hayy Ibn-Yaqzan inspired debates about autodidacticism in a range of historical fields from classical Islamic philosophy through Renaissance humanism and the European Enlightenment. In his book Reading Hayy Ibn-Yaqzan: a Cross-Cultural History of Autodidacticism Avner Ben-Zaken showed how the text travelled from late medieval Andalusia to early modern Europe and demonstrated the intricate ways in which autodidacticism was contested in and adapted to diverse cultural settings. Autodidacticism, apparently, intertwined with struggles over Sufism in twelfth-century Marrakesh; controversies about the role of philosophy in pedagogy in fourteenth-century Barcelona; quarrels concerning astrology in Renaissance Florence in which Pico della Mirandola plead for autodidacticism against the strong authority of intellectual establishment notions of predestination; and debates pertaining to experimentalism in seventeenth-century Oxford. Pleas for autodidacticism echoed not only within close philosophical discussions; they surfaced in struggles for control between individuals and establishments.

In the story of African American self-education, Heather Andrea Williams presents a historical account to examine African American's relationship to literacy during slavery, the Civil War and the first decades of freedom. Many of the personal accounts tell of individuals who have had to teach themselves due to racial discrimination in education.

The working-class protagonist of Jack London's Martin Eden *(1909) embarks on a path of self-learning in order to gain the affections of Ruth, a member of cultured society. By the end of the novel, Eden has surpassed the intellect of the bourgeois class, leading him to a state of indifference and, ultimately, suicide.*

Jean-Paul Sartre's *Nausea* (1938) depicts, as a secondary character, an autodidact.

In *The Ignorant Schoolmaster* (1987), Jacques Rancière describes the emancipatory education of Joseph Jacotot, a post-Revolutionary philosopher of education who discovered that he could teach things he did not know. The book is both a history and a contemporary intervention in the philosophy and politics of education, through the concept of autodidacticism; Rancière chronicles Jacotot's "adventures", but he articulates Jacotot's theory of "emancipation" and "stultification" in the present tense. The 1997 drama film *Good Will Hunting* follows the story of autodidact Will Hunting, played by Matt Damon. Hunting demonstrates his breadth and depth of knowledge throughout the film, but especially to his therapist and in a heated discussion in a Harvard bar.

On the television show *Criminal Minds* (2005–present), Supervisory Special Agent Dr. Spencer Reid is an autodidact with an eidetic memory, meaning that he can remember and easily recall almost everything he sees (this, however, only applies to visual information). He holds doctoral degrees in mathematics, chemistry, and engineering. He also holds bachelor degrees in sociology and psychology, and is working on completing another in philosophy. He is known on the show for being a genius; he has an IQ of 187 and is certainly the smartest member of the FBI's Behavioural Analysis Unit stationed at Quantico, Virginia. Most of his autodidacticism comes from reading books, which he prefers over traditional forms of education, including schooling. He reads at a rate of 20,000 words per minute.

One of the main characters in *The Elegance of the Hedgehog* (2006), by Muriel Barbery, is an autodidact. The story is told from the view point of Renee, a middle-aged autodidact concierge in a Paris upscale apartment house and Paloma, a 12-year-old daughter of one of the tenants who is unhappy with her life. These two people find they have much in common when they both befriend a new tenant, Mr. Ozu, and their lives change forever.

In the Hindu epic, the *Mahabharata*, Ekalayva is depicted as a tribal boy who was denied education in the science of arms from royal teachers from the house of Kuru. Ekalavya went to the forest, where he taught himself archery in front of an image of the Kuru teacher, Drona, that he had built for himself. Later, when the royal family found that Ekalavya had practiced with the image of Drona as his teacher, Drona asked for Ekalavya's thumb as part of his tuition. Ekalavya complied with Drona's request, thus ending his martial career.

Autodidacticism in Architecture

Many successful and influential architects, such as Mies Van Der Rohe, Frank Lloyd Wright, Violet-Le-Duc, and Tadao Ando were self-taught. There are very few countries allowing autodidacticism in architecture today. The practice of architecture, or the use of the title: "architect", are now protected in most countries.

Self-taught architects have generally studied and qualified in other fields such as engineering or arts and crafts. Jean Prouvé was first a structural engineer. Le Corbusier had an academic qualification in decorative arts. Tadao Ando started his career as a draftsman and Eileen Gray studied fine arts.

When a political state starts to implement restrictions on the profession, there are issues related to the rights of established self-taught architects. In most countries the legislation includes a grandfather clause, authorising established self-taught architects to continue practicing. In the UK, the legislation, allowed self-trained architects with 2 years of experience to register. In France, it allowed self-trained architects with 5 years of experience to register. In Belgium, the law allowed experienced self-trained architects in practice to register. In Italy, it allowed self-trained architects with 10 years of experience to register. In The Netherlands, the "*wep op de architectentitel van 7 juli 1987*" along with additional procedures, allowed architects with 10 years of experience and architects aged 40 years old or over, with 5 years of experience, to access the register.

However, other sovereign states made the choice to omit such clause and many established and competent practitioners were stripped of their professional rights. In the Republic of Ireland, a group named "Architects' Alliance of Ireland" is defending the interests of long-established self-trained architects who were recently deprived from their rights to practice as per Part 3 of the Irish Building Control Act 2007.

Theoretical research such as "*Architecture of Change, sustainability and humanity in the built environment*" or older studies like "Vers une Architecture" from Le Corbusier describe the practice of architecture as an environment changing with new technologies, sciences and legislations. All architects must be autodidacts to keep up to date with new standards, new regulations, or new methods.

Self-taught architects like Eileen Gray, Luis Barragán and many others, created a system where working is also learning, where self-education is associated with creativity and productivity within a working environment.

While he was primarily interested in naval architecture, William Francis Gibbs learned his profession through his own study of battleships and ocean liners. Through his life he could be seen examining and changing the designs of ships that were already built, that is, until he started Gibbs and Cox.

Future Impact

The role of self-directed learning continues to be investigated in learning approaches, along with other important goals of education, such as content knowledge, epistemic practices and collaboration. As colleges and universities offer distance learning degree programmes and secondary schools provide cyber school options for K-12 students, technology provides numerous resources that enable individuals to have a self-directed learning experience. Several studies show these programmes function most effectively when the "teacher" or facilitator is a full owner of virtual space to encourage a broad range of experiences to come together in an online format. This allows self-directed learning to encompass both a chosen path of information enquiry, self-regulation methods and reflective discussion among experts as well as novices in a given area.

Alternative Schooling in Different Countries

India: In India, from the early 20th century, some educational theorists discussed and implemented radically different forms of education. Rabindranath Tagore's Visva-Bharati University, and Sri Aurobindo's Sri Aurobindo International Centre of Education are prime examples. In recent years many new alternative schools have formed.

The traditional system of learning in India was for students to stay in Gurukulas, where they received free food, shelter, and education from a "guru" ("teacher" in Sanskrit). Progress was not based on examinations and marks; tests were given by the gurus but not ranks. This system aimed to nurture the students' natural creativity and all-round personality development. While the mainstream education system in India is still based on that introduced by Lord Macaulay, a few projects aim to rejuvenate the early system, Some students in these and similar projects take up research work in the field of Sanskrit studies, Vedic studies, Vedic science, Yoga and Ayurveda. Others after completing their education in a Gurukula continue into regular mainstream education such as Bachelor degrees in Commerce, Science, Engineering etc.

Japan

Japanese education has been run as a nation-wide standardized system under the full control of the Ministry of Education. The only alternative option has been accredited private schools that have more freedom to offer different curriculum including the choice of textbooks (public schools can use only the government approved textbooks) and foreign languages, teaching methods, hiring guidelines. However, almost all of these private schools require competitive entrance examination and tuition with very few scholarships available.

An interest in alternative education was stimulated first by problems of student violence against people and property, since the 1980s by problems of bullying by peers, frequently leading to school refusal, acute social withdrawal and in the worst case, suicide. A desire to enable young people to keep in an increasingly globalized economy provided an independent impetus for alternative educational possibilities.

Ijime and Free Schools

Free school is the term used in Japan to describe a non-profit group or independent school which specialized in the care and education of children who refused to go to school. The first school based on democratic schools was founded in 1985, starting as a shelter for children who avoided the school environment; a number of other schools working on this basis, as well as other schools for school refusers, have since been established. In 1987, the first of what are now seven Waldorf schools in Japan was founded. Other alternatives include a growing homeschooling movement.

In 2003, Japan introduced Special Zones for Structural Reform, based on China's Special Economic Zone policy, which enable the opening of government-accredited schools providing alternative education. In 2005, the first school was founded under the new law.

Globalization and International Schools

Increasingly, parents are interested in sending their children to International schools to acquire a fluent command of a foreign language, usually English.

Although international schools are not legally certified by the Japanese government, many of them are approved by their native country such as the US, Canada, Germany, France, Korea and China, and some offer the International Baccalaureate programme. For the past two decades, international schools, especially American or English-based schools, have been very popular in spite of their costly tuition. A new trend in the early 21st century has been attending Chinese schools.

United Kingdom

In 2003 there were approximately 70 alternative schools in the United Kingdom. Summerhill School was established by A.S. Neill in 1921 as the first of what are now a number of democratic schools. There are a number of Steiner-Waldorf schools in the UK. Homeschooling is also a popular alternative. Though alternative schools were until recently fee-paying, the introduction of state-funded Academies in the last year has been changing the educational landscape.

United States

There are many Montessori and Waldorf schools in the USA; some of these are fee-paying, while others are public or charter schools. There are also many home school programmes.

There are many public and private educational provisions available in the USA for children with autism, attention deficit hyperactivity disorder, Asperger's syndrome, obsessive-compulsive disorder, nonverbal learning disorder, etc.

At the level of higher education several alternative practices have arisen, especially since the late 20th century. St. John's College, for example, is a Great Books school with a standard curriculum culminating in a singular degree for all students, primary source readings, and gently moderated classroom discussions. Other colleges use narrative evaluations rather than standardized grades for assessment or do not have traditional academic departments and are instead organized around interdisciplinary units.

The Netherlands

At the level of higher education there is Intercultural Open University, an alternative education provider for person-centred graduate education. In keeping with the philosophy of alternative education, the university does not issue grades; narrative evaluations are used for assessment. There are no traditional academic departments or paid faculty and staff; its faculty and staff are volunteers. Learners develop a self-directed individualized curriculum under the guidance of a faculty advisor.

Special

In the past, those who were disabled were often not eligible for public education. Children with disabilities were often educated by physicians or special tutors. These early physicians (people like Itard, Seguin, Howe, Gallaudet) set the foundation for special education today. They focused on individualized instruction and functional skills. Special education was only provided to people with severe disabilities in its early years, but more recently it has been opened to anyone who has experienced difficulty learning.

Vocational

Vocational education is a form of education focused on direct and practical training for a specific trade or craft. Vocational education may come in the form of an apprenticeship or internship as well as institutions teaching courses such as carpentry, agriculture, engineering, medicine, architecture and the arts.

Informal Education

Indigenous: Indigenous education refers to the inclusion of indigenous knowledge, models, methods and content within formal and non-formal educational systems. Often in a post-colonial context, the growing recognition and use of indigenous education methods can be a response to the erosion and loss of indigenous knowledge and language through the processes of colonialism. Furthermore, it can enable indigenous communities to "reclaim and revalue their languages and cultures, and in so doing, improve the educational success of indigenous students."

Education Through Recreation

Figure: *An arched bridge being made from blocks at an interactive "Discovery Day" event in Laos*

The concept of education through recreation was first applied to childhood development in the 19th century. In the early 20th century, the concept was broadened to include young adults but the emphasis was on physical activities. L.P. Jacks, also an early proponent of lifelong learning, described education through recreation: "A master in the art of living draws no sharp distinction between his work and his play, his labour and his leisure, his mind and his body, his education and his recreation. He hardly knows which is which. He simply pursues his vision of excellence through whatever he is doing and leaves others to determine whether he is working or playing. To himself he always seems to be doing both. Enough for him that he does it well." Education through recreation is the opportunity to learn in a seamless fashion through all of life's activities. The concept has been revived by the University of Western Ontario to teach anatomy to medical students.

Systems of Higher Education

Higher education, also called tertiary, third stage, or post secondary education, is the non-compulsory educational level that follows the completion of a school providing a secondary education, such as a high school or secondary school. Tertiary education is normally taken to include undergraduate and postgraduate education, as well as vocational education and training.

Colleges and universities are the main institutions that provide tertiary education. Collectively, these are sometimes known as tertiary institutions. Tertiary education generally results in the receipt of certificates, diplomas, or academic degrees.

Higher education generally involves work towards a degree-level or foundation degree qualification. In most developed countries a high proportion of the population (up to 50%) now enter higher education at some time in their lives. Higher education is therefore very important to national economies, both as a significant industry in its own right, and as a source of trained and educated personnel for the rest of the economy. A number of career specific courses are now available to students through the Internet.

University Systems

University education includes teaching, research, and social services activities, and it includes both the *undergraduate* level (sometimes referred to as tertiary education) and the *graduate* (or *postgraduate*) level (sometimes referred to as graduate school). Universities are generally composed of several colleges. In the United States, universities can be private and independent, like Yale University, they can be public and State governed, like the Pennsylvania State System of Higher Education, or they can be independent but State funded, like the University of Virginia.

***Figure:** Lecture at the Faculty of Biomedical Engineering, CTU in Prague.*

Open

Higher education in particular is currently undergoing a transition towards open education, elearning alone is currently growing at 14 times the rate of traditional learning. Open education is fast growing to become the dominant form of education, for many reasons such as its efficiency and results compared to traditional methods. Cost of education has been an issue throughout history, and a major political issue in most countries today. Open education is generally significantly cheaper than traditional campus based learning and in many cases even free. Many large university institutions are now starting to offer free or almost free full courses such as Harvard, MIT and Berkeley teaming up to form edX Other universities offering open education are Stanford, Princeton, Duke, Johns Hopkins, Edinburgh, U.Penn, U. Michigan, U. Virginia, U. Washington, Caltech. It has been called the biggest change in the way we learn since the printing press. Many people despite favourable studies on effectiveness may still desire to choose traditional campus education for social and cultural reasons.

The conventional merit system degree is currently not as common in open education as it is in campus universities. Although some open universities do already offer conventional degrees such as the Open University in the United Kingdom. Currently many of the major open education sources offer their own form of certificate. Due to the popularity of open education these new kind of academic certificates are gaining more respect and equal "academic value" to traditional degrees. Many open universities are working to have the ability to offer students standardized testing and traditional degrees and credentials. There has been a culture forming around distance learning for people who are looking to enjoy the shared social aspects that many people value in traditional on campus education that is not often directly offered from open education. Examples of this are people in open education forming study groups, meetups and movements such as UnCollege.

Liberal Arts Colleges

Figure: Saint Anselm College, a traditional New England liberal arts college.

A liberal arts institution can be defined as a "college or university curriculum aimed at imparting broad general knowledge and developing general intellectual capacities, in contrast to a professional, vocational, or technical curriculum." Although what is known today as the liberal arts college began in Europe, the term is more commonly associated with Universities in the United States.

Community Colleges

A nonresidential junior college offering courses to people living in a particular area.

Learning Modalities

Figure: Students in laboratory, Saint Petersburg State Polytechnical University.

There has been much interest in learning modalities and styles over the last two decades. The most commonly employed learning modalities are:

- Visual: learning based on observation and seeing what is being learned.
- Auditory: learning based on listening to instructions/information.
- Kinesthetic: learning based on movement, e.g. hands-on work and engaging in activities.

Other commonly-employed modalities include musical, interpersonal, verbal, logical, and intrapersonal.

Dunn and Dunn focused on identifying relevant stimuli that may influence learning and manipulating the school environment, at about the same time as Joseph Renzulli recommended varying teaching strategies. Howard Gardner identified a wide range of modalities in his Multiple Intelligences theories. The Myers-Briggs Type Indicator and Keirsey Temperament Sorter, based on the works of Jung, focus on understanding how people's personality affects the way they interact personally, and how this affects the way individuals respond to each other within the learning environment. The work of David Kolb and Anthony Gregorc's Type Delineator follows a similar but more simplified approach.

Some theories propose that all individuals benefit from a variety of learning modalities, while others suggest that individuals may have preferred learning styles, learning more easily through visual or kinesthetic experiences. A consequence of the latter theory is that effective teaching should present a variety of teaching methods which cover all three learning modalities so that different students have equal opportunities to learn in a way that is effective for them. Guy Claxton has questioned the extent that learning styles such as VAK are helpful, particularly as they can have a tendency to label children and therefore restrict learning. Recent research has argued "there is no adequate evidence base to justify incorporating learning styles assessments into general educational practice."

Instruction

***Figure:** Teacher in a classroom in Madagascar*

Instruction is the facilitation of another's learning. Instructors in primary and secondary institutions are often called teachers, and they direct the education of students and might draw on many subjects like reading, writing, mathematics, science and history. Instructors in post-secondary institutions might be called teachers, instructors, or professors, depending on the type of institution; and they primarily teach only their specific discipline. Studies from the United States suggest that the quality of teachers is the single most important factor affecting student performance, and that countries which score highly on international tests have multiple policies in place to ensure that the teachers they employ are as effective as possible. With the passing of NCLB in the United States (No Child Left Behind), teachers must be highly qualified. A popular way to gauge teaching performance is to use student evaluations of teachers (SETS), but these evaluations have been criticized for being counterproductive to learning and inaccurate due to student bias.

Economics

Figure: *Students on their way to school, Hakha, Chin State, Myanmar*

It has been argued that high rates of education are essential for countries to be able to achieve high levels of economic growth. Empirical analyses tend to support the theoretical prediction that poor countries should grow faster than rich countries because they can adopt cutting edge technologies already tried and tested by rich countries. However, technology transfer requires knowledgeable managers and engineers who are able to operate new machines or production practices borrowed from the leader in order to close the gap through imitation. Therefore, a country's ability to learn from the leader is a function of its stock of "human capital". Recent study of the determinants of aggregate economic growth have stressed the importance of fundamental economic institutions and the role of cognitive skills.

At the individual level, there is a large literature, generally related back to the work of Jacob Mincer, on how earnings are related to the schooling and other human capital of the individual. This work has motivated a large number of studies, but is also controversial. The chief controversies revolve around how to interpret the impact of schooling.

Economists Samuel Bowles and Herbert Gintis famously argued in 1976 that there was a fundamental conflict in American schooling between the egalitarian goal of democratic participation and the inequalities implied by the continued profitability of capitalist production on the other.

History

The history of education according to Dieter Lenzen, president of the Freie Universität Berlin 1994, "began either millions of years ago or at the end of 1770". Education as a science cannot be separated from the educational traditions that existed before. Adults trained the young of their society in the knowledge and skills they would need to master and eventually pass on. The evolution of culture, and human beings as a species depended on this practice of transmitting knowledge. In pre-literate societies this was achieved orally and through imitation. Story-telling continued from one generation to the next. Oral language developed into written symbols and letters. The depth and breadth of knowledge that could be preserved and passed soon increased exponentially. When cultures began to extend their knowledge beyond the basic skills of communicating, trading, gathering food, religious practices, etc., formal education, and schooling, eventually followed. Schooling in this sense was already in place in Egypt between 3000 and 500BC.

In the West, Ancient Greek philosophy arose in the 6th century BC. Plato was the Classical Greek philosopher, mathematician and writer of philosophical dialogues who founded the Academy in Athens which was the first institution of higher learning in the Western world. Inspired by the admonition of his mentor, Socrates, prior to his unjust execution that "the unexamined life is not worth living", Plato and his student, the political scientist Aristotle, helped lay the foundations of Western philosophy and science.

The city of Alexandria in Egypt was founded in 330BC, became the successor to Athens as the intellectual cradle of the Western World. The city hosted such leading lights as the mathematician Euclid and anatomist Herophilus; constructed the great Library of Alexandria; and translated the Hebrew Bible into Greek (called the Septuagint for it was the work of 70 translators). Greek civilization was subsumed within the Roman Empire. While the Roman Empire and its new Christian religion survived in an increasingly Hellenised form in the Byzantine Empire centred at Constantinople in the East, Western civilization suffered a collapse of literacy and organization following the fall of Rome in AD 476. In the East, Confucius (551-479), of the State of Lu, was China's most influential ancient philosopher, whose educational outlook continues to influence the societies of China and neighbours like Korea, Japan and Vietnam. He gathered disciples and searched in vain for a ruler who would adopt his ideals for good governance, but his Analects were written down by followers and have continued to influence education in the East into the modern era.

In Western Europe after the Fall of Rome, the Catholic Church emerged as the unifying force. Initially the sole preserver of literate scholarship in Western Europe, the church established Cathedral schools in the Early Middle Ages as centres of advanced education. Some of these ultimately evolved into medieval universities and forebears of many of Europe's modern universities. During the High Middle Ages, Chartres Cathedral operated the famous and influential Chartres Cathedral School. The medieval universities of Western Christendom were well-integrated across all of Western Europe, encouraged freedom of enquiry and produced a great variety of fine scholars and natural philosophers, including Thomas Aquinas of the University of Naples, Robert Grosseteste of the University of Oxford, an early expositor of a systematic method of scientific experimentation; and Saint Albert the Great, a pioneer of biological field research The University of Bologne is considered the oldest continually operating university. Elsewhere during the Middle Ages, Islamic science and mathematics flourished under the Islamic caliphate established across the Middle East, extending from the Iberian Peninsula in the west to the Indus in the east and to the Almoravid Dynasty and Mali Empire in the south.

The Renaissance in Europe ushered in a new age of scientific and intellectual enquiry and appreciation of ancient Greek and Roman civilizations. Around 1450, Johannes Gutenberg developed a printing press, which allowed works of literature to spread more quickly. The European Age of Empires saw European ideas of education in philosophy, religion, arts and sciences spread out across the globe. Missionaries and scholars also brought back new ideas from other civilisations — as with the Jesuit China missions who played a significant role in the transmission of knowledge, science, and culture between China and the West, translating Western works like Euclids Elements for Chinese scholars and the thoughts of Confucius for Western audiences. The Enlightenment saw the emergence of a more secular educational outlook in the West.

In most countries today, education is compulsory for all children up to a certain age. Due to this the proliferation of compulsory education, combined with population growth, UNESCO has calculated that in the next 30 years more people will receive formal education than in all of human history thus far.

The Internationalization of Education

Nearly every country now has universal education. Similarities — in systems or even in ideas — that schools share internationally have led to an increase in international student exchanges. The European Socrates-Erasmus Programme facilitates exchanges across European universities. The Soros Foundation provides many opportunities for students from central Asia and eastern Europe. Programmes such as the International Baccalaureate have contributed to the internationalization of education. The global campus online, led by American universities, allows free access to class materials and lecture files recorded during the actual classes.

Philosophy

As an academic field, philosophy of education is "the philosophical study of education and its problems ... its central subject matter is education, and its methods are those of philosophy". "The philosophy of education may be either the philosophy of the process of education or the philosophy of the discipline of education. That is, it may be part of the discipline in the sense of being concerned with the aims, forms, methods, or results of the process of educating or being educated; or it may be metadisciplinary in the sense of being concerned with the concepts, aims, and methods of the discipline." As such, it is both part of the field of education and a field of applied philosophy, drawing from fields of metaphysics, epistemology, axiology and the philosophical approaches (speculative, prescriptive, and/or analytic) to address questions in and about pedagogy, education policy, and curriculum, as well as the process of learning, to name a few. For example, it might study what constitutes upbringing and education, the values and norms revealed through upbringing and educational practices, the limits and legitimization of education as an academic discipline, and the relation between education theory and practice.

Purpose of Schools

Individual purposes for pursuing education can vary. The understanding of the goals and means of educational socialization processes may also differ according to the sociological paradigm used.

In the early years of schooling, the focus is generally around developing basic Interpersonal communication and literacy skills in order to further ability to learn more complex skills and subjects. After acquiring these basic abilities, education is commonly focused towards individuals gaining necessary knowledge and skills to improve ability to create value and a livelihood for themselves. Satisfying personal curiosities (Education for the sake of itself) and desire for personal development, to "better oneself" without career based reasons for doing so are also common reasons why people pursue education and use schools.

Education is often understood to be a means of overcoming handicaps, achieving greater equality and acquiring wealth and status for all. Learners can also be motivated by their interest in the subject area or specific skill they are trying to learn. Learner-responsibility education models are driven by the interest of the learner in the topic to be studied.

Education is often perceived as a place where children can develop according to their unique needs and potentialities with the purpose of developing every individual to their full potential.

Psychology

Educational psychology is the study of how humans learn in educational settings, the effectiveness of educational interventions, the psychology of teaching, and the social psychology of schools as organizations. Although the terms "educational psychology" and "school psychology" are often used interchangeably, researchers and theorists are likely to be identified as educational psychologists, whereas practitioners in schools or school-related settings are identified as school psychologists. Educational psychology is concerned with the processes of educational attainment in the general population and in sub-populations such as gifted children and those with specific disabilities.

Educational psychology can in part be understood through its relationship with other disciplines. It is informed primarily by psychology, bearing a relationship to that discipline analogous to the relationship between medicine and biology. Educational psychology in turn informs a wide range of specialties within educational studies, including instructional design, educational technology, curriculum development, organizational learning, special education and classroom management. Educational psychology both draws from and contributes to cognitive science and the learning sciences. In universities, departments of educational psychology are usually housed within faculties of education, possibly accounting for the lack of representation of educational psychology content in introductory psychology textbooks (Lucas, Blazek, & Raley, 2006).

Figure: *School children in Laos*

Developing Countries

Development Goals and Issues

Universal Primary Education is one of the eight international Millennium Development Goals, towards which progress has been made in the past decade, though barriers still remain. Securing charitable funding from prospective donors is one particularly persistent problem. Researchers at the Overseas Development Institute have indicated that the main obstacles to receiving more funding for education include conflicting donor priorities, an immature aid architecture, and a lack of evidence and advocacy for the issue. Additionally, Transparency International has identified corruption in the education sector as a major stumbling block to achieving Universal Primary Education in Africa. Furthermore, demand in the developing world for improved educational access is not as high as foreigners have expected. Indigenous governments are reluctant to take on the recurrent costs involved. There is economic pressure from those parents who prefer their children to earn money in the short term rather than work towards the long-term benefits of education.

A study conducted by the UNESCO International Institute for Educational Planning indicates that stronger capacities in educational planning and management may have an important spill-over effect on the system as a whole. Sustainable capacity development requires complex interventions at the institutional, organizational and individual levels that could be based on some foundational principles:

- national leadership and ownership should be the touchstone of any intervention;
- strategies must be context relevant and context specific;
- they should embrace an integrated set of complementary interventions, though implementation may need to proceed in steps;
- partners should commit to a long-term investment in capacity development, while working towards some short-term achievements;
- outside intervention should be conditional on an impact assessment of national capacities at various levels.
- Removal of a certain percentage of students for improvisation of academics (usually practiced in schools, after 10th grade)

Private Schools vs Public Schools in Developing Countries

Research into low cost private schools found that over 5 years to July 2013, debate around low-cost private schools to achieving Education for All (EFA) objectives was polarised and finding growing coverage in international policy. The polarisation was due to disputes around whether the schools are affordable for the poor, reaching disadvantaged groups, provide quality education, supporting or undermining equality, and are financially sustainable. The report examined the main challenges that development organisations which support LCPSs have encountered. Surveys suggest these types of schools are expanding across Africa and Asia and is attributed to excess demand. These surveys also found concern for:

- Equity, widely found in the literature, as the growth in low-cost private schooling may be exacerbating or perpetuating already existing inequalities in developing countries, between urban and rural populations, lower- and higher-income families, and between girls and boys The report says findings are that LCPSs see evidence girls are underrepresented and that they are reaching some low-income families, often in small numbers compared with higher-income families.
- Quality of provision and educational outcomes, you cannot generalise about the quality of private schools, while most achieve better results than government counterparts, even after their social background is taken into account, some studies find the opposite. Quality in terms of levels of teacher absence, teaching activity and pupil to teacher ratios in some countries are better in LCPSs than in government schools.
- Choice and affordability for the poor: parents can choose private schools because of perceptions of better-quality teaching and facilities, and an English language instruction preference. Nevertheless, the concept of 'choice' does not apply in all contexts, or to all groups in society, partly because of limited affordability (which excludes most of the poorest) and other forms of exclusion, related to caste or social status.
- Cost-effectiveness and financial sustainability: Evidence is that private schools operate at low cost by keeping teacher salaries low, but their financial situation may be precarious where they are reliant on fees from low-income households.

The report said there were some cases of successful voucher and subsidy programmes, evaluations of international support to the sector are not widespread. Addressing regulatory ineffectiveness is a key challenge. Emerging approaches stress the importance of underst-anding the political economy of the market for LCPSs, specifically how relationships of power and accountability between users, government and private providers can produce better education outcomes for the poor.

Education and Technology in Developing Countries

Figure: *The OLPC laptop being introduced to children in Haiti*

Technology plays an increasingly significant role in improving access to education for people living in impoverished areas and developing countries. There are charities dedicated to providing infrastructures through which the disadvantaged may access educational materials, for example, the One Laptop per Child project.

The OLPC foundation, a group out of MIT Media Lab and supported by several major corporations, has a stated mission to develop a $100 laptop for delivering educational software. The laptops were widely available as of 2008. They are sold at cost or given away based on donations. In Africa, the New Partnership for Africa's Development (NEPAD) has launched an "e-school programme" to provide all 600,000 primary and high schools with computer equipment, learning materials and internet access within 10 years. An International Development Agency project called nabuur.com, started with the support of former American President Bill Clinton, uses the Internet to allow co-operation by individuals on issues of social development. India is developing technologies that will bypass land-based telephone and Internet infrastructure to deliver distance learning directly to its students. In 2004, the Indian Space Research Organization launched EDUSAT, a communications satellite providing access to educational materials that can reach more of the country's population at a greatly reduced cost.

Career Guidance

Career guidance helps people to reflect on their ambitions, interests, qualifications and abilities. It helps them to understand the labour market and education systems, and to relate this to what they know about themselves. Comprehensive career guidance tries to teach people to plan and make decisions about work and learning. Career guidance makes information about the labour market and about educational opportunities more accessible by organising it, systematising it, and making it available when and where people need it.

In its contemporary forms, career guidance draws upon a number of disciplines: psychology; education; sociology; and labour economics. Historically, psychology is the major discipline that has under-pinned its theories and methodologies. In particular differential psychology and developmental psychology have had an important influence.

One-to-one interviews and psychological testing for many years were seen as its central tools. There are many countries where psychology remains the major entry route into the profession.

However, in most countries today, career guidance is provided by people with a very wide range of training and qualifications. Some are specialists; some are not. Some have had extensive, and expensive, training; others have had very little.

Training programmes are still heavily based upon developing skills in providing help in one-to-one interviews. On the other hand, psychological testing now receives a reduced emphasis in many countries as counselling theories have moved from an emphasis upon the practitioner as expert to seeing practitioners as facilitators of individual choice and development.

Career guidance is provided to people in a very wide range of settings: schools and tertiary institutions; public employment services; private guidance providers; enterprises; and community settings. It is provided unevenly to different groups both within and between countries. In most countries there are large gaps in services. In particular employed adults, those not in the labour market, and students in tertiary education receive more limited services than, for example, students in upper secondary school and the unemployed. In many settings, career guidance is integrated into something else: teaching; job placement; personal and educational counselling; or providing educational information.

Where this is the case, it can have low visibility, be difficult to measure, and clear performance criteria for it can be hard to define. There are parallels between the role that career guidance can play in improving labour market efficiency and the role that information plays in improving the efficiency of other types of market.

Career guidance assumes an even higher profile as countries adopt more active approaches to unemployment and to welfare reform. These normally require the unemployed or welfare recipients to develop proposals for active job search, or education and training, as a condition of continuing to receive income support. This increases the need for personal advice, and for access to information, if such policy approaches are to succeed. In Spain, for example, where adoption of the European Employment Strategy now requires earlier intervention to assist unemployed people, the National Employment Office (INEM) has introduced a much stronger emphasis upon individual action planning in the job placement process. This has required employment office staff to develop new skills. In Denmark, Norway and Sweden, guidance is a central element in locally-managed early intervention programmes for school drop-outs.

These safety net programmes are associated with strong evidence of improved labour market outcomes for youth. Recent Australian research has suggested that intensive interviewing of welfare recipients, including counselling and personal action planning, can increase social integration through increased participation in education and training. In principle, it can help to increase access to learning, and to improve course completion rates. It can assess learning needs and interests, and put people in contact with learning providers so that they enrol in appropriate programmes. Feedback from career guidance practitioners can encourage learning providers to meet the unmet needs of learners and potential learners: for example, by changing their opening hours, modifying their teaching methods, or developing new types of course.

In such ways, career guidance can help to articulate better the scale and nature of demand for learning, as well as its supply, and help improve the match between the two. It can increase the transparency of learning systems, and their responsiveness to consumer demand. In these ways, it can help not only to increase participation, but also reduce dropout rates. American research suggests that comprehensive guidance services can have a positive impact on the quality of students' educational and occupational decisions, and also on their educational performance and the overall climate of the school. Lifelong learning has major implications for career guidance, and vice versa. The European Commission has recognised this, making career guidance one of its six priorities in implementing lifelong learning. The importance of information and advice grows as alternatives and choices within education systems increase, and as the educational choices and labour market consequences that people face become more complex. Countries tend to put more emphasis upon career guidance as they make pathways through education more flexible and more ndividualised. Both trends can be strongly observed, for example, in Denmark and Finland during the 1990s. Consumer-driven learning systems require greater attention to the information and advisory systems needed to support efficient decision making by individuals. This increases the importance of career guidance in helping to manage transitions from one level of education to another, and transitions between education and working life.

Philosophy of Educational Guidance

Philosophy of education is a domain of philosophical enquiry into the nature and aims of education, the diverse normative dimensions of education, aspects of learning, teaching, and curricula, the character and structure of educational theory, and its own place in that theory. It seeks understanding of educational matters and to provide practical guidance for educational practice and policy. Throughout its history, philosophy of education has been shaped by related philosophical developments and by contemporaneous educational, social, economic, and political circumstances. Over the past half century, it has also come to exhibit features associated with its professionalization as a research specialization.

Historical Overview

What we know of the origins of philosophy of education in the West suggests that it began in Greek antiquity in the pedagogical claims and counterclaims of the adult educators we now know as philosophers, orators, and sophists (all of whom claimed the title "philosopher" in their time), and in debates about the role of slave pedagogues, the invention of group lessons for children, and the virtues and limitations of Spartan education. In the aftermath of the Peloponnesian Wars, the philosopher-moralists of Athens called for systematic investments in education and they explored related questions about justice, virtue, happiness, human development, civic friendship, political stability, the relationships between education and law, and the tools of statesmanship. So it was that in the works of Plato and Aristotle many of the perennial problems of philosophy of education were framed: What is education? How does it contribute to human well-being or flourishing? To what extent, and by what means, can the aim of educating children for their own good be reconciled with educating them for the common good? How can education contribute to civic unity? Should education be the same for everyone? Should education be a matter of individual parental choice or publicly controlled?

Through what forms of learning and instruction are virtues of character and intellect acquired? How does rationality develop, and what role does instruction play in that development? To what extent and by what means can education "emancipate" human beings or enhance their freedom? What is knowledge and how is it acquired? Can understanding and knowledge be *transmitted* through teaching? How are methods of enquiry and methods of instruction related to one another? What is the role of the arts in education? What role do practical arts and the development of talents play in a "liberal" education? How are education and work related to one another?

Other questions of enduring interest got their footing in the early modern period, in the midst of the scientific revolution and the seemingly endless religious persecution and wars of the Reformation. Philosophers, from René Descartes and Thomas Hobbes to John Locke and Jean-Jacques Rousseau, were occupied with understanding the new science, reconciling it with religious faith and moral knowledge, and rethinking the relationships between church, state and moral formation: What must be learned through experience to be understood? To what extent is learning through enquiry or discovery feasible? To what extent can education rely on "natural" learning, motivated by curiosity? Should societies forgo the imposition of a state religion and trust the spontaneous activity of human reason to impart the moral prerequisites of good citizenship? In the nineteenth and early twentieth centuries, the industrial revolution, growth of mass schooling, new-found respectability of democracy, and consolidation of the modern system of the arts and aesthetics, cast new light on enduring questions of philosophy of education and prompted some new ones: Is mass schooling desirable? Is it compatible with cultural excellence? Should all students receive the same education? What is the relationship between education and labour? How is education related to socio-economic status and opportunity?

The history of philosophical enquiry concerning education reveals an occupation with the nature, aims, and means of education; with philosophical aspects of teaching and learning; with matters of educational authority, responsibility, equity, and entitlement. Through most of this history, philosophical enquiry concerning education rarely announced itself *as* philosophy of education, no one made a living as a philosopher of education, and no societies or journals of philosophy of education had yet been founded. All of this began to change in the middle of the twentieth century. Philosophy of education constituted itself as a profession employed primarily in faculties of education, and as a scholarly enterprise straddling education and philosophy. Journals and societies were founded, a handful of institutions established Ph.D. programmes in philosophy of education, and the prestige of research stimulated a growing stream of publications, much as it did in other academic domains. As its professional advancement has progressed, philosophy of education has come to exhibit traits associated with the rising costs and diminishing returns on research in a field's established core. One consequence of this is that the nature and limits of philosophy of education are now harder to identify.

Professionalization, Fragmentation, and Strategies of Renewal

Judging from what is presented and published under the aegis of the philosophy of education societies of Australasia, Great Britain, and North America, philosophy of education is exploding in so many directions away from its historic core that one may wonder whether it is simply disintegrating. It seems intent on leaving no far-flung theoretical stone unturned, on what often appears the merest supposition that so important a theory would naturally have *some* educational implications. To write about Derrida or Dualism, Wittgenstein or Whiteness, Levinas or the Other, may be thought so obviously rich in practical implications that education need not be mentioned at all. Are these exploding fragments of a field meaningfully tethered to enduring central questions about education? If so, is there a body of ongoing enquiry into those central questions that informs the diverse fragments?

Similar concerns have been expressed about other philosophical sub-fields in recent decades. Philosophers of law have asked whether their own field, once so plainly defined by a cluster of conceptual and normative questions about the nature and boundaries of law, authority, obligation, responsibility, and liberty, has come to a standstill. Philosophers of science, once similarly focused on the nature of science and logic of scientific laws, explanation, evidence, and theory, have also worried about the fragmentation of their field and the extent to which its far-flung parts are not informed by work on the fundamental questions. All three fields, all of them philosophies of domains of norm-governed human endeavour, have exhibited dramatic out-migration from their centres. As fields of enquiry, law and education have looked beyond themselves for periodic intellectual renewal, and philosophy of law and philosophy of education have followed suit. Yet the patterns of out-migration have been very different. Philosophy of law has advanced and critiqued feminist, neo-Marxist, economic, humanistic, and semiotic analyses of core aspects of law, while moving beyond the field's defining core to investigate diverse, specific legal rules, procedures, and principles. The explosion away from the core has been characterized by detailed engagement with puzzling and controversial features of legal systems and developments pertaining to them, relying on intimate knowledge of law and framed in terms accessible to legal scholars and practitioners who are not philosophers. Aspirations to shape practice are not misplaced. The movement away from the core of philosophy of science has followed a similar pattern to the extent it has occupied itself substantially with what is distinctive in different sciences – their distinctive ontological puzzles and modes of enquiry, confirmation, and explanation. The occupation with one or another diverse science has diminished communication between philosophers of science and collective memory of work in the field's core that could usefully inform their work. These drawbacks of abandoning the core having been recognized and discussed, there has been a significant renaissance of work on the field's central topics in recent years.

Why Should These Patterns Recur Across Diverse Fields of Enquiry?

There is a dynamic of diminishing marginal returns on investment that explains it. As a field constitutes itself as a self-governing professional enterprise, it will begin by addressing the most basic and important problems in its domain, a domain defined by its object of study. It will address the nature of the objects in the domain, their properties, and their variety and relationships to one another. If the domain is one of human practice, it will not only seek understanding, but will identify norms of success and provide guidance on achieving success. Only by starting in this way is a field likely to attract interest and establish the external and internal legitimacy a profession requires. External legitimacy is predicated on a promise of value to the host socio-political system, and internal legitimacy is predicated on intrinsic intellectual rewards and socio-economic return on energy invested in acquiring professional expertise. The pioneers of fields of enquiry establish the starting points of such legitimacy by demonstrating the success of their methods in producing model solutions to fundamental problems. The course of subsequent work within that research paradigm will follow a predictable path. Improvements in the answers to the most basic questions will be increasingly difficult to obtain, as energy invested in mastering increasingly complex debates and methods yields smaller and smaller refinements. Marginal return on investment in further research on the field's defining questions will decline, and this will yield incentives to (1) work on relatively unexplored but increasingly peripheral problems and (2) search outside the field's established parameters for new sources of intellectual "energy" or new research paradigms.

Both strategies for preserving an acceptable return on investment in research are themselves subject to declining marginal returns, but the former is more reliably conducive to maintaining the legitimacy of a professionalized field of enquiry. As the examples of medicine, law, and other fields demonstrate, progress on peripheral problems can be conducive to both external legitimacy and internal legitimacy in the form of intellectual gratification and feasible career paths. Prospecting for transformative theoretical paradigms is more adventuresome. In philosophy of education, literary studies, and some related fields, it also trades on a status hierarchy that honours abstraction. But it is a strategy analogous to prospecting for gold or prospecting for petroleum at a point when energy return on energy invested in petroleum exploration and development is in sharp decline.

Looking Ahead

In order to flourish in the years ahead, philosophy of education must recommit itself to its central problems and find the patience and resourcefulness to do philosophically sound and interesting work *on fundamental and controversial aspects of education.* Only in this way can it replenish itself with talent, bolster its legitimacy, and set itself on a trajectory of accumulating success. In developing its periphery, it would do well to observe the norms of counterpart domains of practical philosophy, such as philosophy of law and biomedical ethics – norms that counsel normative clarity and serious engagement with what can be learned of the institutional and human realities in one's domain of enquiry.

4

Guidance in the Elementary School

An elementary school or primary school is an institution where children receive the first stage of academic learning known as elementary or primary education. Elementary school is the preferred term in some countries, particularly those in North America, where the terms grade school and grammar school are also used. Primary school is the preferred term in the United Kingdom, France, India, Ireland, Pakistan, Bangladesh, Australia, Latin America, Nepal, South Africa, New Zealand, Malaysia and in most publications of the United Nations Educational, Scientific, and Cultural Organization (UNESCO).

United Kingdom

Elementary school was formerly the name given to publicly funded schools in Great Britain which provided a basic standard of education for working class children aged from five to 14, the school leaving age at the time. They were also known as industrial schools.

Elementary schools were set up to enable working class children to receive manual training and elementary instruction. They provided a restricted curriculum with the emphasis on reading, writing and arithmetic (the three Rs). The schools operated on a 'monitorial' system, whereby one teacher supervised a large class with the assistance of a team of monitors, who were quite often older pupils. Elementary school teachers were paid by results. Their pupils were expected to achieve precise standards in reading, writing and arithmetic such as reading a short paragraph in a newspaper, writing from dictation, and working out sums and fractions. Before 1944 around 80 percent of the school population attended elementary schools through to the age of 14. The remainder transferred either to secondary school or junior technical school at age 11. The school system was changed with the introduction of the Education Act 1944. Education was restructured into three progressive stages which were known as primary education, secondary education and further education.

In the UK, schools providing primary education are now known as primary schools. They generally cater for children aged from four to eleven (Reception to Year Six or in Northern Ireland and Scotland P1 to P7). Primary schools are often subdivided into infant schools for children from four to seven and junior schools for ages seven to 11. In the (diminishing) minority of areas where there is a "three-tier" system, children go to lower school or "first school" until about 9, then middle school until about 13, then upper school; in these places, the term "primary school" is not usually used.

United States

In the United States, authority to regulate education resides constitutionally with the individual states. The direct authority of the U.S. Congress and the federal U.S. Department of Education is essentially limited to regulation and enforcement of federal constitutional rights. Great indirect authority is exercised through federal funding of national programmes and block grants; but there is no obligation upon any state to accept these funds, and the U.S. government otherwise may propose but not enforce national goals, objectives and standards, which generally lie beyond its jurisdiction.

Nevertheless, education has had a relatively consistent evolution throughout the United States. All states have historically made a distinction between two genres of K-12 education and three genres of K-12 school. The genres of education are primary and secondary; and the genres of school are elementary school, middle or junior high school, and high school (historically, "senior" high school to distinguish it from the junior school).

Primary education (or "primary school" meaning "primary education") still tends to focus on basic academic learning and socialization skills, introducing children to the broad range of knowledge, skill and behavioural adjustment they need to succeed in life - and, particularly, in secondary school. Secondary education or secondary school has always focused on preparing adolescents for higher education or/and for careers in industries, trades or professions that do not require an academic degree.

The elementary school has always been the main point of delivery for primary education; and the (senior) high school has always been the focal point of secondary education. Originally, elementary school was synonymous with primary education, taking children from kindergarten through grade 8; and secondary school was entirely coextensive with the high school grades 9 - 12. This system was the norm in America until the years following World War I, because most children in most parts of what was then the mostly rural United States could go no further than Grade 8. Even when the high schools were available, they were often not accessible.

As the population grew and became increasingly urban and suburban instead of rural, the one-room schoolhouse gave way to the multi-room schoolhouse, which became multiple schools. This produced the third genre of school - the junior high school - which was designed to provide transitional preparation from primary school to secondary school, thus serving as a bridge between the elementary school and the high school. Elementary schools typically operated grades Kindergarten through 6; the junior high school, often housed in the same building as the senior high school, then covered grades 7 through 9; and the senior high school operated grades 10 through 12. At the same time, grade 9 marked the beginning of high school for the purpose of GPA calculation.

Figure: *A teacher and her students in an elementary school classroom (USA, probably in 2008.)*

It was typical during this period for state departments of education to certify (in California, "credential") teachers to work in either primary or secondary education. A Primary School Certificate qualified the holder to teach any subject in grades K through 8, and his/her major and minor subjects in grade 9. A Secondary School Certificate qualified the holder to teach any subject in grades 7 and 8, and his/her major and minor subjects in grades 9 through 12. Certain subjects, such as music, art, physical, and special education were or could be conferred as K through 12 Teaching Certificates.

By the late 1960s, the lines of transition between primary and secondary education began to blur, and the junior high school started to get replaced by the middle school. This change typically saw reassignment of grade 9 to the (senior) high school, with grade 6 reassigned to the middle school with grades 7 and 8. Subsequent decades in many states have also seen the realignment of teacher certification, with grade 6 frequently now included on the secondary teaching certificate. Thus, whereas 20th-century American education began with the elementary school finishing at grade 8, the 21st century begins with the American elementary school finishing at grade 5 in many jurisdictions.

Nevertheless, the older systems do persist in many jurisdictions. While they are in the minority today, there are still school districts which, instead of adopting the "middle school", still distinguish between junior and senior high schools. Thus, high schools can be either 9-12, which is most common, or 10-12. The transformation of elementary education is evident. With a constant, steady rise in diversity in thousands of country-wide elementary schools, the educational approach of teachers must adapt. While college students of the 21st century took the basic classes in elementary school (Social Studies, Science, Language Arts, Math, etc.), many schools today are changing their curricula and incorporating classes such as Mandarin Chinese education. Even though the usual educational classes are still in practice, a different approach is being met by administrators and teachers in order to effectively teach all students, and keep up with a changing and evolving society.

Saudi Arabia

Brazil

Brazil has recently gone through changes in school grades. Currently, at the age of 6 children attend from the grade 1 to 4 what is called Ensino Primário (Portuguese for Primary Teaching, or Primary School), and afterwards from grade 5 to 9 the Ensino Fundamental (Fundamental Teaching/School). At the age of 15 the teenagers go to Ensino Médio (Mid Teaching/School), which is equivalent High School in other countries, but it is only 3 years long (grades 10 to 12) and can either be a regular or technical course.

Germany

Figure: *Elementary school ("Grundschule") in Treia (Germany).*

Depending on state, elementary schools (usually called *Grundschulen*) provide education from grade 1 to 4 or 1 to 6. Upon graduation from elementary school, students attend either Hauptschule, Realschule or Gymnasium; or a combination of Hauptschule, Realschule and Gymnasium called Gesamtschule.

India

In India, elementary schools provide education from Class 1 to Class 8. The children in these classes are generally aged between 6 to 14 years. It is the next stage after kindergarten (Pre-Nursery, Nursery, Prep or Lower Kindergarten and Upper Kindergarten). The next stage after primary education is Middle School (Class 6th to 8th). In most schools in North India, children in Classes 1st to 3rd are taught English, Hindi, Mathematics, Environmental Science, and General Knowledge. In class 4th and 5th the environmental science subject is replaced by General Science and Social Studies. However some schools may introduce this concept in Class 3 itself. Some schools may also introduce a third language in Class 5th or even in Class 4th.

Sanskrit and French are the most common third languages taught in Indian schools. At some places, primary education is labelled as the education of Class 3rd to Class 5th and up to class 2nd as pre-primary education. This is because many new concepts are introduced in this class. Children are taught painting instead of drawing and colouring, exams are taken, and Word Sum Puzzle in maths are introduced along with geometry.

Japan

South Korea: In South Korea, students attend elementary school from kindergarten to the 6th grade. Students study a wide range of subjects, including: Korean, English, Chinese characters, math, social studies, science, computers, art, physical education, music, health, ethics, and home economics. English instruction generally begins in the 3rd grade. After finishing elementary school, students attend middle school (middle school 1st–3rd grade). The Korean term for elementary school is chodeung hakgyo (Hangul).

Malaysia

The Malaysian term for elementary school is *sekolah rendah*, or as known as primary school.

Indonesia

The Indonesian term for elementary school is *sekolah dasar*.

Philippines: In the Philippines, the Department of Education mandates that elementary school lasts for 6 years in the public school system starting with grade 1 and culminating with grade 6. After successful completion of the 6-year programme shall a student graduate, be awarded an elementary diploma and can move-on to a 4-year high school programme (most private schools will require an entrance examination). However most private schools (which usually call the elementary level as "grade school"), especially exclusive schools and those accredited to have a high degree of autonomy from the Department of Education usually extend their programmes to 7th grade and can also include levels such as nursery, kindergarten or preparatory (prep) as entry levels prior to 1st grade. Subjects usually taken-up include Communication Arts in English (some private schools break this down into Language and Reading) and Filipino, Mathematics, Science, Social Studies (taught in Filipino), Home Economics (HELE - for all-girls schools), Music, Art, and Physical Education (which in some schools is collectively known as MAPE). Students in the 6th grade, whether studying in a public or private school are required to undergo a National (Elementary) Achievement Test (NAT) even if grade 6 isn't the terminal level in that school. The NAT is similar to certain schemes like Primary School Leaving Examination of Singapore (PSLE) except that that NAT score isn't used as a basis to admit students to a high school. Grade 1 and Grade 6 are affected with the K-12 education.

Elementary Guidance Programme: The elementary school counsellor serves the needs of all elementary students, to help them develop, academically, socially and emotionally. The school counsellor"s role is constantly changing, reflecting the needs of the many people in our school community; children, parents, teachers, and administrators. A variety of services are provided:

Guidance Lessons

Elementary counsellors present regularly scheduled classroom lessons to all students in grades one through five. Kindergarten lessons are offered periodically throughout the year. The elementary guidance curriculum is child-centred and developmental - in that it considers the characteristics and needs of each age and grade level. The curriculum encourages students to:

- develop positive self-image
- become more aware of the relationships between themselves and others.
- recognize their own needs and goals.

Individual Counselling Services

Elementary school counsellors meet individually with students to provide support for school-related issues. The counselling strategies vary with each student"s needs and are provided on a short-term basis as determined by the school counsellor. Students can refer themselves to the counsellor or can be referred by parents, teachers, or other school staff.

Group Counselling Services

Elementary school counsellors meet with small groups of students on various topics. Topics are determined by the children's needs and interests.

Consultation

School counsellors, parents, and teachers work together to support children.

Elementary school counsellors work with parents:

- to exchange and gather information
- to provide recommendations; and
- to discuss parenting concerns

Elementary school counsellors work with teachers, administrators, and other staff:

- to provide information, materials and referral assistance
- to address student needs, especially within the Instructional Support Team (IST); and
- to promote a positive learning environment.

Study of Home Environment

A core goal of education is to create lifelong learners. Success in the workplace requires an ability to pick up new high-quality knowledge. The foundation for these learning skills is the study habits that are acquired from early in school. After all, most learning in life takes place outside of the classroom. We use the term *study habits* all the time, but we do not often take both parts of that term seriously. Clearly, we want students to study, but what about the habit component? Habits are actions that people perform automatically and without thinking. The human mind is a habit creation machine that looks for actions performed consistently in a particular environment and allows those actions to be performed again in the same environment without thinking. For example, you don't have to think about where the light switch is in your bedroom, how to press the gas and brake pedals in your car or how to type letters on your computer keyboard. You have done these actions so many times that they have become habits.

The study environment needs to harness the power of habits. We want students to think about the concepts they are learning, but we don't want the environment to suggest other actions that will get in the way of studying. Here are three things that can make studying more effective.

Minimize the Habits of Distraction

In the modern world, children are attached to iPods, smart phones, text messages, Facebook and instant message. From early on, children have developed the habit of checking these sources several times hourly. Those habits break into a child's concentration during study, reminding him or her that it is time to check the phone or computer.

Unfortunately, this multitasking gets in the way of acquiring high quality knowledge. It takes time to shift attention from homework to some other source of information and additional time to shift attention back. Not only does that constant shifting influence the amount of time it takes to get work done, it also affects the quality of the study itself. To create a more effective work environment, create a distraction-free zone during work time. Park the portable technology elsewhere in the house. Keep the smart phones and iPods out of arm's reach. Remove instant messaging from the computer and ban Facebook during study time.

Create a Consistent Work Space for Study

The habits children create reach all the way down to the level of where they should look to find the tools and supplies they need to study. That means children's work space should be set up so that they do not need to search each day for pencils, erasers or calculators. Children who study at a desk should keep that desk set up the same way each day. Children who study at a communal table at home should have a nearby bin or tray with supplies where they can regularly find what they need without having to spend a lot of time thinking about how to prepare for studying.

Find an Effective Location and Posture for Studying

Modern technology is so flexible that it does not place many constraints on where or how children study. It is common to see a child writing briefly at a desk, then working from a laptop computer on the floor, and then lying down on the couch to read a book. It is hard to maintain the same level of concentration when lying on the floor or propped up in bed as when sitting at a desk. The body's habit when lying down is to relax and sleep. It is not helpful for a child to have to fight that tendency when studying. In addition, lying down promotes passive reading. It is hard to take notes or type while lying down. So students who are lying down are playing a less active role in their learning than those who are sitting up. The advantage of promoting these behaviours is that after a while the habit system kicks in. Eventually, sitting in a consistently structured environment free of distracting technology is simply how studying gets done — now and for life.

Physical Needs of Children

Some of the most basic physical needs for children are food, shelter, clothing, and exercise. It doesn't really stop there though.

"Food" can be anything, but it takes a nutritious diet and regular meal times to provide for the real needs in this area. Regular meal times and proper diet promote healthy eating now and later in life. Providing shelter is important, but also taking the necessary precautions to be sure it is a safe, smoke free, fume free, warm, clean, and healthy environment is just as important as the roof they live under. Same goes for clothing. Every season is different. You can't really say "I provide my children with the basic need of clothes" if you're making them wear shorts in the middle of winter. It's important to make sure they have adequate clothing for the weather as well.

At home or at the daycare, children have physical needs that must be met which contribute to their total well being and comfort. Here are some ideas:

One of the important physical needs of children is a suitable environment which provides fresh air to breathe, clean water and a nutritious diet. The inhalation of fresh air is essential for good health and normal development. Consequently lack of fresh air can cause poor mental functioning in a child. It can result in the spread of airborne diseases like whooping cough and measles. Homes and nurseries should be properly ventilated in order to replace expired air with fresh air.

At home the children should not be exposed to paint fumes and dry cleaning solvents, cigarette smoke, chemicals present in detergents, cosmetics, food etc. Likewise, clean water and a nutritious balanced diet are also necessities for the normal development of the child.

Mealtimes in the nursery and at home are a very important aspect of caring for a child. Mealtimes should be set and regular so as to set up good eating habits and food given should be attractive and full of essential nutrients.

A suitable environment should also provide shelter and warmth for the child. Children should not be exposed to unsuitable variations of temperature. The home and nursery should be properly insulated from wild and harsh weather conditions by providing heating and cooling facilities when the need arises.

Physical exercise is important. Children should engage in exercises to encourage optimal development of their muscles, heart and lungs. Also exercises help good posture and co-ordination, as well as promoting a feeling of well being. Simple motor activities like hopping; jumping, skipping, and climbing should be encouraged.

Good and healthy habits are an important responsibility of parents and caregivers. Parents should make sure that their children are vaccinated at the right time. Likewise at school a visit from the school's doctor should be encouraged to create awareness Safety is important. At home and in school the need for safety should be taken seriously. A fire extinguisher should be close by incase of fire accident.

The physical needs of a child are an important part of his/her development and should be taken seriously by parents and caregivers.

Social Needs of Children

Children are constantly learning about their world and how to get along with others. A child's desire to connect with others motivates them to learn and gives the child confidence to try new things. Children's social development is closely related to their emotional development. Children who can control their feelings, such as anger or excitement, are more likely to be able to engage in positive play with other children and negotiate difficulties with others when they arise. Equally, children who understand the feelings of others will be better able to be sensitive to the needs of other children during play.

Children learn about relationships from the ways you relate to them and others.

All children go through different phases of social development. Children develop social skills mostly through games and play. How children play changes with age. As they grow, children move from playing alone to playing alongside other children and finally play co-operatively with other children.

Know Your Child

Children of different ages, backgrounds and personalities experience different challenges in developing social skills. Some children make friends easily and others less so. Some children are shy and others outgoing. Sometimes children have no trouble developing some social skills but do have difficulty with others.

Observe the child in different social situations. Notice how they manage. Do they seem different in different settings? Are they lacking in confidence? Do they need help to join in? What are they doing easily? What, if anything, are they finding more difficult?

Just like learning to walk and talk, a child's developing social skills require support, practice and repetition.

Ways to Help the Child

Create a climate of kindness and generosity at home. Encourage sharing and being considerate of others. Model the social behaviour you want to encourage in the child. Older siblings can also be helpful role models for younger bothers and sisters.

Ask children for help with daily chores and accept their offers of help. Encourage a variety of appropriate relationships between your child and others - both adults and children.

Help children to feel positive about them-selves. Positive self esteem is critical to healthy social development.

Support children to understand their own feelings and the feelings of others.

Help your child to develop skills in knowing how to join in with a group, take turns and follow rules.

Have reasonable expectations about sharing. Some toys may be more difficult than others for a child to share, for example, a favourite toy. Put these things away when your child is playing with friends.

Provide lots of opportunities for children to play with others.

Ask your child's preschool or school who your child spends time with and set up play dates with them.

Keep play dates for young children short, simple and fun. Introduce structured activities to the play for very young children. Gradually extend the length of time children play, increase the number of children involved and decrease the amount of structure you put in place as your child gets older and you can see that they have developed the skills to manage in these situations.

Vocational Rehabilitation

Vocational rehabilitation is a process which enables persons with functional, psychological, developmental, cognitive and emotional impairments or health conditions to overcome barriers to accessing, maintaining or returning to employment or other useful occupation.

Vocational rehabilitation can require input from a range of health care professionals and other non-medical disciplines such as disability employment advisers and career counsellors. Techniques used can include:

- assessment, appraisal, programme evaluation and research.
- goal setting and intervention planning.

- provision of health advice and promotion, in support of returning to work.
- support for self-management of health conditions.
- making adjustments to the medical and psychological impact of a disability.
- case management, referral, and service co-ordination.
- psychosocial interventions.
- career counselling, job analysis, job development, and placement services.
- functional and work capacity evaluations.

Vocational rehabilitation practitioners are often governed by standards of practice. In the United Kingdom these are produced by the Vocational Rehabilitation Association.

Rehabilitation Counselling

Rehabilitation Counselling is focused on helping people who have disabilities achieve their personal, career, and independent living goals through a counselling process.

Rehabilitation Counsellors can be found in private practice, in rehabilitation facilities, hospitals, universities, schools, government agencies, insurance companies and other organizations where people are being treated for congenital or acquired disabilities. While most rehabilitation counsellors focus on vocational services, in some states they qualify as both a Certified Rehabilitation Counsellor (CRC) and a Licensed Professional Counsellor (LPC), enabling them to focus on psychotherapy. Over time, with the changes in social work being more psychotherapy-oriented, rehabilitation counsellors take on more and more community engagement work, especially as it relates to special populations.

History

United States: Historically, rehabilitation counsellors primarily served working-age adults with disabilities. Today, the need for rehabilitation counselling services extends to persons of all age groups who have disabilities. Rehabilitation counsellors also may provide general and specialized counselling to people with disabilities in public human service programmes and private practice settings.

Initially, rehabilitation professionals were recruited from a variety of human service disciplines, including public health nursing, social work, and school counselling. Although educational programmes began to appear in the 1940s, it was not until the availability of federal funding for rehabilitation counselling programmes in 1954 that the profession began to grow and establish its own identity.

Education/Training

Though no specific undergraduate degree is required, the majority of rehabilitation counselling graduate students have undergraduate degrees in rehabilitation services, psychology, sociology, or other human services-related fields. As a Masters degree is required at a minimum, rehabilitation counsellors are trained at the graduate level, with most earning a Masters degree, and a few continuing on to the Doctoral level. The Council on Rehabilitation Education (CORE) accredits qualifying institutions, though not all programmes meet accreditation requirements, prohibiting some graduates from professional certification/licensure. Rehabilitation counsellors are trained in the following areas:

- Individual and group counselling
- Medical and psychosocial information
- Problems and community engagement of special populations
- Evaluation and assessment
- Research utilization
- Employment and occupational choice
- Case and caseload management
- Job development and placement

Accredited rehabilitation counsellor education programmes typically provide 60 credit hours of academic and field-based clinical training. Clinical training consists of at least a semester of practicum and a minimum of 600 hours of supervised internship experience. Clinical field experiences are available in a variety of community, state, federal, and private rehabilitation-related programmes.

Professional Certification/Licensure

The Commission on Rehabilitation Counsellor Certification (CRCC) grants certification to counsellors who meet educational requirements and have passed an examination indicating that they possess the competency and skill to become a Certified Rehabilitation Counsellor, (CRC in the United States; CCRC in Canada). A Masters degree is required to obtain certification. Certification as a rehabilitation counsellor is not mandated by any state or federal laws, however eligibility to sit for the certification exam is mandated by federal law for those wishing to work for state/federal vocational rehabilitation systems. Some states have Licensed Rehabilitation Counsellors (LRC), which places LRCs at the same level as other licensed social service professionals. In other states the CRC qualifies the rehabilitation counsellor to obtain the Licensure as a Professional Counsellor (LPC). Certification is highly desirable to many employers.

Social Relevancy

Community service to a culturally and ethnically diverse population, professional functions, critical thinking, advocacy, applied research activities, and ethical standards are integrated throughout rehabilitation counsellor preparation and development. Though rehabilitation counsellors are adept at understanding medical issues surrounding the disability (as proven by certification/licensure), they are trained in the social model of disability, which identifies systemic barriers, negative attitudes and exclusion by society (purposely or inadvertently) that mean society is the main contributory factor in disabling people. Rehabilitation Counsellors are often advocates in the community for people with disabilities outside of the workplace, with most doing some form of community engagement. As a good portion of counsellors have disabilities themselves, the counselling process often emphasizes self-advocacy skills. Rehabilitation counsellors can be found in the leadership of many prominent organizations that support human rights and civil rights for people with disabilities such as American Coalition of Citizens with Disabilities, National Black Deaf Advocates, etc.

Notable Rehabilitation Counsellors

- Antonia Darder Aguilo - Public Intellectual, Leavey Presidential Endowed Chair in Ethics and Moral Leadership in the School of Education at Loyola Marymount University
- Bill G. Chapman - Air Force Veteran, Blind/Vision-impaired advocate
- Bill Copeland - Award-winning Poet
- Laurence M. Foley - American Diplomat to Jordan
- Patricia Gerard - First female Mayor of Largo, FL
- Juan de Dios Ramírez Heredia - Spanish Romani politician
- Al Jarreau - Grammy-winning Jazz Musician

- Gordon Johnson - Child Welfare Advocate
- Young Woo Kang - First Korean man with vision impairment to earn a PhD, Creator of braille alphabet for the Korean language
- Robert Kelly - Navy Veteran, Film-inspiration
- Kathleen Kenna - Canadian Journalist in Afghanistan
- Erin Pac - U.S. Olympic Bobsledder, 2010 Bronze-medal winner
- Dianne Primavera - U.S. Legislator for the state of Colorado
- Kathleen Hawk Sawyer - Former Director of U.S. Federal Bureau of Prisons
- Alberta Banner Turner - First African-American woman to earn a PhD in Psychology from The Ohio State University
- Ronnie Mae Tyson - First Miss Black Deaf America

Rehabilitation Counselling Careers

Careers in the Profession: In the United States, many rehabilitation counsellors work in a variety of arenas. The predominant placement of rehabilitation counsellors are state rehabilitation programmes as Vocational Counsellors, social service agencies as Administrators, and at the collegiate level as Disability Counsellors/Specialists:

State Rehabilitation Programmes

The predominant need for rehabilitation counsellors is within federal/state funded vocational rehabilitation programmes. While the Veterans Benefits Administration has its own vocational rehabilitation programme, the rest of Federal/State Vocational Rehabilitation Programmes are funded and regulated by the Rehabilitation Services Administration (RSA), a division of the U.S Department of Education. Although policies vary from state to state, rehabilitation counsellors who work in the federal/state systems typically must hold a masters degree in rehabilitation counselling, special education or a related field, and are required to be certified or be eligible to sit for the certification examination. People accepting employment in the federal/state Vocational Rehabilitation programmes do so with the agreement they will meet these qualifications by a specified date to maintain employment.

Social Service Agencies/corporate Sector

Rehabilitation Counsellors can work in the non-profit/corporate sector in various ways. Though the majority start as counsellors, specializing in career counselling, most rehabilitation counsellors that work in the non-profit arena rise to the administration level, either in supervising staff or directing programmes for people with disabilities. Others supervise staff that work in case management programmes that serve people with disabilities. Some rehabilitation counsellors work with Independent Living Centres, doing community engagement, advocacy, outside referrals, and social service provision for people with disabilities. Entrepreneurial rehabilitation counsellors also work as consultants, establishing their own private service agencies. Counsellors in working with corporations focus on community relations or corporate service, serving as liaisons between companies and charities or service programmes.

College disability Counsellors/specialists

By law all community colleges, colleges and universities are required to make reasonable accommodations for students with disabilities. To satisfy this requirement most collegial settings have a Disability Resources Centre, a Special Needs Coordinator or a similar office. Staff are responsible for coordinating services that *may* include but are not limited to: advocacy/liaison, computer access, counselling (academic, personal, vocational), equipment loan, information/referral services, in-service awareness programmes, notetakers, on campus orientation and mobility training for visually impaired students, priority registration assistance, readers, scribes, shuttle (on-campus), sign language interpreters, test proctoring/testing accommodations, and tutors.

Some adaptive technological accommodations *may* include but are not limited to: Adaptive computer technology (including voice activated and speech output), Assistive listening devices, Films/ videotapes about disabilities, Kurzweil personal reader, Large print software,Print enlargers (CCTV), Raised-line drawing kit, Tactile map of campus, Talking calculators, Tape recorders/APH Talking Book Machine, TDD for hearing impaired, Wheelchair, Wheelchair access maps.

Students who have documentation proving their disability status and the staff are trained to access or have knowledge of the necessary services according the students' unique need. As the college level is different from the primary school system, the same services that a student may have received within a special education programme in high school may not be required at the collegiate level. A wide variety of students with disabilities can be served, some examples are individuals with: learning disabilities, sensorial disabilities (hearing loss, vision loss, etc.), physical disabilities (cerebral palsy, etc.) and psychological disabilities.

The Growth of the Field

Job Outlook: As of 2010 there were 129,800 working in the field. Jobs for rehabilitation counsellors are expected to grow by 28 percent, which is much faster than the average for all occupations.

Professional Development

There are several professional organizations Rehabilitation Counsellors and other rehabilitation professionals belong to, including the American Rehabilitation Counselling Association, National Rehabilitation Counselling Association, and American Rehabilitation Action Network. Though there is no nationwide union or lobbying organization supporting rehabilitation counsellors (such as is the case with social workers, or psychologists), the Commission on Rehabilitation Counsellor Certification (CRCC) does a lot of work in organizing rehabilitation counsellors that pursue the professional advancement of the young field.

Career and Vocational Guidance

From the earliest years of our lives, we are asked to consider what we want to be when we grow up. Parents and guardians carefully plan and manage their children's educational experiences in the hope of preparing them for successful careers.

As a caregiver, you are faced with the challenge of helping children and youth identify and achieve their career goals. Young people tend to have limited information about the types of jobs that are available to them. Lack of information leads many to make unrealistic decisions about careers. Many youth are not sure of what they want to do. Some of them are not even aware of their own talents. You can help them get the information they need to make realistic and satisfying career choices. Another of your roles as a caregiver is to help children and youth develop the qualities they need to be successful in the job market. Certain qualities can contribute to success, such as: the willingness to work hard and do more than the bare minimum; good spoken and written communication skills; dependability; and the ability to work well with others. Career guidance becomes more and more challenging as the realities of the workplace change. At one time the types of work available and the skills required changed very little from one generation to another. Now, times are changing so quickly that it's hard to predict what the next 20, 10, or even 5 years will bring. In these rapidly changing times, qualities such as flexibility, creativity, and the desire to be a lifelong learner have become important.

The word "career" is used to refer to one's progress through his/her working life, particularly in a certain profession or line of work. When we talk about a "career in teaching" or a "career in technology" we mean that a person will study and then work in teaching or in technology, perhaps changing jobs from time to time in the interests of advancement. The goals that one has for one's working life are called "career goals," and planning how we will reach them is called setting a "career path." Carpentry, engineering, nursing, hospitality, social work, banking, and farming are just a few of the many possible careers people might choose.

Vocation

In its most usual use, the word "vocation" refers to a strong feeling within an individual that they are meant to do a certain job. Sometimes people feel that they are "called" to a particular kind of life or work, such as nursing or a religious life. The word "vocation" can also be used to refer to a trade or profession.

Vocational Guidance

Vocational guidance is the process through which an individual is helped to choose a suitable occupation, make the necessary preparations for it (such as enrolling in a training programme), enter into it, and develop in it. This is a continuous process since an individual is likely to re-evaluate the career choice at various points in his/her life and may make changes at any point in his/her career.

Life Skills

The term "life skills" refers to the various psychosocial and interpersonal skills that lead people to a healthy and productive life. These skills include the ability to make informed decisions, communicate effectively, cope with life situations, and manage oneself. Life skills may include actions for oneself or towards others, as well as actions to change the surrounding environment in order to make it more conducive to good health.

Life skills competencies are necessary for the total development of children and youth. These competencies are the knowledge, skills, attitudes, and types of behaviour that children and youth need to become healthy, happy, and well-balanced individuals. Children who have these competencies will be able to meet the challenges of work and life in a complex and fast-paced world.

Sources of Information

Following are the possible sources of information about careers.

- Local libraries.
- Media advertising (newspapers, magazines, radio, TV).
- Government labour office.
- Shopping markets with bulletin boards for advertising.
- Local non-governmental organisations (NGOs) in the community.
- Employment bureaus.
- Friends who have careers.
- Current employees of an organisation (a farmer, business person, medical doctor, teacher, builder, radio announcer, etc.).
- Past employees of an organisation.
- Paying visits to an organisation of your career interest (such as a hospital for a physiotherapist, radiographer, or nurse).
- From work sites in the immediate community (such as at a mosque, church, school, or farm).
- Professionals (pilot, engineer, lawyer, etc.).
- Job attachments (such as working with a construction company).
- Internet websites.

Youth and children have a limited knowledge of the range of possible occupations and careers. This can contribute to unrealistic career aspirations. As a caregiver, you will need to ensure that youth have appropriate career information. In order to make an informed choice, youth need to have a realistic picture of occupations they are considering: the working conditions, the tasks that are involved, the qualifications and education required, the salary, the job opportunities, and so on.

Eliminating Gender Bias and Stereotypes in Career Choices

Gender is the social dimension of being male and female. There are two ways of looking at this definition:

- Gender identity is the sense of being male or female, which most children acquire by the time they are three years old.

- Gender roles refer to a set of expectations regarding how females or males should think, act, or feel.

Gender bias begins early in life when parents start dressing children differently depending on whether they are male or female, giving them different toys, treating them differently, and having different expectations for them. The differences are reinforced as children watch and imitate their parents fulfilling these traditional roles. Culture, the schools, peers, and the media reinforce what children have learned from their parents. Gender stereotypes are the beliefs and impressions that people have about males and females. Males are believed to be dominant, aggressive, independent, and enduring go-getters. Females are widely believed to be soft, caring, more helpful, weak, and emotional. It is assumed that females are not ambitious, are unable to do certain jobs, and want to stay at home and nurture children.

The problems with gender biases and stereotypes include the following:

- Girls and women often are not encouraged to use their talents, which deprives them of satisfaction and deprives society of the contributions they could make.
- Men and boys are expected to act in certain ways and do certain kinds of work, so they also face restrictions in the careers they choose.
- Because girls and women are expected to be passive and helpless, they are more vulnerable to abuse and exploitation within and outside of their homes.

Vocational Choice

Early theories of occupational choice were based on an economic perspective and today that is also a large factor in determining the occupation a person chooses.

However, there are psychological and sociological aspects of occupational choice. Many times persons are offered advice that does not take into account religious views, history of one's mother country, and attitudes about work based in the literature of one's home country.

There are several theories of occupational choice - that is what job is right for a person with certain characteristics? The theories are based on the view of a normal person who progresses through stages of human development. Each theory emphasizes certain factors:

- the person has to select his own occupation,
- there are certain factors that influence occupational choice,
- choosing an occupation is a very distinct event in one's life.

One of the most popular theories is trait-factor. This means that a person has certain distinct traits that are needed for success in a certain job. For example, a bookkeeper should be a person who likes accuracy, detail, mathematics, and quiet work area. If a person's traits can be measured, there is a direct way to predict success in certain job.

When this theory is applied to helping people find jobs, there are the following implications:

1. Each person has traits that are for one or a few correct occupations.
2. If left alone, a person should naturally make the correct occupational choice.
3. Without assistance though, a person might choose the wrong occupation and waste his time.
4. During the teen-age years, a person should learn what traits he has.
5. When the person knows his traits and the jobs that correlate with his traits, his educational choices should be based on those traits.
6. The choice of occupation and decisions that affect achieving that occupation should remain constant over a period of time. For example, if a young person decides to become a doctor, he will make decisions about his education (which medical institute is best, what speciality interests him the most, and what is necessary for him to know to pass entry exams) so that he will eventually be the doctor he wants to be.

Another theory is that a person has certain needs that drive him toward a certain job. The motivation to satisfy these needs may be logical or emotional, conscious or unconscious, and directly or indirectly expressed in words. It is said that work is a way to satisfy one's needs. For example, a person may have a need for stability so that he finds a job that pays him well, and he stays in that job all of his life. He is content to be in one place and have reliable pay every month. Some vocational scientists have developed six basic interests or needs that can be measured. They are:

1. Theoretical - An overriding interest in the discovery of truth and an experimental, rational, and intellectual approach.
2. Economic - This is an emphasis on practical values and doing business activities.
3. Aesthetic - Placement of highest value on form and harmony; evaluating experience from its gracefulness, symmetry, or fitness.
4. Social - Emphasizing altruism and philanthropy
5. Political - An interest in personal power, influence, and renown.
6. Religious - Interest in unity of experience and in attempting to understand people and the universe in a whole system.

Theory of Early Parent-Child Relationships

Ann Roe developed three types of psychological climates that affect the work children eventually choose. If a parent is focuses on the emotional aspects of a child's growth, the result is an over-protecting or over-demanding atmosphere for the child. For example, the parent may be so concerned that the child has quiet, non-threatening life experiences as he grows, the child grows up in an over-protecting environment, not one that usually helps him adapt to different types of people and experiences. These children may choose occupations that have to do with emphasis on their own importance such as a political or governmental occupation.

The avoidance of a child results in his growing up in a neglectful or rejecting climate. Oftentimes these children have difficult behaviour as babies and their parents try everything to satisfy them without being very successful. These children tend to choose those jobs that involve objects (technology), animals (outdoor life occupations), or ideas (science). The parent who is relaxed and accepting of his child tries to provide a loving atmosphere for growth. These children tend to choose those professions that relate to people such a teachers, professors, doctors, social workers, and church workers.

Question:

1. Which theory of occupational choice is most reasonable to you? Are there other factors to consider when making an occupational choice?

Vocational Development

The main idea of all the theories of occupational choice is that one, several, or a group of factors influence the person and at some point in live each person chooses an occupation in association with these factors or as a reaction to them. There is another group of theories that states that a person proceeds through various stages in life with vocation as only one part of his human development. For example, as people age and gain life experience, they may turn to another occupation. An engineer may become a teacher or pastor. A person does not choose an occupation for the whole of life, but chooses a series of occupations related to his life stage. People are not designated for a correct occupation - everyone can be satisfied with many jobs. These theories are known as theories of vocational development.

For example, each person goes through a course of development psychologically and socially. Through what he experiences, he grows in different ways. There are some basic assumptions about vocational development:

1. Individual development is continuous, and there are distinct life stages.
2. People in each stage of life have certain common traits.
3. Most people in a specific culture pass through similar developmental periods.
4. Society places certain demands on individuals and they are similar for all people in that society.
5. Developmental crises occur when people become aware of the need to change current behaviour and learn new coping skills.
6. As individuals learn new skills, they become more mature.
7. Preparations for overcoming a developmental crisis are made in the stage prior to next new crisis.
8. The crisis must be met successfully before the individual can pass to another developmental stage.
9. Learning required tasks gives the individual approval from society and helps a person pass through other crises successfully.

There may be a series of different tasks for a person to complete in society. An adolescent faces the task of choosing an occupation, but he must also master several other tasks concurrently:

- Accept his physical appearance,
- Accept the masculine or feminine role,
- Establish relationships with both sexes,
- Depend less on his parents for emotional support,

- Develop socially responsible behaviour,
- Prepare for marriage and family,
- Establish his own life values.

Another theory is that occupational choice is a long-term process that becomes progressively irreversible. A final choice in occupations is the compromise of an ideal and the available realistic alternatives. For example, a person may want to become a doctor after having an illness from which he recovered. However, his age may limit him since medical study requires long preparation. Instead, he may become a laboratory researcher or help with funding a research group that is trying to conquer a certain disease. Also, when an occupational choice is made, other choices are eliminated. As time goes by, the ability to change professions is limited. The responsibilities of family, finances, and use of one's energies limits choices. Other factors that affect occupational choice are role models, coping with reality of certain occupational environments, and if a person thinks of work as enjoyment or a task.

Question:

2. Think about the role model, occupational environments, and how you see work. Write an example for each.

Another theory is that a person develops an image of himself as he works. Through different work activities, people learn about their own unique style and similarity to others. Sensations, perceptions, and experiences all help a person to build an adult image of himself. People work to earn a living, to gain recognition as a person, to express themselves, and for satisfaction. So vocational development occurs in a social and economic sphere of work.

How Do These Theories Relate to Disabled Persons?

Disabilities affect a person's ability to do a certain type of work. Adjustment to disability affects how a person works. For example, a person who loses a leg may not have the ability to return to his former job assembling cars. He must find other work where he is not required to stand for long periods of time. Adjustment to a disability may be positive in that a person strives to work after the disability occurs. It may be negative because a person sees himself as unable to work and must sit at home for the rest of his life.

The vocational development of the person before his disability has a direct effect on how he sees himself after the disability happens.

The rehabilitation specialist needs to know what residual abilities the person has after an accident and identify the disabled persons needs (independence, adequate income, care for family, etc.). By knowing these abilities and needs, the specialist can help a person find work that fits abilities and needs. How do we know if a person is successful in a new job or in training? In a new job, we see that he is using his abilities and gaining some new ones. His work pleases him and he is a stable worker. If he decides on training, we verify that he attends classes, he finishes his course of training, and finds a job that gives him stability.

There are four potential problem areas for the individual with a disability as he begins his search for work.

1. Most kinds of work are done away from home and require travel to the place of work
2. Work is done in a public place, so that privacy from others is limited.
3. The work situation is impersonal and work is done regardless of a person's personal characteristics.
4. Work is bound by time commitments, that is, a person has to be on a job for so many hours per day or complete so many tasks per day.

Each work situation is special in that there are certain customs, rules, and traditions that come from the culture a person lives in and from the specific work place's history and place in society. For example, a car repairman has certain procedures he follows in fixing a car and there are certain prices paid for his knowledge and expertise. The car repairman's work place may be his own yard by his own home, which is not a high level place in society, or it may be with a dealer repairing BMW cars which is more prestigious.

3. What factors affect a person after his disability in getting work?

(Only one of the following answers is correct.)

a) depression and adjustment,

b) abilities and needs,

c) training and work situation.

How Do We Help a Person Understand How to Look for Different Work?

As we get to know the person, we are able to collect data about his medical history, his level of education, interest inventories, behaviour descriptions of himself and what others think of him, his likes and dislikes, and his sense of values. From all this information, we have a picture of who the person is and help him understand himself.

The process of finding a good job or career is not exact, but then neither is the choice of a marriage partner. Both of these choices maybe emotionally influenced, based on inadequate sampling of what is available, and scientifically unsound, but they can produce happy outcomes.

In many developing countries in the world, types of work are constantly changing. Professions we never heard of 10 years ago are now established. Many older types of work are vanishing as machines now do them or there is not a need for this work anymore. People with or without disabilities need to think about the type of work they do because the world of work is always changing. It changes drastically after an accident. For example, a person who is injured as a builder may not be able to work at his former job anymore. Therefore, he needs to find a job that will use his skills from earlier jobs. He may become a building inspector or order supplies for a builder.

In the modern world, the idea of having a job for all of one's life is no longer an option. Persons may change jobs every few years since the needs of a country change. The types of jobs that may be practiced over a lifetime are those associated medicine and government. Most other jobs will change in form over the years. For example, many engineers and university researchers lost their jobs in Russia during the 1990's. Some of these people became drivers since they have a good work record and ability to learn new habits. Some of these people have gone on to other jobs, but others have remained in their work as drivers and make a good income.

Why Does a Person Need to Understand Himself?

(Only one of the following answers is correct.)

a. Because he then knows better what his strengths are,

b. He knows what he wants and does not want in his life,

c. He avoids making mistakes in choosing a job.

How Do We Find Information About Jobs?

There are local information centres in each region that provide information about jobs available. The disadvantage about this system is that the information may be out of date and the bureaucracy is not willing to help you find the information you need. However, that may be the first place to begin looking for jobs for your client.

There is also local information in your towns. There maybe employers who list job needs in their offices of personnel. For example, Perekriostik, a grocery store chain in Moscow, lists needs for persons with disability near their manager's office. When looking at such a job, you must observe the workers in this job while they are at work, find out how much training is needed for the job, find out about the rate of pay, and hours of work. Sometimes people with disabilities are hired simply as a tax break for an employer. The disabled worker gets very little pay and very little time actually working.

Newspapers and television are also sources of information. For example, there are ads in newspapers for work and special newspapers about types of jobs that need workers. Sometimes special announcements are made on television or radio about new businesses or factories that are opening. If the business is legitimate, it is good to keep a file of each one, its location, and telephone number.

How can you help the client know about a specific job? Gathering information becomes specific when one needs to know about a specific job. There are:

- legal qualifications - is a license required to do this job, are there legal restrictions that prevent a disabled person from doing this job?
- medical qualifications - what are the specific physical demands for this job? For example, a watch repairman needs finger dexterity to do his job. By actually looking at a person doing the job, you can observe what physical demands are made on his body to do this job.
- social skill requirements - one must be able to get along with others in a job, especially, the boss, co-workers, and supervisors.
- education - usually the completion of high school is necessary to get any type of job, however, once a person is in a job, advancement depends on practical learning rather then educational credentials
- job duties - analyze what is each mini-task of a job is, for example, working on an assembly line is not merely one big job, but may involve putting a certain number of items in a box, closing a box, and putting it on a different conveyer.

- working conditions - this includes the amount of time spent on the job each day, special hazards of the job, the social climate of the job meaning that certain types of clothing may be necessary or certain relationships are important in doing one's job, and accessibility to transport to a job.
- payment for work
- availability of this job over a period of time - is it a short term job that will be finished in a period of months, does it depend on weather conditions (such as construction work), or would it be better for a person to have his own independent work?

Question:

5. How did you gather information about the job or profession you have? How many choices did you have?

How Does a Person Make a Choice of a Job or Occupation?

A person must be familiar with his own strengths and liabilities. He must know about the job he wants to do. His goals must fit with the job he wants to do. If a person is over the age of 35 years and enjoyed his former work, he can use the skills he has now and apply them to another job. For example, if he worked on a construction site, he may be able to use the skills he learned there in a store or market helping people estimate the quantity of materials needed for a certain remodelling job or he may simply work in a place that sells building materials.

There are several types of decision-making processes that can be taught to help a person make a decision. Here is one of them:

1. The person must be willing to make a decision to solve a problem.
2. The problem must be defined and the goals identified - for example, a problem could be "finding a job that is suitable for me" and the goal would be to find the job in 2 months.
3. Alternatives to the decision are identified - for example, a person could say that actually working on a job is not his choice and he would rather take a government pension and play cards or watch television for the rest of his life.
4. Information is collected about the decision through interviews with prospective employers, other workers in the same jobs, or written materials.

5. The results of this data and the various possible choices are reviewed and compared.
6. There is a comparison of the person's values, family situation, and practicality of a job with the choices. For example, a man may want to drive a truck for a living, but if he has children, what kind of driving will he choose: does he want to be away from his family for weeks or does he want to drive locally and be at home every night?
7. The person makes a choice.
8. The chosen alternative is tried and the person evaluates whether or not he needs to change his situation or stay with the job he chose.

5

Psychology and Vocational Guidance

Career counselling, career guidance and career coaching are similar in nature to other types of counselling or coaching, e.g. marriage or psychological counselling. What unites all types of professional counselling is the role of practitioners, who combine giving advice on their topic of expertise with counselling techniques that support clients in making complex decisions and facing difficult situations. The focus of career counselling is generally on issues such as career exploration, career change, personal career development and other career related issues.

Around the globe, countless definitions, concepts and terminology exist for career counselling - particularly due to cultural and linguistic differences. This even affects the most central term *counselling* (or: *counselling* in British English) which is often substituted with the word *guidance* as in *career guidance*. For example, in the UK, *career counselling* would usually be referred to as *careers advice* or *guidance*. Due to the widespread reference to both *career guidance* and *career counselling* among policy-makers, academics and practitioners around the world, references to *career guidance and counselling* are becoming common. Accordingly, this article emphasizes a *broad understanding* of career counselling which involves a variety of professionals activities commonly associated with career counselling, guidance, coaching, and advise. More specific roles and activities associated with career counselling are explained below.

Related Professional Activities

Career counselling or career guidance includes a wide variety of professional activities which focus on supporting people in dealing with career-related challenges - both preventively and in difficult situations (such as unemployment). Career counsellors work with people from various walks of life, such as adolescents seeking to explore career options, experienced professionals contemplating a career change, parents who want to return to the world of work after taking time to raise their child, or people seeking employment. Career counselling is also offered in various settings, including in groups and individually, in person or by means of digital communication.

Several approaches have been undertaken to systemize the variety of professional activities related to career guidance and counselling. In the most recent attempt, the Network for Innovation in Career Guidance and Counselling in Europe (NICE) - a consortium of 45 European institutions of higher education in the field of career counselling - has agreed on a system of professional roles for guidance counsellors. Each of these five roles is seen as an important facet of the *career guidance and counselling profession.* Career counsellors performing in any of these roles are expected to behave professionally, e.g. by following ethical standards in their practice. The NICE Professional Roles (NPR) are:

- The *Career Educator* "supports people in developing their own career management competences"
- The *Career Information & Assessment Expert* "supports people in assessing their personal characteristics and needs, then connecting them with the labour market and education systems"
- The *Career Counsellor* "supports individuals in understanding their situations, so as to work through issues towards solutions"
- The *Programme & Service Manager* "ensures the quality and delivery of career guidance and counselling organisations' services"
- The *Social Systems Intervener & Developer* "supports clients (even) in crisis and works to change systems for the better"

The description of the NICE Professional Roles (NPR) draws on a variety of prior models to define the central activities and competences of guidance counsellors. The NPR can, therefore, be understood as a state-of-the-art framework which includes all relevant aspects of career counselling. For this reason, other models haven't been included here so far. Models which are reflected in the NPR include:

- BEQU: "Kompetenzprofil für Beratende" (Germany, 2011)
- CEDEFOP "Practitioner Competences" (2009)

- ENTO: "National Occupational Standards for Advice and Guidance" (Great Britain, 2006)
- IAEVG: "International Competences for Educational and Vocational Guidance" (2003)
- Savickas, M.: "Career Counselling" (USA, 2011)

Benefits

Professional career counsellors can support people with career-related challenges in many ways. Through their expertise in career development and labour markets, they can put a person's qualification, experience, strengths and weakness in a broad perspective taking into consideration their desired salary, personal hobbies and interests, location, job market and educational possibilities. Through their counselling and teaching abilities, career counsellors can additionally support people in gaining a better understanding of what really matters for them personally, how they can plan their careers autonomously, or help them in making tough decisions and getting through times of crisis. Finally, career counsellors are often capable of supporting their clients in finding suitable placements/ jobs, in working out conflicts with their employers, or finding the support of other helpful services. It is due to these various benefits of career counselling that policy-makers in many countries of the world publicly fund guidance services. For example, the European Union understands career guidance and counselling as an instrument to effectively combat social exclusion and increase citizens' employability.

History

Frank Parson's *Choosing a Vocation* (1909) was perhaps the first major work which is concerned with careers guidance. While until the 1970s a strongly normative approach was characteristic for theories (e.g. of Donald E. Super's *life-span approach*) and practice of career counselling (e.g. concept of *matching*), new models have their starting point in the individual needs and transferable skills of the clients while managing biographical breaks and discontinuities. Career development is no longer viewed as a linear process. More consideration is now placed on nonlinear, chance and unplanned influences.

Training

Up until now there is no standardized qualification path for professional career counsellors, although various certificates are offered nationally and internationally (e.g. by professional associations), and the number of academic degree programmes in career guidance and/ or career counselling is growing worldwide. Still, in most countries, basically anybody could call themselves a "career counsellor" (unlike engineers or psychologists whose professions are protected legally). At the same time, policy makers agree that the competence of career counsellors is one of the most important factors in ensuring that people receive high quality support in dealing with their career questions. Depending on the country of their education, career counsellors may have a variety of academic backgrounds: In Europe, for instance, degrees in (vocational/ industrial/ organization) psychology and educational sciences are among the most common, but backgrounds in sociology, public administration and other sciences are also frequent. At the same time, many training programmes for career counsellors are becoming increasingly multidisciplinary.

Professional Career Guidance Centres

There are many career guidance and counselling centres all over the world. They give services of guidance and counselling on higher studies, possibilities, chances and nature of courses and institutes. Also that these services are offered either fixing up a meeting with the Experts or having telephonic conversations with the guide or even the online guidance which is very common these days with the people getting services on click of their mouse. There are many such service providers all over the world providing online counselling to people about their career or conducting a psychometric test to know the persons aptitude as well as interests.

Career Testing

People who participate in career counselling can benefit from the use of aptitude tests, or career testing. Career testing is often done online and provides insightful and relatively objective information about which jobs may be suitable for the test taker based on combination of their interests, values and skills. Career tests usually provide a list of recommended jobs that match the test takers attributes with those of people with similar personalities who enjoy/are successful at their jobs. There are various ways to test an individual for which field he is suitable, psychometric testing being one among them.

Psychometric testing covers a wide range of skills, interests and values of people and can be of use in career counselling in different ways. For example, the information won from such tests can be of help for the professionals who mentor, coach or counsel individuals. With psychometric testing, there is no pass or fail, but the quality of the information won from the tests can vary. Psychometric testing uses in-depth psychological profiles to assess personality and intellectual levels. Different test companies use different theoretical approaches to testing, such as the psychometric approach, the psychodynamic approach, the social learning approach and the humanist approach. Different test companies have their own methods of testing, some of them being protected with copyrights. Two commonly used assessments are the Strong Interest Inventory and the MBTI, for example. Usually, psychometric testing uses multiple sets of questions relating to personality type, how the test taker would handle aspects of work and home life, what his or her goals are for the future and his or her strengths and weaknesses. If the test taker is honest and the employed tests follow scientific standards, the results should be fairly accurate and useful for career counselling activities.

Challenges

One of the major challenges associated with career counselling is encouraging participants to engage in the process. For example in the UK 70% of people under 14 say they have had no careers advice while 45% of people over 14 have had no or very poor/limited advice.

In a related issue some client groups tend to reject the interventions made by professional career counsellors preferring to rely on the advice of peers or superiors within their own profession. Jackson et al. found that 44% of doctors in training felt that senior members of their own profession were best placed to give careers advice. Furthermore it is recognised that the giving of career advice is something that is widely spread through a range of formal and informal roles. In addition to career counsellors it is also common for teachers, managers, trainers and Human Resources (HR) specialists to give formal support in career choices. Similarly it is also common for people to seek informal support from friends and family around their career choices and to bypass career professionals altogether. Today increasingly people rely on career web portals to seek advice on resume writing and handling interviews; as also to research on various professions and companies. It has even become possible to take vocational assessments online.

Preparing Counsellors

A school counsellor is a counsellor and an educator who works in elementary, middle, and high schools to provide academic, career, college readiness, and personal/social competencies to all K-12 students through a school counselling programme. The four main school counselling programme interventions used include: developmental school counselling core curriculum classroom lessons and annual academic, career/college readiness, and personal/social planning for every student; and group and individual counselling for some students.

Older, outdated terms for the profession were "guidance counsellor" or "educational counsellor" but "school counsellor" is preferred due to professional school counsellors' advocating for every child's academic, career, and personal/social success in every elementary, middle, and high school . In the Americas, Africa, Asia, Europe, and the Pacific, the terms school counsellor, school guidance counsellor, and guidance teacher are also used with a traditional emphasis on career development. Countries vary in how a school counselling programme and school counselling programme services are provided based on economics (funding for schools and school counselling programmes), social capital (independent versus public schools), and School Counsellor certification and credentialing movements in education departments, professional associations, and national and local legislation. The largest accreditation body for Counsellor Education/School Counselling programmes is the Council for the Accreditation of Counselling and Related Educational Programmes (CACREP). International Counsellor Education programmes are accredited through a CACREP affiliate, the International Registry of Counsellor Education Programmes (IRCEP).

In some countries, school counselling is provided by educational specialists (for example, Botswana, China, Finland, Israel, Malta, Nigeria, Romania, Taiwan, Turkey, United States). In other cases, school counselling is provided by classroom teachers who either have such duties added to their typical teaching load or teach only a limited load that also includes school counselling activities (for example-India, Japan, Mexico, South Korea, Zambia). The IAEVG focuses primarily on career development with some international school counselling articles and conference presentations.

School Counselling History

Canada: In Canada, most provinces have adapted K-12 comprehensive school counselling programmes similar to those initiated by and adapted in the ASCA National Model. School counsellors reported in 2004 at a conference in Winnipeg on issues such as budget cuts, lack of clarity about school counsellor roles, high student to school counsellor ratios, especially in elementary schools, and how using a comprehensive school counselling model helped to clarify school counsellor roles with teachers and administrators and strengthen the profession. In 2009, The Canadian Counselling Association (CCA) became the Canadian Counselling and Psychotherapy Association (CCPA).

China

In China, discussed the main influences on school counselling as being Chinese philosophers Confucius and Lao-Tsu, who provided early models of child and adult development that later influenced the work of Abraham Maslow and Carl Rogers. China also developed mental testing over 3,000 years ago, which was used for civil service examinations initially and eventually adopted by the British in the mid-19th century and later in the USA.

Only 15% of high school students are admitted to college in China, so the entrance exams are fiercely competitive and those who do enter university graduate at a rate of 99%.

Much pressure is put on children and adolescents to study and be able to attend college and this pressure is a central school counselling focus in China. An additional stressor is that there are not enough places for students to attend college, and over 1/3 of college graduates cannot find jobs, so career and employment counselling and development are central in school counselling.

There is a stigma related to personal or emotional problems and even though most universities and many schools now have counsellors, there is a reluctance by many students to seek counselling for issues such as anxiety and depression.

There is no national system of certifying school counsellors. Most are trained in Western-developed cognitive methods including REBT, Rogerian, Family Systems, Behaviour Modification, and Object Relations and also recommend Chinese methods such as qi-gong (deep breathing), acupuncture, and music therapy.

Shared that Chinese school counsellors always work within a traditional Chinese world view of a community and family-based system that lessens the primacy of focus on the individual. In Hong Kong, Hui (2000) discussed work on moving toward comprehensive whole-school counselling programmes and away from a remediation-style model.

Finland

In Finland, legislation has been passed in terms of the school counselling system. The Basic Education Act of 1998 states that every student must receive school counselling services. All Finnish school counsellors must have a teaching certificate as well as master's degree in a specific subject and a specialized certificate in school counselling.

Ireland

In Ireland, school counselling began in County Dublin in the 1960s and went countrywide in the 1970s. However, legislation in the early 1980s severely curtailed the movement due to budget constraints. The main organization for school counselling profession is the IGC or Institute of Guidance Counsellors, which has a code of ethics.

Israel

In Israel, a 2005 study by Erhard & Harel of 600 elementary, middle, and high school counsellors found that a third of school counsellors were delivering primarily traditional individual counselling services, about a third were delivering preventive classroom counselling curriculum lessons, and a third were delivering both individual counselling services and school counselling curriculum lessons in a more balanced or comprehensive developmental school counselling programme; school counsellor roles varied due to three elements: the school counsellor's personal preferences, school level, and the principal's expectations. Erhard & Harel stated that the profession in Israel, like many other countries, is transforming from various marginal and ancillary services to a comprehensive school counselling approach integral in the total school's education programme.

Japan

In Japan, school counselling is a very recent phenomenon with school counsellors being introduced only in the mid-1990s and then often only part-time with a strong emphasis on assisting with behavioural issues.

Lebanon

In Lebanon, the government sponsored the first training of school counsellors for public elementary and middle schools in 1996. There are now school counsellors in about 1/5 of the elementary and middle schools in Lebanon and none in the high schools. They have been trained in delivering preventive, developmental, and remedial services.

Private schools have some school counsellors serving all grade levels but the focus is exclusively individual counselling and primarily remedial. Challenges include regular violence and wartime strife and not enough resources and a lack of a professional school counselling organization, assignment of school counsellors to cover more than one school at a time, and only two school counselling graduate programmes in the country. Last, for persons trained in Western models of school counselling there are dangers of overlooking unique cultural and family aspects of Lebanese society.

Malta

In Malta, school counselling services began in 1968 in the Department of Education based on recommendations from a UNESCO consultant and used these titles: Education Officer, School Counsellor, and Guidance Teacher. Through the 1990s they included school counsellor positions in primary and trade schools in addition to secondary schools. Guidance teachers are mandated at a 1:300 teacher to student ratio.

Nigeria

In Nigeria, school counselling began in 1959 and exists in some high schools. It rarely exists at the elementary school level. Where there are federally funded secondary schools, there are some professionally trained school counsellors. However, in many cases, there are only teachers who function as career masters/mistresses. School counsellors often have teaching and other responsibilities that take time away from their school counselling tasks. The Counselling Association of Nigeria (CASSON) was formed in 1976 to promote the profession, but there is no code of ethics. However, a certification/licensure board has been formed. Aluede, Adomeh, & Afen-Akpaida (2004) discussed the overreliance on textbooks from the USA and the need for school counsellors in Nigeria to take a whole-school approach and lessen the focus on individual approaches and honour the traditional African world view that values the family and community's roles in decision-making as paramount for effective decision-making in schools.

Philippines

In the Philippines, the Congress of the Philippines passed the Guidance and Counselling Act of 2004, with a specific focus on Professional Practice, Ethics, National Certification, and the creation of a Regulatory Body, and specialists in school counselling are subject to this law.

South Korea

In South Korea, school counsellors must teach a subject besides counselling, and not all school counsellors are appointed to counselling positions, even though Korean law requires school counsellors in all middle and high schools.

Taiwan

In Taiwan, school counselling traditionally was done by "guidance teachers." Recent advocacy by the Chinese Guidance and Counselling Association pushed for licensure for school counsellors in Taiwan's public schools. Prior to this time, the focus had been primarily individual and group counselling, play therapy, career counselling and development, and stress related to national university examinations.

United States

Christopher Farms Elmentary School Counsellor Elizabeth Prince working with students in Virgina Beach, Virginia, USA In the United States, the school counselling profession began with the vocational guidance movement at the beginning of the 20th century now known as career development. Jesse B. Davis was the first to provide a systematic school guidance programme. In 1907, he became the principal of a high school and encouraged the school English teachers to use compositions and lessons to relate career interests, develop character, and avoid behavioural problems. Many others during this time also focused on what is now called career development. For example, in 1908, Frank Parsons, "Father of Vocational Guidance" established the Bureau of Vocational Guidance to assist young people in making the transition from school to work.

From the 1920s to the 1930s, school counselling grew because of the rise of progressive education in schools. This movement emphasized personal, social, moral development. Many schools reacted to this movement as anti-educational, saying that schools should teach only the fundamentals of education. This, combined with the economic hardship of the Great Depression, led to a decline in school counselling. In the 1940s, psychologists and counsellors selected, recruited, and trained military personnel. This propelled the school counselling movement in schools by providing ways to test students and meet their needs. Schools accepted these military tests openly. Also, Carl Rogers' emphasis on helping relationships and a move away from directive "guidance" to nondirective or person-centred "counselling" influenced the profession of school counselling.

In the 1950s the government established the Guidance and Personnel Services Section in the Division of State and Local School Systems. In 1957, the Soviet Union launched Sputnik I. Out of concern that the Russians were winning the space race and that there were not enough scientists and mathematicians, the government passed the National Defence Education Act, spurring growth in vocational counselling through larger funding. In the 1960s, new legislation and professional developments refined the school counselling profession (Schmidt, 2003).

The 1960s was also a time of great federal funding for land grant colleges and universities in establishing Counsellor Education programmes. School counselling shifted from an exclusive focus on career development and added personal and social issues paralleling the rise of social justice and civil rights movements. In the early 1970s, Dr. Norm Gysbers began shifting the profession from school counsellors as solitary professionals into having a comprehensive developmental school counselling programme for all students K-12. He and his colleagues' research evidenced strong correlations between fully implemented school counselling programmes and student academic success; a critical part of the evidence base for the profession based on their work in the state of Missouri. Dr. Chris Sink & associates showed similar evidence-based success for school counselling programmes at the elementary and middle school levels in Washington State.

But school counselling in the 1980s and early 1990s was absent from educational reform efforts. The profession was facing irrelevance as the standards-based educational movement gained strength with little evidence of systemic effectiveness for school counsellors. In response, consulted with elementary, middle, and high school counsellors and created the ASCA Student Standards with three core domains (Academic, Career, Personal/Social), nine standards, and specific competencies and indicators for K-12 students. A year later, the first systemic meta-analysis of school counselling was published focused on outcome research in academic, career, and personal/social domains.

In the late 1990s, a former mathematics teacher, school counsellor, and administrator, Pat Martin, was hired by The Education Trust to focus the school counselling profession on closing the achievement gap that harmed children and adolescents of colour, poor and working class children and adolescents, bilingual children and adolescents and children and adolescents with disabilities. Martin developed focus groups of K-12 students, parents, guardians, teachers, building leaders, and superintendents, and interviewed professors of School Counsellor Education. She hired a school counsellor educator from Oregon State University, Dr. Reese House, and they co-created what emerged in 2003 as the National Centre for Transforming School Counselling (NCTSC).

The NCTSC focused on both changing school counsellor education at the graduate level and changing school counsellor practice in local districts to teach school counsellors how to prevent, intervene with, and close achievement and opportunity gaps. In the focus groups, they found what Hart & Jacobi had indicated—-too many school counsellors were gatekeepers for the status quo instead of advocates for the academic success of every child and adolescent. Too many school counsellors used inequitable practices, supported inequitable school policies, and were unwilling to change.

This professional behaviour kept many students from non-dominant backgrounds (i.e., students of colour, poor and working class students, students with disabilities, and bilingual students) from getting the rigorous coursework and academic, career, and college access skills needed to successfully graduate from high school and pursue post-secondary options including college. They funded six $500,000 grants for six Counsellor Education/School Counselling programmes, with a special focus on rural and urban settings, to transform their school counselling programmes to include a focus on teaching school counsellor candidates advocacy, leadership, teaming and collaboration, equity assessment using data, and culturally competent programme counselling and coordination in 1998 (Indiana State University, University of Georgia, University of West Georgia, University of California-Northridge, University of North Florida, and Ohio State University) and then over 25 other Counsellor Education/School Counselling programmes joined as companion institutions in the following decade. By 2008, NCTSC consultants had worked in over 100 school districts and major cities and rural areas to transform the work of school counsellors.

In 2002, the American School Counsellor Association released the first edition of the ASCA National Model: A framework for school counselling programmes, written by Dr. Trish Hatch and Dr. Judy Bowers (2003), comprising key school counselling components: the work of Drs. Norm Gysbers, Curly & Sharon Johnson, Robert Myrick,

Carol Dahir & Cheri Campbell's ASCA National Standards, and the skill-based focus for closing achievement and opportunity gaps from the Education Trust's Pat Martin and Dr. Reese House into one document. In 2003, the Centre for School Counselling Outcome Research and Evaluation (CSCORE) was developed as a clearinghouse for evidence-based practice with regular research briefs disseminated and original research projects developed and implemented with founding director Dr. Jay Carey. One of the research fellows, Dr. Tim Poynton, developed the EZAnalyze software programme for all school counsellors to use as free-ware to assist in using data-based interventions and decision-making.

In 2004, the ASCA Ethical Standards for School Counsellors was revised to focus on issues of equity, closing achievement and opportunity gaps, and ensuring all K-12 students received access to a school counselling programme. Also in 2004, Pat Martin moved to the College Board and hired School Counsellor Educator Dr. Vivian Lee. They developed an equity-focused entity on school counsellors' role in college readiness and admission counselling, the National Office for School Counsellor Advocacy (NOSCA). NOSCA developed research scholarships for research on college counselling by K-12 school counsellors and how it is taught in School Counsellor Education programmes. On January 1, 2006, the USA Congress declared the first week of February National School Counselling Week, which grew out of advocacy from ASCA members.

In 2008, the first NOSCA study was released by Dr. Jay Carey and colleagues focused on innovations in selected College Board "Inspiration Award" schools where school counsellors collaborated inside and outside their schools for high college-going rates and strong college-going cultures in schools with large numbers of students of non-dominant backgrounds. In 2008, ASCA released School Counselling Competencies focused on assisting school counselling programmes to effectively implement the ASCA Model.

Also in 2008, in support of the ASCA Model and new vision school counselling, Dr. Rita Schellenberg introduced *standards blending* as a cross-walking approach to align school counselling with the academic achievement mission of schools as well as two data-based reporting systems, SCORE and SCOPE. In 2009, NOSCA released a national study under the leadership of Dr. Vicki Brooks-McNamara addressing the school counsellor/principal connection with specific recommendations for best practices in collaborative leadership in school counselling. In 2010, the Centre for Excellence in School Counselling and Leadership (CESCAL) co-sponsored the first school counsellor and educator conference devoted to the needs of lesbian, bisexual, gay, and transgendered students in San Diego, California.

In 2011, *Counselling at the Crossroads: The perspectives and promise of school counsellors in American education,* the largest survey of high school and middle school counsellors in the United States (over 5,300 interviews), was released by the College Board's National Office for School Counsellor Advocacy, the National Association of Secondary School Principals, and the American School Counsellor Association. The study shared school counsellors' views on educational policies, practices, and reform, and how many of them, especially in urban and rural school settings, are not given the chance to focus on what they were trained to do, especially career and college access counselling and readiness for all students, in part due to high caseloads and inappropriate tasks that take up too much of their time. School counsellors made strong suggestions about their crucial role in accountability and success for all students and how school systems need to change so that school counsellors can be key players in student success. Implications for public policy and district and school-wide change are addressed. The National Centre for Transforming School Counselling at The Education Trust released a brief, *Poised to Lead: How School Counsellors Can Drive Career and College Readiness,* challenging all schools to utilize school counsellors for equity and access for rigorous courses for all students and ensuring college and career access skills and competencies be a major focus of the work of school counsellors K-12.

In 2012, the CSCORE assisted in evaluating and publishing six statewide research studies assessing the effectiveness of school counselling programmes based on statewide systemic use of school counselling programmes such as the ASCA National Model and their outcomes in *Professional School Counselling*. Research indicated strong correlational evidence between lower school counselling ratios and better student success academically, in terms of career and college access/readiness/admission, and for various personal/social issues including school safety, reduced disciplinary issues, and better attendance in schools with fully implemented school counselling programmes.

Also in 2012, the American School Counsellor Association released the third edition of the ASCA National Model. Also, the National

Centre for Transforming School Counselling (NCTSC) created a School Counsellor Educator Coalition to further transform graduate School Counsellor Education programmes in the new vision of school counselling for K-12 school counsellors. Twenty universities were represented and four School Counsellor Educator faculty mentors were named: Dr. Carolyn Stone, University of North Florida, Dr. Trish Hatch, San Diego State University, Dr. Stuart Chen-Hayes, City University of New York/Lehman College, and Dr. Erin Mason, DePaul University.

Both the IAEVG and the Vanguard of Counsellors have promoted school counselling internationally.

School Counsellor Roles, School Counselling Programme Framework, Professional Associations, and Ethics

Professional school counsellors ideally implement a school counselling programme that promotes and enhances student achievement (Hatch & Bowers, 2003, 2005; ASCA, 2012). A framework for appropriate and inappropriate school counsellor responsibilities and roles is outlined in the ASCA National Model (Hatch & Bowers, 2003, 2005; ASCA, 2012). School counsellors, in most USA states, usually have a Master's degree in school counselling from a Counsellor Education graduate programme.

In Canada, they must be licensed teachers with additional school counselling training and focus on academic, career, and personal/social issues. China requires at least three years of college experience. In Japan, school counsellors were added in the mid-1990s, part-time, primarily focused on behavioural issues. In Taiwan, they are often teachers with recent legislation requiring school counselling licensure focused on individual and group counselling for academic, career, and personal issues. In Korea, school counsellors are mandated in middle and high schools.

School counsellors are employed in elementary, middle, and high schools, and in district supervisory settings and in counsellor education faculty positions (usually with an earned Ph.D. in Counsellor Education in the USA or related graduate doctorates abroad), and post-secondary settings doing academic, career, college readiness, and personal/social counselling, consultation, and programme coordination. Their work includes a focus on developmental stages of student growth, including the needs, tasks, and student interests related to those stages(Schmidt, 2003).

Professional school counsellors meet the needs of student in three basic domains: academic development, career development, and personal/social development (Dahir & Campbell, 1997; Hatch & Bowers, 2003, 2005; ASCA, 2012) with an increased emphasis on college access. Knowledge, understanding and skill in these domains are developed through classroom instruction, appraisal, consultation, counselling, coordination, and collaboration. For example, in appraisal, school counsellors may use a variety of personality and career assessment methods (such as the or (based on the) to help students explore career and college needs and interests.

School counsellor interventions include individual and group counselling for some students. For example, if a student's behaviour is interfering with his or her achievement, the school counsellor may observe that student in a class, provide consultation to teachers and other stakeholders to develop (with the student) a plan to address the behavioural issue(s), and then collaborate to implement and evaluate the plan. They also provide consultation services to family members such as college access, career development, parenting skills, study skills, child and adolescent development, and help with school-home transitions. School counsellor interventions for all students include annual academic/career/college access planning K-12 and leading classroom developmental lessons on academic, career/college, and personal/social topics. The topics of character education, diversity and multiculturalism (Portman, 2009), and school safety are important areas of focus for school counsellors. Often school counsellors will coordinate outside groups that wish to help with student needs such as academics, or coordinate a programme that teaches about child abuse or drugs, through on-stage drama (Schmidt, 2003).

School counsellors develop, implement, and evaluate school counselling programmes that deliver academic, career, college access, and personal/social competencies to all students in their schools. For example, the ASCA National Model (Hatch & Bowers, 2003, 2005; ASCA, 2012) includes the following four main areas:

- Foundation - a school counselling programme mission statement, a beliefs/vision statement, SMART Goals; ASCA Student Standards & ASCA Code of Ethics;
- Delivery System - how school counselling core curriculum lessons, planning for every student, and individual and group counselling are delivered in direct and indirect services to students (80% of school counsellor time);

- Management System - calendars; use of data tool; use of time tool; administrator-school counsellor agreement; advisory council; small group, school counselling core curriculum, and closing the gap action plans; and
- Accountability System - school counselling programme assessment; small group, school counselling core curriculum, and closing-the-gap results reports; and school counsellor performance evaluations based on school counsellor competencies.

The model (ASCA, 2012) is implemented using key skills from the Education Trust's Transforming School Counselling Initiative: Advocacy, Leadership, Teaming and Collaboration, and Systemic Change.

School Counsellors around the world are affiliated with national and regional school counselling associations including: Asociacion Argentina de Counsellors (AAC-Argentina), American Counselling Association (ACA-USA), African Counselling Association (AfCA), American School Counsellor Association (ASCA-USA), Associacao Portuguesa de Psicoterapia centrada na Pessoa e de Counselling (APPCPC-Portugal), Australian Guidance and Counselling Association (AGCA), British Association for Counselling and Psychotherapy (BACP-UK), Canadian Counselling Association (CCA)/Association Canadienne de Counselling (ACC), Centre for Excellence in School Counselling and Leadership(CESCaL) (USA), Centre for School Counselling Outcome Research (CSCOR-USA) Council for the Accreditation of Counselling and Related Educational Programmes (CACREP-USA and international), Counselling Children and Young People (BACP affiliate, UK), Counselling & Psychotherapy in Scotland (COSCA), Cypriot Association of School Guidance Counsellors (OELMEK), European Counselling Association (ECA), France Ministry of Education, Federacion Espanola de Orientacion y Psicopedagogia (FEOP-Spain), Department of Education-Malta, Hellenic Society of Counselling and Guidance (HESCOG-Greece), Hong Kong Association of Guidance Masters and Career Masters (HKAGMCM), Institute of Guidance Counsellors (IGC) (Ireland), International Association for Educational and Vocational Guidance (IAEVG)/Association Internationale d'Orientation Scolaire et Professionnelle (AIOSP)/ Internationale Vereinigung für Schul- und Berufsberatung (IVSBB)/Asociación Internacional para la Orientación Educativa y Profesional(AIOEP), International Baccalaureate (IB), International Vanguard of

Counsellors (IVC), Kenya Association of Professional Counsellors (KAPC), National Board for Certified Counsellors (NBCC, USA), National Centre for Transforming School Counselling (NCTSC) at The Education Trust (USA), National Office for School Counsellor Advocacy (NOSCA) at The College Board (USA), New Zealand Association of Counsellors/Te Roopu Kaiwhiriwhiri o Aotearoa (NZAC), Counselling Association of Nigeria (CASSON), Philippine Guidance and Counselling Association (PGCA), Overseas Association of College Admissions Counsellors (OACAC, an affiliate of National Association of College Admissions Counsellors-USA), Singapore Association for Counselling (SAC), and the Taiwan Guidance and Counselling Association (TGCA).

School Counsellors are expected to follow a professional code of ethics in many countries. For example, In the USA, they are the American School Counsellor Association (ASCA) School Counsellor Ethical Code, the American Counselling Association (ACA) Code of Ethics., and the National Association for College Admission Counselling (NACAC) Statement of Principles of Good Practice (SPGP).

Elementary School Counselling

Elementary school counsellors provide academic, career, college access, and personal and social competencies and planning to all students, and individual and group counselling for some students and their families to meet the developmental needs of young children K-6. Transitions from pre-school to elementary school and from elementary school to middle school are an important focus for elementary school counsellors.

Increased emphasis is placed on accountability for closing achievement and opportunity gaps at the elementary level as more school counselling programmes move to evidence-based work with data and specific results.

School counselling programmes that deliver specific competencies to all students help to close achievement and opportunity gaps. To facilitate individual and group school counselling interventions, school counsellors use developmental, cognitive-behavioural, person-centred (Rogerian) listening and influencing skills, systemic, family, multicultural, narrative, and play therapy theories and techniques. released a research study showing the effectiveness of elementary school counselling programmes in Washington state.

Middle School Counselling

Middle school counsellors provide school counselling curriculum lessons on academic, career, college access, and personal and social competencies, advising and academic/career/college access planning to all students and individual and group counselling for some students and their families to meet the needs of older children/early adolescents in grades 7 and 8.

Middle School College Access curricula have been developed by The College Board to assist students and their families well before reaching high school. To facilitate the school counselling process, school counsellors use theories and techniques including developmental, cognitive-behavioural, person-centred (Rogerian) listening and influencing skills, sytemic, family, multicultural, narrative, and play therapy. Transitional issues to ensure successful transitions to high school are a key area including career exploration and assessment with seventh and eighth grade students. Sink, Akos, Turnbull, & Mvududu released a study in 2008 confirming the effectiveness of middle school comprehensive school counselling programmes in Washington state.

High School Counselling

High school counsellors provide academic, career, college access, and personal and social competencies with developmental classroom lessons and planning to all students, and individual and group counselling for some students and their families to meet the developmental needs of adolescents (Hatch & Bowers, 2003, 2005, 2012). Emphasis is on college access counselling at the early high school level as more school counselling programmes move to evidence-based work with data and specific results that show how school counselling programmes help to close achievement, opportunity, and attainment gaps ensuring all students have access to school counselling programmes and early college access activities. The breadth of demands high school counsellors face, from educational attainment (high school graduation and some students' preparation for careers and college) to student social and mental health, has led to ambiguous role definition. Summarizing a 2011 national survey of more than 5,300 middle school and high school counsellors, researchers argued: "Despite the aspirations of counsellors to effectively help students succeed in school and fulfill their dreams, the mission and roles of counsellors in the education system must be more clearly defined; schools must create measures of accountability to track their effectiveness; and policymakers and key stakeholders must integrate counsellors into reform efforts to maximize their impact in schools across America".

Transitional issues to ensure successful transitions to college, other post-secondary educational options, and careers are a key area. The high school counsellor helps students and their families prepare for post-secondary education including college and careers (e.g. college, careers) by engaging students and their families in accessing and evaluating accurate information on what the National Office for School Counsellor Advocacy calls the 8 essential elements of college and career counselling: (1) College Aspirations, (2) Academic Planning for Career and College Readiness, (3) Enrichment and Extracurricular Engagement, (4) College and Career Exploration and Selection Processes, (5) College and Career Assessments, (6) College Affordability Planning, (7) College and Career Admission Processes, and (8) Transition from High School Graduation to College Enrollment. Some students turn to private college admissions advisors but there is no research evidence that private college admissions advisors have any effectiveness in assisting students attain selective college admissions.

Lapan, Gysbers & Sun showed correlational evidence of the effectiveness of fully implemented school counselling programmes on high school students' academic success. Carey et al.'s 2008 study showed specific best practices from high school counsellors raising college-going rates within a strong college-going environment in multiple USA-based high schools with large numbers of students of nondominant cultural identities.

Education and Professional Credentials Including Certification for School Counsellors

The education of school counsellors (school counsellors) around the world varies based on the laws and cultures of countries and the historical influences of their educational and credentialing systems and professional identities related to who delivers academic, career, college readiness, and personal/social information, advising, curriculum, and counselling and related services.

In Canada, school counsellors must be certified teachers with additional school counselling training.

In China, there is no national certification or licensure system for school counsellors. Korea requires school counsellors in all middle and high schools.

In the Philippines, school counsellors must be licensed with a master's degree in counselling.

Taiwan instituted school counsellor licensure for public schools (2006) through advocacy from the

In the USA, a school counsellor is a certified educator with a master's degree in school counselling (usually from a Counsellor Education graduate programme) with school counselling graduate training including qualifications and skills to address all students' academic, career, college access and personal/social needs.

About half of all Counsellor Education programmes that offer school counselling are accredited by the Council on the Accreditation of Counselling and Related Educational Programmes (CACREP) and all are in the USA with one in Canada and one under review in Mexico as of 2010. CACREP maintains a current list of accredited programmes and programmes in the accreditation process on their website. CACREP desires to accredit more international counselling university programmes.

According to CACREP, an accredited school counselling programme offers coursework in Professional Identity and Ethics, Human Development, Counselling Theories, Group Work, Career Counselling, Multicultural Counselling, Assessment, Research and Programme Evaluation, and Clinical Coursework—a 100-hour practicum and a 600-hour internship under supervision of a school counselling faculty member and a certified school counsellor site supervisor (CACREP, 2001).

When CACREP released the 2009 Standards, the accreditation process became performance-based including evidence of school counsellor candidate learning outcomes. In addition, CACREP tightened the school counselling standards with specific evidence needed for how school counselling students receive education in foundations; counselling prevention and intervention; diversity and advocacy; assessment; research and evaluation; academic development; collaboration and consultation; and leadership in K-12 school counselling contexts.

Certification practices for school counsellors vary around the world. School counsellors in the USA may opt for national certification through two different boards. The National Board for Professional Teaching Standards (NBPTS) requires a two-to-three year process of performance based assessment, and demonstrate (in writing) content knowledge in human growth/development, diverse populations, school counselling programmes, theories, data, and change and collaboration. As of February, 2005, 30 states offer financial incentives for this certification.

Also in the USA, The National Board for Certified Counsellors (NBCC) requires passing the National Certified School Counsellor Examination (NCSC), including 40 multiple choice questions and seven simulated cases assessing school counsellors' abilities to make critical decisions. Additionally, a master's degree and three years of supervised experience are required. NBPTS also requires three years of experience, however state certification is required (41 of 50 states require a master's degree). At least four states offer financial incentives for the NCSC certification.

Job Growth and Earnings

The rate of job growth and earnings for school counsellors depends on the country that one is employed in and how the school is funded—public or independent. School counsellors working in international schools or "American" schools globally may find similar work environments and expectations to the USA. School counsellor pay varies based on school counsellor roles, identity, expectations, and legal and certification requirements and expectations of each country. According to the Occupational Outlook Handbook (OOH), the median salary for school counsellors in the USA in 2010 was (USD) $53,380 or $25.67 hourly. The USA has 267,000 employees in titles such as School Counsellor or related titles in education and advising and college and career counselling. The projected growth for school counsellors is 14-19% or faster than average than other occupations in the USA with a predicted 94,000 job openings from 2008-2018. " In Australia, a survey by the Australian Guidance and Counselling Association found that school counsellor salary ranged from (AUD) the high 50,000s to the mid 80,000s.

Among all counselling speciality areas, public elementary, middle and high school counsellors are (2009) paid the highest salary on average of all counsellors. Budget cuts, however, have affected placement of public school counsellors in Canada, Ireland, the United States, and other countries due to the global recession in recent years. In the United States, rural areas and urban areas traditionally have been under-served by school counsellors in public schools due to both funding shortages and often a lack of best practice models. With the advent of No Child Left Behind legislation in the USA and a mandate for school counsellors to be working with data and showing evidence-based practice, school counsellors able to show and share results in assisting to close gaps are in the best position to argue for increased school counselling resources and positions for their programmes

Play Therapy

Play therapy is generally employed with children aged 3 through 11 and provides a way for them to express their experiences and feelings through a natural, self-guided, self-healing process. As children's experiences and knowledge are often communicated through play, it becomes an important vehicle for them to know and accept themselves and others.

General

Play therapy is a form of counselling or psychotherapy that uses play to communicate with and help people, especially children, to prevent or resolve psychosocial challenges. This is thought to help them towards better social integration, growth and development. Play therapy can also be used as a tool of diagnosis. A play therapist observes a client playing with toys (play-houses, pets, dolls, etc.) to determine the cause of the disturbed behaviour. The objects and patterns of play, as well as the willingness to interact with the therapist, can be used to understand the underlying rationale for behaviour both inside and outside the session..

According to the psychodynamic view, people (especially children) will engage in play behaviour in order to work through their interior obfuscations and anxieties. In this way, play therapy can be used as a self-help mechanism, as long as children are allowed time for "free play" or "unstructured play." Normal play is an essential component of healthy child development. One approach to treatment is for play therapists use a type of desensitization or relearning therapy to change disturbing behaviour, either systematically or in less formal social settings. These processes are normally used with children, but are also applied with other pre-verbal, non-verbal, or verbally-impaired persons, such as slow-learners, or brain-injured or drug-affected persons.

History

Play has been recognized as important since the time of Plato (429-347 B.C.) who reportedly observed, "you can discover more about a person in an hour of play than in a year of conversation." In the eighteenth century Rousseau (1762/1930), in his book 'Emile' wrote about the importance of observing play as a vehicle to learn about and understand children. Friedrich Fröbel, in his book *The Education of Man* (1903), emphasized the importance of symbolism in play. He observed, "play is the highest development in childhood, for it alone is the free expression of what is in the child's soul.... children's play is not mere sport. It is full of meaning and import." (Fröbel, 1903, p. 22) The first documented case, describing the therapeutic use of play, was in 1909 when Sigmund Freud published his work with "Little Hans." Little Hans was a five-year-old child who was suffering from a simple phobia. Freud saw him once briefly and recommended that his father take note of Hans' play to provide insights that might assist the child. The case of "Little Hans" was the first case in which a child's difficulty was related to emotional factors.

Hermine Hug-Hellmuth (1921) formalized the play therapy process by providing children with play materials to express themselves and emphasize the use of the play to analyze the child. In 1919, Melanie Klein (1955) began to implement the technique of using play as a means of analyzing children under the age of six. She believed that child's play was essentially the same as free association used with adults, and that as such, it was provide access to the child's unconscious. Anna Freud (1946, 1965) utilized play as a means to facilitate positive attachment to the therapist and gain access to the child's inner life.

In the 1930s David Levy (1938) developed a technique he called release therapy. His technique emphasized a structured approach. A child, who had experienced a specific stressful situation, would be allowed to engage in free play. Subsequently, the therapist would introduce play materials related to the stress-evoking situation allowing the child to reenact the traumatic event and release the associated emotions.

In 1955, Gove Hambidge expanded on Levy's work emphasizing a "Structured Play Therapy" model, which was more direct in introducing situations. The format of the approach was to establish rapport, recreate the stress-evoking situation, play out the situation and then free play to recover.

Jesse Taft (1933) and Frederick Allen (1934) developed an approach they entitled relationship therapy. The primary emphasis is placed on the emotional relationship between the therapist and the child. The focus is placed on the child's freedom and strength to choose.

Carl Rogers (1942) expanded the work of the relationship therapist and developed non-directive therapy, later called client-centred therapy (Rogers, 1951). Virginia Axline (1950) expanded on her mentor's concepts. In her article entitled 'Entering the child's world via play experiences' Axline summarized her concept of play therapy stating, "A play experience is therapeutic because it provides a secure relationship between the child and the adult, so that the child has the freedom and room to state himself in his own terms, exactly as he is at that moment in his own way and in his own time" (Progressive Education, 27, p. 68).

In 1953 Clark Moustakas wrote his first book Children in Play Therapy. In 1956 he compiled Publication of The Self, the result of the dialogues between Abraham Maslow, Carl Rogers, Clark Moustakas and others, forging the Humanistic Psychology movement.

Filial therapy, developed by Bernard and Louise Guerney, was a new innovation in play therapy during the 1960s. The filial approach emphasizes a structured training programme for parents in which they learn how to employ child-centred play sessions in the home. In the 1960s, with the advent of school counsellors, school-based play therapy began a major shift from the private sector. Counsellor-educators such as Alexander (1964); Landreth (1969, 1972); Muro (1968); Myrick and Holdin (1971); Nelson (1966); and Waterland (1970) began to contribute significantly, especially in terms of using play therapy as both an educational and preventive tool in dealing with children's issues.

1973 Clark Moustakas continues his journey into play therapy and publishes his novel "The child's discovery of himself". Clark Moustakas' work as being concerned with the kind of relationship needed to make therapy a growth experience. His stages start with the child's feelings being generally negative and as they are expressed, they become less intense, the end results tend to be the emergence of more positive feelings and more balanced relationships. Today, his daughter Kerry Moustakas continues his legacy as an author and president of The Michigan School of Professional Psychology. 2004 Clark and Kerry Moustakas publish Loneliness, Creativity and Love: Awakening Meanings in Life.

Growth of Organizations

In 1982, the Association for Play Therapy (APT) was established marking not only the desire to promote the advancement of play therapy, but to acknowledge the extensive growth of play therapy. Currently, the APT has almost 5,000 members in twenty-six countries (2006). Play therapy training is provided, according to a survey conducted by the Centre for Play Therapy at the University of North Texas (2000), by 102 universities and colleges throughout the United States.

In 1985, the work of two key Canadians in the field of child psychology and play therapy, Mark Barnes and Cynthia Taylor, resulted in the establishment of Certification Standards through the non-profit Canadian child psychotherapy and play therapy association. A fledgling group of practising Canadian child psychotherapists and play therapists worked on developing an organization to meet professional needs. It gradually expanded and eventually a Board of Directors was formed; objects and by-laws were designed, revised, re-revised and finally approved by the Government of Canada. The Canadian association was eventually recognized as a non-profit organization in 1986.

During 1995/1996, a whole new horizon opened up for the profession of play therapy as a result of the Canadian Play Therapy Institute's pioneering efforts on an International basis. Play Therapy International was founded from the Canadian Play Therapy Institute and there now existed a mutually supportive recognition between Play Therapy International/The International Board of Examiners of Certified Play Therapists, The Canadian Play Therapy Institute, as well as a number of other professional bodies throughout the world.

In the UK, The United Kingdom Society for Play and Creative Arts Therapies Limited (known in short as PTUK) was originally set up in October 2000 as Play Therapy UK with the encouragement of Play Therapy International. Meanwhile the British Association of Play Therapists was distinguished from its American counterpart in 1996 and was granted charity status within the UK in 2006 by the UK Charities Commission. By 2010 Play Therapy International has partnered sister organisations in Ireland, Canada, Australasia, France, Spain, Wales, Malaysia, Romania, Russia, United Kingdom, Slovenia, Germany, New Zealand, Hong Kong, Korea and Ethiopia.

Models of Play Therapy

Play therapy can be divided into two basic types: nondirective and directive. Nondirective play therapy is a non-intrusive method in which children are encouraged to work toward their own solutions to problems through play.

Figure: *An individual engaging in sandplay therapy.*

Figure: *Equipment used for sandplay therapy.*

It is typically classified as a psychodynamic therapy. In contrast, directive play therapy is a method that includes more structure and guidance by the therapist as children work through emotional and behavioural difficulties through play. It often contains a behavioural component and the process includes more prompting by the therapist. Directive play therapy is more likely to be classified as a type of cognitive behavioural therapy. Both types of play therapy have received at least some empirical support. On average, play therapy treatment groups when compared to control groups improve by .8 standard deviations.

Nondirective Play Therapy

Nondirective play therapy, also called client-centred and unstructured play therapy, is guided by the notion that if given the chance to speak and play freely under optimal therapeutic conditions, troubled children and young people will be able to resolve their own problems and work toward their own solutions. In other words, nondirective play therapy is regarded as non-intrusive. The hallmark of nondirective play therapy is that it has few boundary conditions and thus can be used at any age. This therapy originates from Carl Rogers's non-directive psychotherapy and in his characterization of the optimal therapeutic conditions. Virginia Axline adapted Carl Rogers's theories to child therapy in 1946 and is widely considered the founder of this therapy. Different techniques have since been established that fall under the realm of nondirective play therapy, including traditional sandplay therapy, family therapy, and play therapy with the use of toys. Each of these forms is covered briefly below.

Play therapy using a tray of sand and miniature figures is attributed to Margaret Lowenfeld (UK), who established her "World Technique" in 1929. Dora Kalff (Swiss.) studied with Lowenfeld on the recommendation of her mentor, C.G. Jung, when Kalff studied at the Jung Institute in Zurich. Kalff combined Lowenfeld's World Technique with Jung's idea of the collective unconscious and received Lowenfeld's permission to name her version of the work "sandplay" (Kalff, 1980). In the US, training and certification in the Jungian-Kalffian method is provided by Sandplay® Therapists of America™ (STA) which received US trademark protection for the term in March, 2012. Therapists working in sand who are not certified by STA may legally term their work "sand tray" therapy or play therapy with sand.

As in traditional nondirective play therapy, research has shown that allowing an individual to freely play with the sand and accompanying objects in the contained space of the sandtray (22.5" x 28.5") can facilitate a healing process as the unconscious expresses itself in the sand and influences the sand player. When a client creates in the sandtray, little instruction is provided and the therapist offers little or no talk during the process. This protocol emphasizes the importance of holding what Kalff (1980) referred to as the "free and protected space" to allow the unconscious to express itself in symbolic, non-verbal play. Upon completion of a tray, the client may or may not choose to talk about his or her creation, and the therapist, without the use of directives and without touching the sandtray, may offer supportive response that does not include interpretation. The rationale is that the therapist trusts and respects the process by allowing the images in the tray to excerpt their influence without interference.

Sand tray therapy can be used during family therapy. The limitations presented by the boundaries of the sandtray can serve as physical and symbolic limitations to families in which boundary distinctions are an issue. Also observance by the therapist of a family working together on a sandtray may show evidence of unhealthy alliances, depending on who works with who, which objects are selected to be incorporated into the sandtray, and who chooses which objects. A therapist may assess these choices and intervene in an effort to guide the formation of healthier relationships.

Using toys in nondirective play therapy with children is another common method therapists employ, a method which was derived from the creative toys used in Freud's theoretical orientations. The idea behind this method is that children will be better able to express their feelings toward themselves and their environment through play with toys than through verbalization of their feelings. Through these actions, then, children may be able to experience catharsis, gain more or better insight into their consciousness, thoughts, and emotions, and test their own reality. Popular toys used during therapy are animals, dolls, hand puppets, crayons, and cars. Therapists have deemed toys such as these more likely to encourage dramatic play or creative associations, both of which are important in expression.

Efficacy of Nondirective Play Therapy

Play therapy has been considered to be an established and popular mode of therapy for children for over sixty years. Critics of play therapy have questioned the effectiveness of the technique for use with children and have suggested using other interventions with greater empirical support such as cognitive behavioural therapy. They also argue that therapists focus more on the institution of play rather than the empirical literature when conducting therapy Classically, Lebo argued against the efficacy of play therapy in 1953, and Phillips reiterated his argument again in 1985. Both claimed that play therapy lacks in several areas of hard research. Many studies included small sample sizes, which limits the generalizeability, and many studies also only compared the effects of play therapy to a control group. Without a comparison to other therapies, it is difficult to determine if play therapy really is the most effective treatment. Recent play therapy researchers have worked to conduct more experimental studies with larger sample sizes, specific definitions and measures of treatment, and more direct comparisons.

Research is lacking on the overall effectiveness of using toys in nondirective play therapy. Dell Lebo found that out of a sample of over 4,000 children, those who played with recommended toys vs. non-recommended or no toys during nondirective play therapy were not more likely to verbally express themselves to the therapist. Examples of recommended toys would be dolls or crayons, while example of non-recommended toys would be marbles or a checker game. There is also ongoing controversy in choosing toys for use in nondirective play therapy, with choices being largely made through intuition rather than through research. However, other research shows that following specific criteria when choosing toys in nondirective play therapy can make treatment more efficacious. Criteria for a desirable treatment toy include a toy that facilitates contact with the child, encourages catharsis, and lead to play that can be easily interpreted by a therapist.

Several meta analyses have shown promising results toward the efficacy of nondirective play therapy. Meta analysis by authors LeBlanc and Ritchie, 2001, found an effect size of 0.66 for nondirective play therapy. This finding is comparable to the effect size of 0.71 found for psychotherapy used with children, indicating that both nondirective play and non-play therapies are almost equally effective in treating children with emotional difficulties. Meta analysis by authors Ray, Bratton, Rhine and Jones, 2001, found an even larger effect size for nondirective play therapy, with children performing at 0.93 standard deviations better than non-treatment groups. These results are stronger than previous meta-analytic results, which reported effect sizes of 0.71, 0.71, and 0.66. Meta analysis by authors Bratton, Ray, Rhine, and Jones, 2005, also found a large effect size of 0.92 for children being treated with nondirective play therapy. Results from all meta-analyses indicate that nondirective play therapy has been shown to be just as effective as psychotherapy used with children and even generates higher effect sizes in some studies. There are several predictors that may also influence the effectiveness of play therapy with children. Number of sessions is a significant predictor in post-test outcomes, with more sessions being indicative of higher effect sizes. Although positive effects can be seen with the average 16 sessions, there is a peak effect when a child can complete 35-40 sessions. An exception to this finding is children undergoing play therapy in critical-incident settings, such as hospitals and domestic violence shelters.

Results from studies that looked at these children indicated a large positive effect size after only 7 sessions, which provides the implication that children in crisis may respond more readily to treatment Parental involvement is also a significant predictor of positive play therapy results. This involvement generally entails participation in each session with the therapist and the child. Parental involvement in play therapy sessions has also been shown to diminish stress in the parent-child relationship when kids are exhibiting both internal and external behaviour problems. Despite these predictors which have been shown to increase effect sizes, play therapy has been shown to be equally effective across age, gender, and individual vs. group settings.

Directive Play Therapy

Directive play therapy is guided by the notion that using directives to guide the child through play will cause a faster change than is generated by nondirective play therapy. The therapist plays a much bigger role in directive play therapy. Therapists may use several techniques to engage the child, such as engaging in play with the child themselves or suggesting new topics instead of letting the child direct the conversation himself. Stories read by directive therapists are more likely to have an underlying purpose, and therapists are more likely to create interpretations of stories that children tell. In directive therapy games are generally chosen for the child, and children are given themes and character profiles when engaging in doll or puppet activities. This therapy still leaves room for free expression by the child, but it is more structured than nondirective play therapy. There are also different established techniques that are used in directive play therapy, including directed sandtray therapy and cognitive behavioural play therapy. Directed sandtray therapy is more commonly used with trauma victims and involves the "talk" therapy to a much greater extent. Because trauma is often debilitating, directed sandplay therapy works to create change in the present, without the lengthy healing process often required in traditional sandplay therapy. This is why the role of the therapist is important in this approach. Therapists may ask clients questions about their sandtray, suggest them to change the sandtray, ask them to elaborate on why they chose particular objects to put in the tray, and on rare occasions, change the sandtray themselves. Use of directives by the therapist is very common. While traditional sandplay therapy is thought to work best in helping clients access troubling memories, directed sandtray therapy is used to help people manage their memories and the impact it has had on their lives.

Roger Phillips, in the early 1980s, was one of the first to suggest that combining aspects of cognitive behavioural therapy with play interventions would be a good theory to investigate. Cognitive behavioural play therapy was then developed to be used with very young children between two and six years of age. It incorporates aspects of Beck's cognitive therapy with play therapy because children may not have the developed cognitive abilities necessary for participation in straight cognitive therapy. In this therapy, specific toys such as dolls and stuffed animals may be used to model particular cognitive strategies, such as effective coping mechanisms and problem-solving skills. Little emphasis is placed on the children's verbalizations in these interactions but rather on their actions and their play. Creating stories with the dolls and stuffed animals is a common method used by cognitive behavioural play therapists in order to change children's maladaptive thinking.

Efficacy of Directive Play Therapy

The efficacy of directive play therapy has been less established than that of nondirective play therapy, yet the numbers still indicate that this mode of play therapy is also effective. In 2001 meta analysis by authors Ray, Bratton, Rhine, and Jones, direct play therapy was found to have an effect size of .73 compared to the .93 effect size that nondirective play therapy was found to have. Similarly in 2005 meta analysis by authors Bratton, Ray, Rhine, and Jones, directive therapy had an effect size of 0.71, while nondirective play therapy had an effect size of 0.92. Although the effect sizes of directive therapy are statistically significantly lower than those of nondirective play therapy, they are still comparable to the effect sizes for psychotherapy used with children, demonstrated by Casey, Weisz, and LeBlanc. A potential reason for the difference in the effect size may be due to the amount of studies that have been done on nondirective vs. directive play therapy. Approximately 73 studies in each meta analysis examined nondirective play therapy, while there were only 12 studies that looked at directive play therapy. Once more research is done on directive play therapy, there is potential that effect sizes between nondirective and directive play therapy will be more comparable.

Parent/child Play Therapy

Several approaches to play therapy have been developed for parents to use in the home with their own children. Training in nondirective play for parents has been shown to significantly reduce mental health problems in at-risk preschool children. One of the first parent/child play therapy approaches developed was Filial Therapy, in which parents are trained to facilitate nondirective play therapy sessions with their own children. Filial therapy has been shown to help children work through trauma and also resolve behaviour problems.

Another approach to play therapy that involves parents is Theraplay, which was developed in the 1970s. At first, trained therapists worked with children, but Theraplay later evolved into an approach in which parents are trained to play with their children in specific ways at home. Theraplay is based on the idea that parents can improve their children's behaviour and also help them overcome emotional problems by engaging their children in forms of play that replicate the playful, attuned, and empathic interactions of a parent with an infant. Studies have shown that Theraply is effective in changing children's behaviour, especially for children suffering from attachment disorders.

In the 1980s, Stanley Greenspan developed Floortime, a comprehensive, play-based approach for parents and therapists to use with autistic children. There is evidence for the success of this programme with children suffering from autistic spectrum disorders.

Lawrence Cohen has created an approach called Playful Parenting, in which he encourages parents to play with their children to help resolve emotional and behavioural issues. Parents are encouraged to connect playfully with their children through silliness, laughter, and roughhousing.

More recently, Aletha Solter has developed a comprehensive approach for parents called Attachment Play, which describes evidence-based forms of play therapy, including nondirective play, more directive symbolic play, contingency play, and several laughter-producing activities. Parents are encouraged to use these playful activities to strengthen their connection with their children, resolve discipline issues, and also help the children work through traumatic experiences such as hospitalization or parental divorce.

Becoming a School Counsellor

School counsellors can play pivotal roles in shaping the lives of students. They help students choose which courses to take, plan for the future, and work through difficult times. The occupation can present great challenges, but also tremendous rewards.

Responsibilities

School counsellors are often the main source of in-school support for students (especially high school students). Ideally, counsellors spend most of their time helping students academically. They administer and interpret career interest and aptitude tests to help students plan a career or post-secondary path. They also provide resources for getting into a post-secondary institution, or for getting a job. At the college level, counsellors help students choose a career path and prepare for employment. Larger schools and private schools are sometimes able to employ additional support staff that can perform some of these duties, such as administering tests or keeping records.

Students who are struggling with social, academic, or personal issues cannot focus on achieving their academic potential and their dreams.Socounsellors also work with students, teachers, administrators, and parents to catch potential problems early, before they turn into major issues. For example, they may hold group counselling sessions to help students deal with grief after a tragic event. Or, they may recommend professional psychiatric counselling for students with severe problems. They can help parents and teachers communicate effectively, and they can help bullies and victims settle their differences.

Unfortunately, school district budget constraints and a general misunderstanding of the role of counsellors means that many spend their time performing non-essential tasks, including substitute teaching, bus duty, disciplining students, and calculating grade point averages (rather than interpreting and applying them).

The American Counselling Association estimates that counsellors spend 10-20% of their time, on average, on these system support tasks, which detracts from the quality of their work and their ability to reach students. Some school districts are working to reverse this trend, but for many areas, it will likely only get worse before it gets better. "A counsellor's main role is to be an advocate for students... unfortunately, fiscal constraints sometimes limit the amount of advocacy work that can be done," says Judy Hingle, director of professional development for the National Association for College Admission Counselling.

Work Environment

Some school counsellors follow the traditional teacher's schedule of a 9- to 10-month school year. They often spend summer vacations doing graduate course work for re-certification. An increasing number of schools, however, employ their counsellors full-time, and most work 8:30 to 4:00 or similar hours. College counsellors are more likely to work year-round and to have heavier work loads.

As with teachers and other administrators, the job may not end when that last bell rings. According to Paula Davis, a counsellor with Canandaigua Academy in western New York, "The job is very time consuming...not a 7:30-3:00 day at all...you will need to put in many extra hours in order to accomplish all that is expected of you." When asked if it is worth it, Paula says, "The real rewards are seeing students overcome academic or personal difficulties to achieve their goals." Counsellors may travel as much as administrators (much more than teachers) to attend conferences and training. Many districts and schools pay for required training, while others offer time off or tuition reimbursement. Opportunities for career advancement include moving on to bigger or better school districts; becoming the main administrator of guidance programmes for a school; teaching; moving onto other counselling positions; or school administration.

To succeed in this field, counsellors must have high physical and emotional energy and a supreme ability to handle stress. They must be organized, willing to continue training over their career, and good communicators. Of course, the desire to work with kids is essential. The stress levels of this job are obvious when one considers the high initial attrition rate; 60% of new school counsellors leave the field within two years. Those that stay, however, report some of the highest rates of job satisfaction of any field.

6

Government Interest in Vocational Education

Guidance helps people accomplish the following goals whether they are learners planning their education, training and careers, or adults planning their careers or further training, or preparing to become more employable.

- Identify own talents, strengths and weaknesses, family expectations and national requirements to sort out the personal relevance of the educational and vocational options available;
- Understand the available education and training options and the requirements for admission and success, and select an appropriate field of study;
- Understand the work options that are available, the qualifications required, the means of gaining entry, the life of the worker and the rewards of the jobs;
- Translate information about self, educational opportunities and the world of work into short-range and long-range career goals;
- Learn effective job-search procedures;
- Develop career adaptability to be able to take advantage of opportunities as they occur;
- Overcome self-defeating behaviours, gain self-confidence and learn life skills;
- Cope with the reactions to job loss of anger, depression, frustration and apathy, and learn to take continuing positive action to become employed again;

- Identify alternative occupations when current employment is in jeopardy.

Guidance is more than giving information. It is a blend of self-development and of the learning and assimilation of career, providing educational and labour market information. The development of self-confidence is often a prerequisite for taking action for one's career. The goals of guidance may be achieved via individual counselling, self-preparation, career development courses, computer-assisted guidance and Internet-based guidance systems.

Challenges of the Twenty-first Century

As the third millennium approaches, there is a growing recognition that guidance contributes to the personal, educational, economic and social development of individuals and nations.

State of the Economy

The first seven years of the 1990s were years of economic expansion in significant parts of Europe, North America and Asia, yet many countries worried about how well they could compete in the face of the globalization of trade. They examined their economic and educational policies and programmes to ensure that they would have competent, competitive and even entrepreneurial work forces. Typically, their recipes for future economic success included strengthening the career guidance services for learners and for workers in the labour force. As the international economy grew more worrisome and as economic management became a priority within an increasing range of countries, the development of competent labour forces was seen as increasingly important to the future economic well being of countries.

In the past a number of countries have followed policies that did not particularly welcome the private sector as an important part of society, but now as some governments downsize they look more and more to the private sector to provide growth in employment and to be good 'corporate citizens'. The years of neglect of the private sector is reflected in the lack of knowledge about basic labour market information (e.g., occupational descriptions, occupational classification system, job requirements, pay rates, hiring practices and job forecasts). The lack of this information and the lack of occupational structures for the gathering and classification of the information have presented problems to technical and vocational educators in deciding what programmes to offer. It also presents a problem to counsellors to provide vocational guidance when very little vocational information is available.

Innovations at the Turn of the Millennium

Guidance was first conducted through group talks and individual interviews with students, but increasingly it has been recognized that adults are in need of guidance as much as youth. It has also been accepted that career development is a cumulative learning often requiring more than an interview or two at significant transition points such as school leaving, preparation for higher education or at the time of job loss. Several current innovations are briefly described below.

Several countries are formulating career development guidelines to specify the characteristics of vocational maturity that people should be able to exhibit at each level of education and employment. These guidelines are then used as specifications for guidance programmes and for the evaluation of programmes. (Australian Education Council, 1992; National Occupational Information and Co-ordinating Committee; National Life Work Centre, 1998.)

Career and personal development courses typically address the following goals:

- Understand the importance of values, work, friends, family, income and self-fulfilment to personal and career development;
- Develop a sense of control over one's own life and work and explore one's own abilities, potential, needs, aspirations, self-monitoring, self-defeating behaviours, self-help skills and use of resources;
- Strengthen one's orientation to the future and identify steps to be taken, anticipate opportunities and barriers, timetable steps to the future, seek and identify opportunities, and take action;
- Examine a variety of occupations, learn about the education and training, licensing, certification or registration, working conditions and work-life style of the occupations;
- Learn decision-making and apply it to one's own career decisions including setting specific targets;
- Examine own self-awareness and tendency to analyse past experience, including what one has and has not accomplished and the reasons for successes and disappointments;

- Learn the job-search skills of preparing résumés, completing application forms, seeking interviews and being interviewed; and,
- Develop the transition skills of continuously developing one's competencies in the face of adversity and opportunity, obtain information on the transferability of one's skills to new opportunities, and of engage in continuous learning. Guidance courses are often taught by regular teachers with but a few days specialized training in the subject.

Career education, the infusion of career and labour market information into the regular subjects of the curriculum helps make the course material more relevant to everyday life and also instills the skills of research, thinking and questioning into education (rather than teaching them separately).

The past two decades have witnessed the growth of computer-assisted educational and career guidance systems that use: interest, aptitude and preference surveys; ed educational and occupational information; person-occupation matching systems; and educational and vocational planning systems. A requirement of such systems is a classification and description of occupations in a jurisdiction.

To make guidance available to adult populations, a number of governments established career centres providing a full range of guidance services including individual and group counselling, labour market information, and job search training. In addition, an increasing number of major employers have career centres for the use of their own staff. The companies actively encourage and assist their employees to acquire advanced skills to make them more promotable. Part of this service often includes personal career planning offered on a confidential basis.

Equity has become an increasingly important focus of career guidance and promises to continue to be more and more evident in career education and guidance. UNESCO is a major international influence in this movement (UNESCO, 1987; Bingham and Martin, 1989; Miller and Vetter, 1996) particularly as it relates to girls and women. Guidance programmes for persons with disabilities (Conger, 1997) and for aboriginals (Peavy, 1994, Charter et al., 1994) are becoming more and more important.

Peer helping is becoming very popular in some school systems because it has been demonstrated to be effective in creating a positive peer pressure in contrast to negative peer pressure. Peers help each other in learning, social activities and career planning. Life-skills training to inculcate problem-solving abilities and their appropriate and responsible use in the management of one's life in such areas as personal, family, education, work and leisure is becoming a feature of many programmes for youth and adults. People who feel that they can influence their own lives, communicate better, have good relationships in the home and community, and exhibit social skills appropriate to the learning and workplaces are more employable and more likely to create opportunities for self-employment. (Allen et al., 1995.)

School guidance programmes in a number of countries now include the preparation by each student of a personal portfolio (National Occupational Information and Coordinating Committee that contains a record of achievement and action plans. These documents are drawn up by students as a basis for self-assessment and future planning. They also provide a medium for the recording of significant career information and relating it to one's plans.

Simulations of working life prompt the participants to obtain knowledge of themselves, occupations, education and training, pay and working conditions, living costs and other factors and integrate them into alternative career plans. Simulations are popular with learners and counsellors alike because they provide a realistic opportunity to test out expectations for the future (e.g. Barry, 1998).

Visits to work sites students in the ninth year are invited to spend the day in the workplace with either a parent, friend, relative or volunteer host. A true 'show and tell' experience for adults, in a multitude of different workplace settings including airports, police departments, civic centres, industrial enterprises, banks, restaurants, universities, radio stations, machine shops and hospitals. The initiative provides opportunities for students to see workers in different roles and responsibilities, and aims to enhance students' understanding of individual jobs in the context of the working community, while linking classroom and workplace experiences directly. The programme aims to create opportunities for students to see the realities of the workplace.

Internet

In an effort to make guidance available to all, and noting the increasing popularity of the Internet, a few affluent countries provide a full range of career, educational and labour-market information, and also career and personal planning courses, via the World Wide Web. In addition to information, some systems include inventories of interests and aptitudes, occupational choice systems, instructions on job search techniques, a resume generator, and even simulated job interviews. These countries like the idea of "self-serve" career guidance. The information provided by governments is often supplemented by information offered by educational institutions, employers, professional and trade associations, and other groups. In a few jurisdictions the Internet guidance programmes are supplemented with electronic mail communication with a counsellor and, in some cases, with other users through open discussion forums. Some experimentation is now underway to provide vocational counselling via interactive video conferencing on the Internet.

A by-product of Internet-based systems is that people in any country with access to the Internet can see the educational and occupational structures and opportunities in other countries and also use the guidance instruments (interest inventories, etc.) on-line. It is relevant to note that some of the users of Canadian Internet-based career systems access them from outside that country.

A more planned effort to provide international guidance on the Internet is found in the European ESTIA project which provides information about education, work and the labour market in four countries, soon to expand to fourteen countries. Internet connections are far from being available to most people in most countries. However, the Internet delivery of career guidance will be increasingly common in the next century. On-line counselling has some distinct advantages: to reach people in rural and remote areas; to serve persons with disabilities that make it difficult for them to attend an office; and to accommodate people who are apprehensive about receiving counselling face to face.

Educational Reform

Some ministries of education are in the process of major educational reform because the emergence of a more 'learning-intensive' economy poses new challenges. Employment is becoming increasingly fluid, work is increasingly complex, occupational boundaries are changing or dissolving, and more jobs are temporary. For these reasons, continual learning is a more important part of work. Five main elements characterize an education system that is likely to prepare students effectively for this new environment:

- emphasis on science and technology;
- skill standards;
- close connection between vocational and academic education to meet the requirements of learning-intensive work;
- links between employers and school, and;
- workplace learning.

These changes present difficulties for the learners and many students (and their parents) are in need of a better understanding of the changes, the implications in terms of career prospects, the skills to adjust to a scientific mode of thinking and the cultures of new industrial working life. This situation calls for a special version of the guidance curriculum and programme generally to provide the orientation and to teach the learning skills.

School Dropouts

Students who prematurely discontinue their studies represent a major potential loss to themselves, the economy and the society. In some countries there is considerable pressure on students to quit school and help with the farm-work or otherwise bring supplemental income into their parents' household. Recently some countries have become increasingly active in attempting to lessen the number of dropouts - and this is quite feasible because dropping out is seldom done without prior notice on the part of the student's behaviour.

A number of mechanisms have been put in place: guidance curriculum; diagnostic surveys intended to help identify students likely to drop out so that remedial steps may be taken; remedial programmes for students falling behind in their studies; teaching of study skills; the implementation of peer helping programmes to make use of positive peer pressure and to combat negative peer pressure; combined work and study programmes; and changes in school management practices to give students the same rights of grievance and appeal that is common in the workplace. Guidance counsellors are often at the heart of these programmes.

School-to-work Transition

The articulation of school-based learning and work-based learning follows significantly different patterns from country to country. In some jurisdictions there is an almost seamless transition from the school to apprenticeship programmes. In other jurisdictions there is a complete separation between school and work. The role of guidance varies significantly according to the system. In the former it is the task of counsellors to assist students to select the appropriate types of work-based training programme and to prepare them for entry. In jurisdictions without this articulation, the school guidance programme has often been more geared to preparing the most academically inclined students for university than to help students who will go immediately into the labour force. Frequently in cultures that separate secondary education and apprenticeship programmes parents want their children to go to university and not to prepare for the trades even though the children have indicated a preference for a trade. Counsellors have a particular responsibility to explain to parents the many favourable aspects of a career in the trades.

Increasingly in jurisdictions that do not articulate school and work-based learning, schools integrate work experience assignments as an integral part of the curriculum and seek the co-operation of local employers, unions and professional associations. According to Stasz (1998) "the power of the work based learning is that authentic work experiences give learners opportunities to apply knowledge in useful contexts. They thereby can gain a deeper understanding of both their abilities and the opportunities they can create for themselves through experience and/or education. In the end, learning is a personal, developmental transformation, so it is crucial to pay attention to whether that transformation occurs, as well as to the context that will enable such a transformation. It is this context that teachers and counsellors, in and out of school, have the most ability to shape".

Guidance for Unemployed Workers

The following practices have been found (Bysshe, 1998 and others) to be helpful in preparing unemployed workers for new employment:

- Identify the "employability skills" that employers expect of workers and train workers in these skills;
- Use income-support programmes to train unemployed workers and to get them appropriate work experience to qualify for new employment;
- Teach job search techniques;
- Identify the information, assessment, guidance and training needs of individuals to help them become employed with-in a realistic time;
- Use an action plan, where the responsibilities of the client and the counsellor are clear;

- Provide ongoing help so that agreed plans are reviewed in the light of progress made and that necessary support can be given to deal with inevitable disappointments and failures;
- Address issues such as bolstering confidence and self-esteem, through appropriate measures;
- Develop and foster self-help to maximize the learning for the individual and ensure that all barriers to effective transition are being addressed; and,
- Act as the link between the individual, and learning and employment opportunities they wish to enter, including advocating on behalf of the individual.

Training of Counsellors

Although there are common elements in vocational guidance wherever practised, there are also important differences in terms of culture, education, employment practices and occupational structures from country to country. Consequently, guidance practitioners generally need to be trained in the country in which they will practise.

As has been already mentioned, when guidance is conducted by a course in career development, it is not unusual to have the course taught by regular classroom teachers who have had special preparation to teach the course. Whether it is to teach a career development curriculum or to conduct courses infused with career education the professional development of teachers should give them a basic framework for career planning and how to connect activities in the classroom to the events unfolding in the labour market. As early as 1974 UNESCO recommended that teachers have "an introduction to educational and occupational guidance methods" (Revised Recommendations for Vocational and Technical Education, Paris, UNESCO, art. 84 g).

When guidance is provided through individual counselling, however, the counsellor is expected to have specialized training in such areas as: counselling techniques; career, educational and labour market information; assessment techniques to measure skills, abilities, aptitudes, interests, values, and personality; needs assessment techniques; computer and Internet systems of guidance; organizing career development programmes; teaching job search techniques; establishing linkages with community-based organizations; and, public relations techniques to promote career development activities and services. Some training for counsellors is beginning to appear on the Internet and may be expected to become increasingly available through that means. Currently there are no internationally accepted standards for guidance counsellors but the International Association for Educational and Vocational Guidance (IAEVG) is in the process of establishing a committee to draft such a standard. International standards are increasingly important as on-line career counselling can be provided across national boundaries and therefore be immune from regulation by most, if not all, countries.

Guidance consultants in ministries usually have the same training as counsellors plus competencies in programme planning and adoption strategies; guidance curriculum development; differing cultural values and their relationship to work values; unique career planning needs of minorities, women, persons with disabilities, and older persons; and alternative approaches to career planning for learners with specific needs.

Many countries do not have "counsellors" although they do have psychologists, sociologists or others performing some of the functions of a counsellor. The unique training of educational and vocational counsellors typically is instruction in: the functioning of the labour market; the structure of the educational and training systems; how to use labour market information in the counselling interview; employability skills; and, job-search techniques. In some countries, training in these areas is needed by those who otherwise have relevant competencies.

Developing National Systems

Ministries of education, labour and social affairs that deal with different aspects of career guidance are expected to provide leadership in the development of policy, programmes, methods and materials, organization structure for delivery, counsellor training and procedures for evaluation. The guidance materials often include classification and description of occupations; brochures describing various educational options and occupations; and computer-assisted guidance systems.

In countries where the private sector has been traditionally ignored by the government, counsellors in the ministries have a particular responsibility to establish collaborative contacts with firms to learn about their occupations, required training, pay structures, employment practices (for example the use of application forms by international companies represents an unexpected innovation in many locations), working conditions, work culture, etc. in order to prepare relevant and useful guidance programmes.

Lifelong learning is important as a means to personal, social and economic development. In many communities there is a variety of formal and non-formal education opportunities for part-time learners. Perhaps the majority of both formal and non-formal learning projects undertaken by adults relates to work. This, it appears, is the prime motive for adult learning. Governments that want their citizens to enrol in learning projects to increase their employability might take this notion and promote a career development culture emphasizing personal achievement. A career development culture would be characterized by elements such as widespread publicity about future job opportunities and the knowledge and skills that they will require; promotion of learning opportunities; and promotion of career guidance services. Increasingly, governments are involving the voluntary and private sectors in promoting the creation of a culture of competence.

Recommendations For Future Strategies

A number of recommendations can be made on the basis of the forgoing. In some cases the responsibility for action is that of government, in other cases technical and vocational education and training institutions and associations of counsellors could initiate action. Government support for guidance is important because:

- Economic development is fast becoming the overarching concern of most governments;
- Economic growth is based increasingly on the availability of highly skilled workers;
- Technical and vocational education and training are very important means to developing a skilled labour force;
- Guidance helps individuals develop their full potential, identify the most appropriate training, and succeed in their education and placement in the labour market. A British study (Killeen, White and Watts, 1992.) indicated that the "learning outcomes" of guidance (self-awareness, opportunity awareness, decision-making skills and transition skills) have been demonstrated to be the precursors of socio-economic outcomes of guidance; and,
- guidance supports the UNESCO values of increasing the educational and labour market accomplishments of girls and

women, of people of all cultures and regions, and of persons with disabilities, and thereby promotes the use of the full talents of a country.

National Action

It is recommended that governments implement the following steps:

1. Establish an office with responsibility to:
   - provide funding for vocational guidance programmes and services;
   - develop and provide methods and materials for guidance;
   - prepare the career guidance curriculum;
   - provide training and continuing education for guidance counsellors and teachers;
   - conduct research and development to create new, more comprehensive and better ways of conducting educational and vocational guidance;
   - design promotional campaigns to interest learners, including girls and women, in science and technology;
   - develop programmes to increase the retention of learners by schools and thus reduce the numbers of drop-outs;
   - design campaigns to develop a career development culture that encourages all people to participate in lifelong learning; and,
   - promote the infusion of career development concepts into academic subjects to help learners understand how the course work fits together and forms a body of knowledge and skills related to performance in work and other aspects of life.
2. Enact legislation that defines the goals of guidance describes the range of services to be provided and stipulates the level of resourcing. The legislation should apply to the services to be provided to learners in educational institutions and to adults in the labour market.
3. Provide employment counselling and placement services for learners completing their studies and for all people in the labour force.
4. Adopt policies on guidance that include the following requirements:

- all learners receive curriculum-based guidance;
- learners who require individual counselling for satisfactory achievement shall receive it;
- individual counselling is a specialized function which must be performed by staff members who possess the required competencies;
- the responsibilities of school principals, teachers and counsellors in respect of the guidance programme development and delivery are specified;
- qualifications that teachers and counsellors in guidance should have; and, provision of guidance services to unemployed workers.

5. Enact legislation to authorize the collection, classification and publishing of labour market information that is useful to economic development efforts, technical and vocational training programmes, and educational and vocational guidance.

Associations of Counsellors

Counsellor's associations have an important part to play in the development of guidance by:

- advocating that all citizens who need and want educational and vocational guidance and counselling can receive it from a competent professional;
- recommending the basic nature and quality of service to be provided to students and adults;
- recommending the essential training and other qualifications that all counsellors in educational and vocational guidance should have;
- organizing continuing education programmes for counsellors;
- requiring all members to adhere to a code of ethics; and,
- certifying or licensing counsellors.

Technical and Vocational Education Institutions

In some jurisdictions, ministries of education observe the innovations undertaken by leading institutions and in time adopt or recommend the more successful ones to other schools in the system. There is, therefore, an important role to be played by institutions themselves in leading the way for national improvement. There are several steps that technical and education and training institutions can undertake in providing guidance to learners:

Hire a counsellor. The tasks of the counsellor include:

- Conduct a needs assessment to determine what needs to be addressed, the characteristics of the learners and how they can be reached and served;
- Build partnerships within the school and community of educators, administrators, business and industry representatives, parents and post-secondary officials to work as a team to effectively assist the learners in realizing their educational and career aspirations;
- Design comprehensive programmes that include integrating guidance activities within the regular curriculum;
- Organize and supervise work-based learning activities, including job shadowing, internships, career simulations and on-the-job training;
- Tap available services and seek assistance (e.g., funding, equipment);
- Plan professional development activities for school staff to orient them to their roles of successfully assisting learners in educational and career planning; and,
- Conduct an ongoing evaluation of the programme (adapted from Stern, Bailey and Merritt, 1996.) The counsellor should endeavour to meet with every potential student to help him/her select the most appropriate programme, and to meet with every student at least once every three months to discuss their education and career plans;
- Prepare descriptions of occupations related to the training being offered. The descriptions might include: brief description of the work, working conditions, education and training required, registration, certification or licensing requirements, average pay, and future outlook. These may be printed. They may also be entered into computers for learners to search. A consortium of technical and vocational education and training institutions in collaboration with UNESCO might prepare a standard format for computerized information;
- Prepare descriptions of the courses and programmes available in the technical and vocational education and training

institutions. These may be printed. They may also be entered into computers for students in more junior levels of education to search. As suggested in the previous recommendation, a consortium of technical and vocational education and training institutions in collaboration with UNESCO might prepare a standard format for computer information;

- Approach companies or other organizations with Internet connections to provide access to career guidance resources on the Internet through their connections. Corporate assistance in translating the material might also be obtained, if necessary;
- Adopt or adapt a career development curriculum and ensure that teachers are competent to conduct the course;
- Organize relevant work experience assignments with local employers.

Enterprises and Vocationaleducation and Training: Expenditure and Expected Returns

Government interest in expenditure (investment) by enterprises in vocational education and training provided a basis for the analysis. As foreshadowed above, this interest is linked to the dual policy goals of attempting to increase the quantum of national VET activity and to transfer the cost of that provision to the enterprises which derive benefit from VET. Reference to VET in this paper encompasses both 'formal' (e.g. participation in accredited courses or courses organised by enterprises) and also 'informal' (e.g. learning on-the-job) provisions, although the majority of the research has focused on surveys and case studies of formal provisions. In the sections which follow, the analysis of recent research literature is presented under two headings:

Enterprise expenditure on VET, and Enterprises and returns.

Enterprise Expenditure on VET

The expenditure by enterprises on training remains uneven across and within industry sectors. Some enterprises will or are expected to bear the full cost of training while other enterprises' skill development are furnished through programmes funded largely from the public purse (Moran,

1994). However, all enterprises, whether they intend it or not, make a contribution through the provision of learning experiences which are often referred to as 'informal'.

Participation in structured entry-level training (e.g. apprentices and traineeships) which includes both on- and off-the-job experiences is another kind of contribution with apprentices not always covering the costs of their employment. A key change that has taken place in VET provisions in countries such as Australia and New Zealand which needs to be acknowledged. Public utilities, such a railways, power generation and transmission departments, have traditionally provided more apprenticeships than their needs warranted thereby contributing to the pool of available skilled workers. Recently, this community service has largely ceased as these utilities have become corporatized and/or privatised. The provision of an internal training role, comprising staff and facilitates dedicated to training, represents another kind of expenditure which often results from particular enterprise needs. However, in order to understand further the variables which influence enterprises' expenditure on training, categorises of (i) size,(ii) specialisation and (iii) location are used.

Size

The literature indicates that larger enterprises typically expend more on VET than smaller enterprises. The evidence suggests simply that the larger the enterprise the greater the likelihood of it expending funds in VET. In data gathered by the Australian Bureau of Statistics (ABS) (1995) it is reported that 97% of businesses with more than a hundred employees, and 79% of enterprises with between 20 and 99 employees reported expenditure on training.

However, only 18% of small businesses, those with fewer than 20 employees, reported expenditure. Using this data, Gibb (1997) claims that 82% of small businesses, which comprise 50% of the private sector workforce, do not spend money on training.

Admittedly, this evidence reflects 'formal' VET provisions and may not fully account for the 'informal' VET provisions which occur in both small and large enterprises. However, this data presents a stark picture of the differentiation in those enterprises that expend funds on training. Yet other differences exist which are not evident in the ABS data. For example, Baker & Wooden (1995) reports that large firms provide more training in management and support functions than small firms who focus their training on activities which are directly related to increased production of goods or services.

Catts also found that the formal training employees received in four small- to medium-sized enterprises (SME) was highly specific, provided by product suppliers (vendor training), and took the form of product knowledge sessions and training concerned with the installation, maintenance and repair of specific equipment.

The ongoing low level of expenditure on training by small businesses, who are the key employers in Australia, presents a difficult and enduring problem for policy makers. Factors such as the required level of skills, lack of incentive, other priorities and a preference for recruitment rather than training are proposed as reasons why smaller enterprises do not invest heavily in VET. A contributing factor is a lack of knowledge within small business about training activities and networks.

Guthrie & Barnett's study reports a lack of understanding by enterprises about the formal accreditation of training programmes and highlights perceptions of excessive bureaucracy associated with formal training provisions.

Schofield and Callus suggest these imposts have discouraged some enterprises from participation in the formal training process. Compliance costs for apprenticeship are also reported as falling disproportionately on small business. However, when incentives for work-based training were offered few small businesses made use of them. Given governments' ongoing interest in maintaining and developing small business as a key sector of the economy, further work is required to determine how best the impasses which inhibit small business involvement in VET can be overcome. Such work may well benefit from examining the local-regional professional/occupational support strategies that have been adopted in countries such as Germany and Australia. These arrangements emphasise voluntarism of a kind which is reminiscent of the community obligation in which large private and public sector enterprises used to engage.

The form of participation in training most commonly reported by enterprises is unstructured on-the-job training with this type of training being significantly low only in enterprises with fewer than 10 employees.

Seventy-eight per cent of workers in these size enterprises reported receiving informal training compared with 84% of workers in large enterprises.

Misko also reports that a majority of small enterprises surveyed indicated that although they were not involved in any formal work-based training, practical training was provided by experienced employees who explain, demonstrate and supervise as new employees learn their tasks. The importance of informal training at enterprise level has not been fully recognised and is undervalued. In one study the benefits of expenditure on formal training in one enterprise were overshadowed by the reported contributions of everyday learning in the workplace guided by experts and others in the workplace.

However, an emerging concern is that the interest in training by small to medium enterprises is not being sustained in new enterprise-based industrial agreements. Callus (1994) reporting the results of a study of 119 enterprise agreements covering fewer than 20 employees found that only 44% of agreements made any reference to training compared with 69% of agreements covering 20 employees or more.

Misko (1996) concluded that the provision of formal work-based training is not widespread in Australian enterprises. Smith (1997) also reported low levels of training provisions in enterprise bargaining negotiations among the enterprises. Moreover, similar but more comprehensive and alarming findings are reported by Guthrie & Barnett. Only one-third of 1913 recent enterprise agreements they examined mentioned training arrangements and only a quarter of these agreements referred to structured training. When this data is added to the downturn in apprentice numbers in some Australian states and the emerging preference by employers for 1-year traineeship arrangements in preference for 3- or 4-year apprenticeship programmes a disturbing picture emerges of a significant decline in the commitment by enterprises to expenditure on training. Together, these data suggest that enterprise commitment to training is stalling.

Specialisation

Enterprises make different levels of contribution to their skill development needs based on their specialisation. Those whose training needs can be met by the existing publicly-funded VET provisions, which are dominated by particular groupings (e.g. metal, construction, hospitality), are required to make a lower level of contribution than those enterprises whose specialisation is outside these provisions. The obvious inequity of some enterprises sponsoring the public provision training of other enterprises skill development through taxation-funded programme is of concern. This inequity in VET provisions, may also result in enterprises within strategically important or emerging industries being expected to make higher levels of contributions to VET, thereby potentially inhibiting the development of these industries.

Consequently, the development of the very skills which should be a national priority may be inhibited. Equally, inequities in demands upon enterprises may well suppress levels of VET activity, with recruitment and in-house preparation being preferred. An issue for national policy arising from this situation is whether the different levels of expenditure being expected of enterprises influence their contribution.

This raises the question of whether national goals for the maintenance and development of a skilful workforce are best addressed by arrangements which favour one industry sector over another based on historical grounds.

Location

In a vast country such as Australia access to publicly-funded VET provisions is not evenly distributed. Hence, the location of enterprises is likely to influence decisions about their expenditure. For example, enterprises in remote locations or those which are distant from

appropriate publicly-funded VET programmes may have to make a high level of expenditure on training given the costs associated with these provisions or else recruit the required skilled workers from the labour market [Food Industry Training Board (FITB)]. Given, that many key exporting enterprises are based on remote localities (e.g. mining and secondary processing) this may be a factor in how and to what degree they expend on training. It seems that these enterprises will expend funds on training when training is needed to secure core business goals, which are often enterprise-specific. For instance, because of problems with moving skilled labour into provincial centres, a number of key infrastructure projects (power station) and enterprises (secondary processing) have elected to develop the skills of local people.

This expenditure, which has been quite extensive in some cases, has been required because of the location and the shortage of skilled workers in the particular location.

Need for Vocationalisation of Education in India

Vocational Education and Training (VET) is an important element of the nation's education initiative. In order for Vocational Education to play its part effectively in the changing national context and for India to enjoy the fruits of the demographic dividend, there is an urgent need to redefine the critical elements of imparting vocational education and training to make them flexible, contemporary, relevant, inclusive and creative. The Government is well aware of the important role of Vocational education and has already taken a number of important initiatives in this area.

The objective of this note is to assess and describe the need for introducing Vocational education at higher and tertiary levels and for establishing a Vocational University. The note also summarizes the present Indian and International Vocational Education scenario and its problems. The note also puts up recommendation for policies with the need for implementation at State and National Level and suggests possible models to introduce Vocational Education at the higher / tertiary levels.

Problem Areas in present Vocational Education and Training System

Through, the study of the prevalent Vocational Education System in India the following problem areas have been identified -:

1. There is a high drop out rate at Secondary level. There are 220 million children who go to school in India. Of these only around 12% students reach university. A large part of the 18-24 years age group in India has never been able to reach college. Comparing India to countries with similar income levels – India does not under perform in primary education but has a comparative deficit in secondary education.
2. Vocational Education is presently offered at Grade 11, 12th – however students reaching this Grade aspire for higher education. Since the present system does not allow vertical mobility, skills obtained are lost. Enrollment in 11th & 12th Grade of vocational education is only 3% of students at upper secondary level. About 6800 schools enroll 400,000 students in vocational education schemes utilizing only 40% of the available student capacity in these schools.
3. International experience suggests that what employers mostly want are young workers with strong basic academic skills and not just vocational skills. The present system does not emphasize general academic skills. The relative wages of workers with secondary education are increasing.
4. Private & Industry Participation is lacking. There are no incentives for private players to enter the field of vocational education.

5. Present regulations are very rigid. In-Service Training is required but not prevalent today. There is no opportunity for continuous skill up-gradation.
6. There is a lack of experienced and qualified teachers to train students on vocational skills. In foreign countries Bachelors of Vocational Education (BVE) is often a mandatory qualification for teachers. However, in India no specific qualifications are being imparted for Vocational Education teachers.
7. Vocationalization at all levels has not been successful. Poor quality of training is not in line with industry needs.
8. There is no definite path for vocational students to move from one level / sector to another level / sector. Mobility is not defined and hence students do not have a clear path in vocational education.
9. No clear policy or system of vocational education leading to certification / degrees presently available for the unorganized / informal sector. No Credit System has been formulated for the same. Over 90% of employment in India is in the Informal sector. JSS offers 255 types of vocational courses to 1.5 million people, Community Polytechnics train about 450,000 people within communities annually and NIOS offers 85 courses through 700 providers. None of these programs have been rigorously evaluated, till date.
10. Expansion of vocational sector is happening without consideration for present problems.

Trends Related to Labour Market

An analysis of the labour market has brought the following issues to the fore-:

1. Labour market requirement for skilled workers without general education skills is declining.
2. Labour force participation is declining while student participation is increasing. Thus more students are joining higher secondary education and looking for vertical mobility.

Government Initiatives

National Vocational Qualification Framework: To stimulate and support reforms in skills development and to facilitate nationally standardized and acceptable, international comparability of qualifications, a "National Vocational Qualifications Framework" is being established by the Central Government. Central Advisory Board of Education (CABE) has resolved to set up an inter-ministerial group which would also include representatives of State Governments to develop guidelines for such a National Framework.

The unified system of national qualification will cover schools, vocational education and training institutions and higher education sector. NVQF will be based on nationally recognized occupational standards which details listing of all major activities that a worker must perform in the occupation or competency standards – a detailed listing of the knowledge, skills and attitude that a worker should possess to perform a task written by the particular employment-led sector skills council.

The National Skill Development Policy 2009 has proposed the following features for the framework:-

a) Competency based qualifications and certification on the basis of nationally agreed standards and criteria;
b) Certification for learning achievement and qualification;
c) A range of national qualification levels – based on criteria with respect to responsibility, complexity of activities, and transferability of competencies;
d) The avoidance of duplication and overlapping of qualifications while assuring the inclusion of all training needs;
e) Modular character where achievement can be made in small steps and accumulated for gaining recognizable qualification;
f) Quality Assurance regime that would promote the portability of skills and labour market mobility;
g) Lifelong learning through an improved skill recognition system; recognition of prior learning whether in formal, non-formal or informal arrangements;
h) Open and flexible system which will permit competent individuals to accumulate their knowledge and skill through testing & certification into higher diploma and degree;
i) Different learning pathways – academic and vocational – that integrate formal and non-formal learning, notably learning in the workplace, and that offer vertical mobility from vocational to academic learning;
j) Guidance for individuals in their choice of training and career planning;

k) Comparability of general educational and vocational qualifications at appropriate levels;

l) Nationally agreed framework of affiliation and accreditation of institutions;

m) Multiple certification agencies/institutions will be encouraged within NVQF.

Analysis of National Vocational Education Framework in Other Countries

Australia

Australia, a country that has had an NQF for many years, has re-introduced vocational courses into schools (entitled 'VET in Schools') but the courses have been developed as 'foundation' vocational skills already defined and standardized by the Australian National Training Authority, the single tripartite body responsible for training standards.

Level-I Certificates from the VET system are regarded as educationally equivalent to Senior Certificates from secondary schools, and Diplomas and Advanced Diplomas may be issued by the VET system or by higher education institutes. Depending on the courses of study, credits may be allowed to be accumulated as participants choose to move between the three sectors. Some VET certificates may now be issued with little or no formal training, for example, to enterprise workers who have obtained their skills over a number of years on the job.

United Kingdom

The National Qualifications Framework (NQF) in UK is a credit transfer system developed for qualifications in England, Wales, Namibia and Northern Ireland.

The Framework has nine levels covering all levels of learning in secondary education, further education, vocational, and higher education. Different qualifications are divided into different levels, according to three important frameworks namely, the National Qualification Framework (NQF), the Qualification and Credit Framework (QCF) and last, but not least, the Framework for Higher Education qualifications.

Proposed Education Model for India

Based on the comparison of various education models across the world, the following education model is recommended for us-:

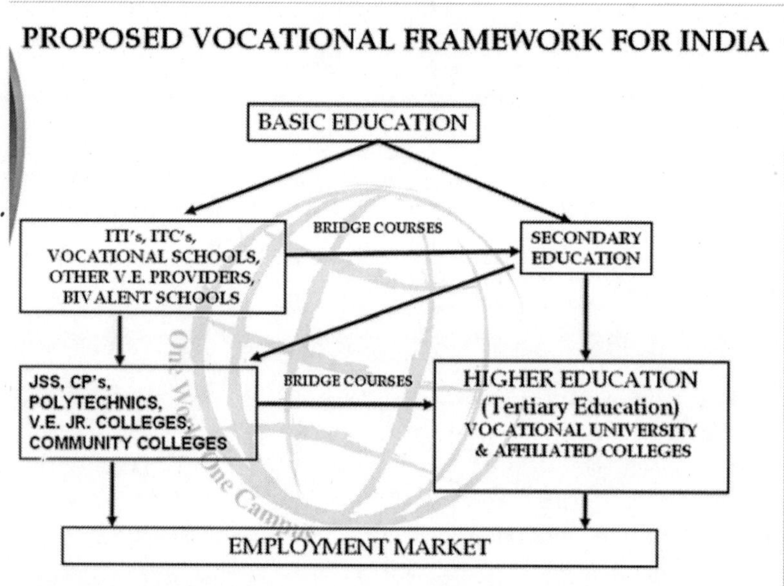

Figure: *Recommendations regarding Vocational Education*

National Board for Vocational Education

1. A national level Board for vocational education should be established, called as National Board for Vocational Education.

For Example, In Australia, there is a similar authority established by the state and federal government called Australian National Training Authority (structure may vary) which plays a major role in :-

a) developing a national TVET system and national strategies with respect to vocational education
b) ensuring close interaction between industries and TVET providers
c) developing effective training market for public and private needs
d) enhancing efficiency and productivity of TVET providers

National Vocational Education Policy

2. A National Vocational Policy should be formulated. The policy should establish equivalence for degrees, diplomas and certifications in the vocational education sector for lateral and vertical mobility across various learning sectors that is, secondary, vocational and higher education.

National Vocational Education Assessment and Accreditation Council

3. National Vocational Assessment & Accreditation Council should be established to formulate a regulatory and quality/standards framework.

Introduction of SSC (Vocational)

4. SSC (vocational) or its equivalent 10th grade certification in vocational stream should be created on similar lines as HSC (Vocational) at both national and state level. Vocational Stream should be introduced at 8th Grade through Bivalent Schools which may provide both conventional and vocational stream of education at secondary level. Presently, in India only sporadic courses as electives are being offered to students under bifocal scheme. However, a separate vocational stream offered by means of bivalent schools does not exist. Statistics reveal that employers prefer students with some general education skills in addition to vocational skills. Thus, in all schemes related to SSC (Vocational) general education courses should be emphasized. Eg. Problem Solving, English, Soft Skills, Business Management etc

For Eg, In China, there are three levels of vocational education: junior secondary, senior secondary and tertiary. Junior vocational education refers to the vocational and technical education after primary school education and is a part of the 9-year compulsory education i.e from age group of 13-15 years.

Credit Banking and Accumulation

In ITI's and ITC's or other vocational education providers, a credit banking system can be established to accumulate required credits in order to grant SSC certificate. This will be especially useful for non-formal and unorganized sectors who do not have any prior formal education. These students in non formal sector may be allowed to take courses worth requisite credit points to obtain SSC Vocational.

In Philippines, the Non-Formal Education - Accreditation and Equivalency (NFE A&E) System enables Filipinos who are unable to avail education through the formal school system or who have dropped out of formal school, obtain elementary and secondary education. NFE A&E test is a standardized paper- and pencil-based test featuring multiple-choice questions based on the expected learning outcomes articulated in the five learning strands of the NFE A&E Curriculum framework which enables students to obtain secondary level certification.

Lateral/Vertical Mobility

5. To ensure vertical mobility, ITIs, MSBVs, Community Colleges and other State Vocational Education Institutions may be granted recognition and accreditation from the respective State Board for Vocational Education to award SSC (Vocational) certification. Vocational Education Providers, Community Colleges, JSS, CP's, Vocational Junior Colleges may also be allowed to award Diplomas and Associate Degrees in addition to HSC (Vocational) certification. Students from Vocational Institutions can be given opportunity for lateral mobility into conventional stream by providing bridge (preparatory) courses. The proposed mobility structure is as indicated below-:

Industrial Participation

7. Private Participation from Industry and other players must be encouraged and is critical for the success of the vocational education growth in India. Industry participation must be at all levels especially in Governance, Curriculum Design, Placements and Funding, Monitoring Outcome. Industry participation is also required for creating production oriented Research and Innovation Labs. A PPP Model can be also created where GOI and Industry can come together to invest in infrastructure and train students in latest skills

For Example, Penang Skills Development Centre is a joint company training centre. The Government invests in the centre and uses it to carry out public training programmes.

The State provided the infrastructure and the industry partners donate equipment, labs, training modules and trainers. Industry thus has access to shared training facilities for in-service employees training. The Government uses the centre as a training institute.

In India, National Skill Development Corporation India (NSDC) is a one of its kind, Public Private Partnership in India. It aims to promote skill development by catalyzing creation of large, quality, for-profit vocational institutions. Three business models established till date are as under-:

B-Able - Tie ups with corporate like L&T and Tata dealers have been established. Six centres providing classroom training and guaranteed 4 week apprenticeship with a prospective employers have been established.

Gram Tarang - Targeting tribal/naxal affected areas. 4 training centres created to train people in Auto CAD, advanced welding on advance machinery funded by NSDC.

8. Teachers training is an important aspect for ensuring quality education in vocational stream. Vocational Educational Qualifications should be insisted (eg. BVE). Higher salaries must be offered to attract skilled teachers. Additional income incentive can also be given through in-service training programmes which can be conducted by teachers for industry employees. Continuous skill development and up-gradation of teachers can be done through Teachers Training Programmes conducted by Teacher Training Centres

Salient Features of a Vocational University

1. A Society registered under the Societies Registration Act, 1860 (Central Act No. 21 of 1860); or Any Public Trust registered under the State Public Trusts Act, or the Indian Trusts Act, 1882 (Central Act No. 2 of 1882) or under the relevant laws in any other State or Union Territory or a Company registered under Sec 25 Companies Act 1956. The University may be established by State Government or by Private players (self-financed)
2. Land, construction and infrastructure requirement may focus on the need for creation of production oriented labs, training centres, innovation/testing labs, latest industry specific equipment etc.
3. Authorities of the University shall have active Industry participation. The administers of the University must have industrial experience.
4. Vocational University will offer all kinds of degree and diploma programmes in vocational higher education sector (Bachelor, Masters, Doctoral) – New Degrees should be created eg. Bachelors in Vocational Studies

For example, In Germany, some of the examples of vocational degrees offered by Vocational Universities are as under-:

(a) Bachelor in Automotive engineering, Clothing design by Berlin School of Applied Sciences (HTW),

(b) Bachelor of Jewellery and Objects of Daily Life by Pforzheim University of Applied Sciences.

(c) Bachelor of Motor Vehicle Industry, Bachelor of Printing and Media by Munich University of Applied Sciences

(d) Bachelor of Arts in Facilities Air Conditioning by Biberach University of Applied Sciences.

5. Vocational University will emphasize on a different teaching – learning pedagogy with a special focus on skill based and hands-on learning and training. Vocational University may offer vocational programmes through online, distance and life-long learning mode.
6. Vocational University Curriculum will emphasize life coping skills and general educational skills such as Liberal arts subjects, English competency, entrepreneur skills, problem solving, team work, leadership, management courses etc.
7. Vocational Education Junior Colleges offering HSC (Vocational), Agencies / Community Colleges offering Associate Degrees or Diplomas may be given affiliation to the Vocational University to provide entry into the Bachelors Programmes.
8. The University shall have a well defined Credit Banking and Transfer System. The Credit System will allow multi-entry and multi-exit to students. The Credit System will also enable students to pursue opportunity for life-long learning and skill development.

For example, in Scotland, the Scottish Credit and Qualification Framework (SCQF) is a credit framework that promotes mobility and credit transfer within and between sectors of learning. Similarly, in UK, the National Vocational Qualification Framework simplifies credit transfer between different awarding bodies, especially for vocational qualifications.

9. Industry participation shall be sought on the Board of Management. Industry representatives will be involved in governance and curriculum design. Production oriented Research and Innovation Labs will be setup in collaboration with Industry to promote regional economic growth. Industry collaboration shall be sought for funding, placements and apprenticeship for students. Department of In-Service Training shall be setup to encourage industry to send employees for regular skill development and up-gradation (this will also gain additional income for teachers).

10. Teachers training will be given special emphasis by the University. The Vocational University will setup a separate department for Teachers Training and Development in order to build teaching resources and research component. Continuous teacher training programmes shall be emphasized by the University Management. A separate degree called Bachelor in Vocational Education (B.V.Ed) or B.Ed with specialization in vocational education is proposed to be introduced. This would be a mandatory requirement for hiring teachers for vocational education and training.

Vocations and Training Available for Students in Schools

In India, we believe that education is the key to the task of nation-building. It is also a well-accepted fact that providing the right knowledge and skills to the youth can ensure the overall national progress and economic growth. The Indian education system recognizes the role of education in instilling the values of secularism, egalitarianism, respect for democratic traditions and civil liberties and quest for justice.

Combine the thought with the fact that India is a nation of young people - out of a population of above 1.1 billion, 672 million people are in the age-group 15 to 59 years, - which is usually treated as the "working age population". It is also being predicted that India will see a sharp decline in the dependency ratio over the next 30 years, which will constitute a major 'demographic dividend' for India. In the year 2001, 11% of population of the country was in age group of 18-24 years which is expected to rise to 12% by the end of XI Five Year Plan. This young population should be considered as an invaluable asset which if equipped with knowledge and skills, can contribute effectively to the development of the national as well as the global economy. The vision is to realize India's human resource potential to its fullest in the education sector, with equity and inclusion.

The Report of the Education Commission (Kothari, 1964-66) which was titled 'Education and National Development', set a number of goals to be pursued. One of them was "to vocationalise secondary education."

Hon'ble Prime Minister of India addressing the nation on Independence Day (2006), spoke of the need for a Vocational Education Mission and in Independence Day speech (2007) announced that 1600 new industrial training institutes (ITIs) and polytechnics, 10,000 new vocational schools and 50,000 new Skill Development Centres would be opened to ensure that annually, over 100 lakh students get vocational training, which would be a four-fold increase. The Finance Minister in his budget speech (2007) also mentioned the emerging shortages in the reservoir of skilled and trained manpower in a number of sectors. There is thus a need to expand the VET programmes to take advantage of the demographic dividend of the country and to fulfill the aspirations and right of the youth to gainful employment and contribute to national productivity.

System of Vocational Education and Training (VET) in India

The technical and vocational education and training system (TVET) in India develops human resource through a three-tier system:

- Graduate and post-graduate level specialists (e.g. IITs, NITs, engineering colleges) trained as engineers and technologists.
- Diploma-level graduates who are trained at Polytechnics as technicians and supervisors.
- Certificate-level for higher secondary students in the vocational stream and craft people trained in ITIs as well as through formal apprenticeships as semi-skilled and skilled workers.

There are more than 17 Ministries/Departments of Govt of India providing or funding formal/non-formal VET programmes. The total annual training capacity of VET programmes thus offered is estimated to be about 25 lakh. However there is a lot of variation among the various programmes in terms of duration, target group, entry qualifications, testing and certification, curriculum, etc. which has resulted in problems related to recognition of qualifications, equivalence and vertical mobility.

The programmes for promoting vocational education currently underway are placed at

Annexure I.

Need for Strengthening Vocational Education Programmes

India is referred to as a 'young nation' with 28 million population of youth being added every year. Only about 2.5 million vocational training seats are available in the country whereas about 12.8 million persons enter the labour market every year. About 90 per cent of employment opportunities require vocational skills, something that is not being imparted on a large scale in schools and colleges. The major reforms proposed for bringing about necessary 'flexibility' in the offering of vocational courses and development of 'modular competency based curricula' in collaboration with industry to suit the needs of both target groups and the employers (industry) will be useful in reducing the shortage of skilled manpower.

In addition the high drop out rate of students after Class X is significant and a cause of worry, as evident from the following statistics:

...	...
No of secondary schools (Cl IX- X)	1,23,265
No of higher secondary schools (Cl XI –XII)	60,383
No of students in secondary schools	2.89 cr
No of students in higher secondary schools	1.66 cr
Projected population of 14-16 age group	4.84 cr
Projected population of 16-18 age group	4.86 cr

Source: Selected Educational Statistics (2008-09) – provisional data. Population projections are based on census data compiled by Registrar General of India

It would be beneficial if these children, as also a large number of children who have the inclination, but are compelled to join formal secondary schooling, to be channelized into vocational education. This would lead to a system of education which is more meaningful and relevant in the local context. Gradually the ambit would be expanded to address the needs and aspirations of those engaged in traditional means of livelihoods too. The contribution of such educated youth would boost the state of the Indian economy through the thrust of the Govt on universalisation of secondary education, skill development and social justice through inclusive education and training.

National Vocational Education Qualification Framework (NVEQF)

The process of development of a National Vocational Education Qualifications Framework (NVEQF) is presently underway. The NVEQF would set common principles and guidelines for a nationally recognized qualification system, covering schools, vocational education institutes and institutes of higher education with qualifications ranging from secondary to doctorate level, leading to international recognition of national standards. Students would have the scope for vertical and horizontal mobility with multiple entry and exits. This would be especially useful to promote the creative genius of every child including children with special needs. The corner stone of the NVEQF would be the close partnership and collaboration with the industry/ potential employers at all stages starting from identification of courses, content development, training and provision of resource persons, assessment, accreditation, certification and placement

Extensive consultations with the State Govts have been carried out. A group of State Education Ministers from 12 States has been constituted to prepare the NVEQF. The working document on NVEQF prepared by a Coordination Committee was presented to the Group of State Education Ministers on 30thMay 2011. Detailed discussions were held on the issues and concerns from the perspective of the States. Further consultations are continuing to prepare a roadmap for implementation of the NVEQF.

There was unanimous endorsement of the Framework being developed by the Central Advisory Board of Education (CABE) in the 58th meeting held on 7th June 2011.

Centrally Sponsored Scheme of Vocationalisation of Secondary Education: The Centrally Sponsored Scheme of Vocationalisation of Secondary Education was launched in year 1988. The Scheme was implemented through State/UTs and NGOs /VA in the formal and non-formal sector respectively. The Scheme envisaged selection of vocational courses on the basis of assessment of manpower needs. The main objectives of the scheme, as spelt out in the National Policy on Education 1986, were to provide diversification of educational opportunities so as to enhance individual employability, reduce the mismatch between demand and supply of skilled manpower and to provide an alternative for those pursuing higher education. Vocational Education was made a distinct stream intended to prepare students for identified occupations spanning several areas of activities.

The Scheme provides broad guidelines in respect of management structure, curriculum design, infrastructure development, vocational surveys, instructional material, teachers and their training, school-industry linkage, examination and certification, modification of recruitment rules, financial assistance to NGOs and other aspects.

Since inception of the scheme, 9,619 schools with about 21,000 sections have been created with an intake capacity of about 10.03 lakhs students. About 150 vocational courses were being offered. According to the evaluation conducted by Operations Research Group (1996) the proportionate share of vocational students vis-a vis total enrolment at the higher secondary stage was 4.8% and 28% of vocational pass outs were employed/self employed. Rs. 765.00 crore has been released to the State Governments and Non-Government Organiza-tions. During 10th Plan an allocation of Rs. 350.00 crore was given under the scheme. An expenditure of Rs. 63.69 crore was incurred during 10th Plan Period.

The existing scheme is presently under revision to address the issue of enhancement of employability of youth through competency based modular vocational courses, to maintain their competitiveness through provision of multi entry and multi exit learning opportunities and vertical mobility /interchangeability in qualifications, to fill the gap between educated and employable and to decrease the pressure on academic higher education.

Central Board of Secondary Education (CBSE): CBSE is offering 34 Vocational courses consisting of 107 subject in its about 500 government and government aided schools across the country. During the academic session 2007 - 08, Financial Market Management was introduced as vocational package in class 11.

CBSE launched three new vocational courses, namely, "Hospitality and Tourism," "Mass Media Studies & Media Production" and "Geospatial Technology" from the academic session 2010-11. CBSE is making efforts to introduce more such courses in collaboration with relevant industry/organization, and has facilities for joint certification.

National Institute of Open Schooling (NIOS): NIOS offers 82 vocational education courses through its accredited vocational Institutes which include Government Institutes, NGOs and Registered Societies. 1063 Accredited Vocational Institute (AVI) provide training to neo literates upto pre-degree level. NIOS.

Sub-Mission on Polytechnics: Under the scheme, it is proposed to establish 1000 Polytechnics in the country, the breakup of which is as under:

i. 300 Polytechnics to be set up by the State governments/Union Territories with assistance from government of India in unserved areas (district).
ii. 300 Polytechnics to be set up through Public Private Partnership by the State Governments/Union Territories. These 300 polytechnics will be selected in consultation with State Governments/Union Territories, various industrial organization such as CII, FICCI, ASSOCHAM and PHD Chamber of Commerce, etc.

iii. It is proposed to facilitate the creation of 400 additional Polytechnics by the private sector.

Establishment of New Polytechnics: Under the scheme, it is proposed to establish 1000 Polytechnics in the country, the breakup of which is as under:

i. 300 Polytechnics to be set up by the State governments/Union Territories with assistance from government of India in unserved areas (district).

ii. 300 Polytechnics to be set up through Public Private Partnership by the State Governments/Union Territories. These 300 polytechnics will be selected in consultation with State Governments/Union Territories, various industrial organization such as CII, FICCI, ASSOCHAM and PHD Chamber of Commerce, etc.

iii. It is proposed to facilitate the creation of 400 additional Polytechnics by the private sector.

Strengthening of Existing Polytechnics: It is proposed to upgrade infrastructure of existing diploma level, public funded Polytechnics by (i) providing financial assistance for modern equipment and replacement of obsolete equipments, (ii) providing modern facilities for application of IT in teaching, learning and testing processes and (iii) creating infrastructure facilities as well as introduction of new diploma courses.

7

Industrial Training Institute

Industrial Training Institutes & "Industrial Training Centres" are training institute which provide training in technical field and constituted under Directorate General of Employment & Training (DGET), Ministry of Labour & Employment, Union Government of India.

Figure: *Industrial Training Institute or ITI at Ballygunge, Kolkata.*

Structure

Industrial Training Institutes (ITIsd) are government-run training organisations. Industrial Training Centres (ITCs) are privately run equivalents. They provide post-school technical training. In 2002 there were 1800 ITIs, providing 373 000 training places, and 2850 ITCs providing 305 000 places. c vb 400 ITIs in India, covered under the scheme – Upgradation into Centres of Excellence Its a Vocational Training Improvement Project with World Bank Assistance.

Access to ITIs

Normally a person who has passed 10 standard (SSLC) is eligible for admission to ITI. The objective of opening of ITI is provide technical manpower to industries. These persons are trained in basic skills required to do jobs of say operator or a craftsman. The course in ITI is designed in way to impart basic skill in the trade specified. The duration of course may vary from one year to three years depending upon trade opted. After completion of desired period of training the person is eligible to appear in the AITT (All India Trade Test) conducted by NCVT (National Council for Vocational training). After passing AITT, the person is awarded NATIONAL TRADE CERTIFICATE (NTC) in concerning trade by NCVT. After passing ITI course a person may opt to undergo practical training in his trade in an industry for a year or two. Again the person has to appear & pass in a test to be conducted by NCVT to get the NATIONAL APPRENTICESHIP CERTIFICATE . There are both government funded and private (self-financing) ITI's in India. Most of ITI's impart training in technical trades like instrument mechanic, electrician, fitter, plumber, diesel mechanic, Computer Operator & Programming Assistant (COPA), electrical mechanic, Information Technology, Mechanic Computer Hardware, Refrigeration & Air Conditioning, Turner, Welder, etc. Industrial Training Centre (ITC's) are self-financing and provide same courses as ITI's. Trade test for ITI and ITC trainees are common. The certificate issued by NCVT are of same standard whether one had a training in Government owned ITI or privately owned ITC.

A 2003 study of the ITIs conducted under the auspices of the International Labour Organisation found that a significant imbalance had developed between the needs of the Indian economy and the training activities of the ITIs, which were producing too many graduates for skills affected by industrial decline, and too few in the emerging and informal areas of the economy.

Opportunities After ITI

People of engineering trade can go for higher studies like diploma in engineering. There are also specialised short term courses in Advanced Training Institute (ATI) which enhances the skills of candidates. ITI qualified persons can set up their own garage, motor/ generator/transformer winding shops or fabrication shops depending upon trade opted. Also candidates can apply for jobs in private sector and public sectors. Government organisations like Indian Army, Navy, Airforce and also paramilitary forces like BSF, CRPF provide opportunities for ITI passed candidates of different trades.

Access to COE, ITIs

Criteria/eligible for admission is same as an ITI.

- The objective of the scheme is to upgrade the existing 400 ITIs into "Centres of Excellence (CoE)" for producing multi skilled workforce of world standard.
- The highlights of the scheme are introduction of multiskilling courses (BBBT- Broad Based Basic Training) of one year duration, followed by Advanced/Specialized Modular courses subsequently by adopting industry wise cluster approach, multi entry and multi exit provisions, and Public-Private-Partnership in the form of Institute Management Committees (IMCs) to ensure greater & active involvement of industry in all aspects of training.

Criteria of Selection of ITI

The identification of ITIs within a State/UT is to be done by the State/UT Government, keeping in view the following guidelines:

- A cluster of specific category of industry like Information Technology, Electronics, Electrical, Automobile, Chemical, Fabrication etc. should preferably be available in the surrounding areas of the selected ITIs
- Academic, administrative, financial and management autonomy will have to be provided to the selected ITIs for upgradation as Centres of Excellence.
- The selected ITI should have constituted/ constitute Institute Management Committees in order to create a public-private partnership model for implementing the scheme.
- The selected ITI should have proper surroundings, sufficient area for landscaping, well constructed buildings with adequate

space for additions/alterations and other infrastructural facilities. The institte should be well connected by road / railway station.

- States are required to sign an MOU with Central Government before funds are released. Detailed guidelines have been issued in this regard

Skill Development

A skill is the learned ability to carry out a task with pre-determined results often within a given amount of time, energy, or both. In other words the abilities that one possesses. Skills can often be divided into domain-general and domain-specific skills. For example, in the domain of work, some general skills would include time management, teamwork and leadership, self motivation and others, whereas domain-specific skills would be useful only for a certain job. Skill usually requires certain environmental stimuli and situations to assess the level of skill being shown and used.

People need a broad range of skills in order to contribute to a modern economy. A joint ASTD and U.S. Department of Labour study showed that through technology, the workplace is changing, and identified 16 basic skills that employees must have to be able to change with it.

Labour Skills

Skilled workers have long had historical import as masons, carpenters, blacksmiths, bakers, brewers, coopers, printers and other occupations that are economically productive. Skilled workers were often politically active through their craft guilds.

Life Skills

Life skills are problem solving behaviours used appropriately and responsibly in the management of personal affairs. They are a set of human skills acquired via teaching or direct experience that are used to handle problems and questions commonly encountered in daily human life. The subject varies greatly depending on societal norms and community expectations.

Enumeration and Categorization

UNICEF states "there is no definitive list" of life skills but enumerates many "psychosocial and interpersonal skills generally considered important." It asserts life skills are a synthesis: "many skills are used simultaneously in practice. For example, decision-making often involves critical thinking ("what are my options?") and values clarification ("what is important to me?"). Ultimately, the interplay between the skills is what produces powerful behavioural outcomes, especially where this approach is supported by other strategies..." Life skills can vary from financial literacy, substance abuse prevention, to therapeutic techniques to deal with disabilities, such as autism. Life skills curricula designed for K-12 often emphasizes communications and practical skills needed for successful independent living for developmental disabilities/special education students with an Individualized Education Programme (IEP). However, some programmes are for general populations, such as the Overcoming Obstacles programme for middle schools and high schools.

Parenting 2.0 (P2.0), LinkedIn's largest parenting group with more than 2,700 members (as of March, 2013), defines Life Skills as all the non-academic foundational skills human beings learn and use to thrive individually and live optimally in community with others. P2.0's founder, Marlaine Paulsen Cover created a Life Skills Report Card that lists five basic skills categories:

- Personal care
- Organization
- Respect for self and others
- Communication
- Social skills and proposes that life skills should be considered as important as academic skills.

Parenting

Life skills are often taught in the domain of parenting, either indirectly through the observation and experience of the child, or directly with the purpose of teaching a specific skill. Yet skills for dealing with pregnancy and parenting can be considered and taught as a set of life skills of themselves. Teaching these parenting life skills can also coincide with additional life skills development of the child. Many life skills programmes are offered when traditional family structures and healthy relationships have broken down, whether due to parental lapses, divorce or due to issues with the children (such as substance abuse or other risky behaviour). For example, the International Labour Organization is teaching life skills to ex-child labourers and risk children in Indonesia to help them avoid the worst forms of child labour.

Youth: Behaviour Prevention vs. Positive Development

While certain life skills programmes focus on teaching the prevention of certain behaviours the Search Institute has found those programmes can be relatively ineffective. Based upon their research The Family and Youth Services Bureau, a division of the U.S. Department of Health and Human Services advocates the theory of Positive Youth Development as a replacement for the less effective prevention programmes. Positive Youth Development, or PYD as it's come to be known as, focuses on the strengths of an individual as opposed to the older methods which tend to focus on the "potential" weaknesses that have yet to be shown. The Family and Youth Services Bureau has found that individuals who developed life skills in a positive, rather than preventive, manner feel a greater sense of competence, usefulness, power, and belonging.

Life Skill Development in Adults

Beyond the K-12 domain, other life skills programmes are focused on social welfare and social work programmes, such as Casey Life Skills. This programme covers diverse topics: career planning, communication, daily living, home life, housing and money management, self care, social relationships, work and study skills, work life, pregnancy and parenting.

People Skills

According to the *Portland Business Journal*, people skills are described as:

- understanding ourselves and moderating our responses
- talking effectively and empathizing accurately
- building relationships of trust, respect and productive interactions.

A British definition is "the ability to communicate effectively with people in a friendly way, especially in business." The term is not listed yet in major US dictionaries. The term people skills is used to include both psychological skills and social skills, but is less inclusive than life skills.

Social Skills

Social skill is any skill facilitating interaction and communication with others. Social rules and relations are created, communicated, and changed in verbal and nonverbal ways. The process of learning such skills is called socialization.

According to the *Portland Business Journal*, people skills are described as:

- understanding ourselves and moderating our responses
- talking effectively and empathizing accurately
- building relationships of trust, respect and productive interactions.

A British definition is "the ability to communicate effectively with people in a friendly way, especially in business." The term is not listed yet in major US dictionaries.

The term people skills is used to include both psychological skills and social skills, but is less inclusive than life skills.

History

Guidelines relating to what later generations eventually dubbed "people skills" have been recorded from very early times. Two examples of early human guidelines appear in the Old Testament. Leviticus 19:18 advises: "Do not seek revenge or bear a grudge against your people, but love your neighbour as yourself"; and Solomon's wisdom in Proverbs 15:1 includes: "A gentle answer turns away wrath, but a harsh word stirs up anger." However the Bible also condemns 'flattery' (Psalms 5:9). Human-relations studies became a movement in the 1920s, as companies became more interested in the "soft skills" and interpersonal skills of employees. In organizations, improving people skills became a specialized role of the corporate trainer. By the mid-1930s, Dale Carnegie popularized people skills in *How to Win Friends and Influence People* and *How to Stop Worrying and Start Living* throughout the United States of America and later throughout the world.

In the 1960s, US schools introduced people-skills topics and methods—often as a way to promote better self-esteem, communication and social interaction. These encompassed psychologist Thomas Gordon's "Effectiveness Training" variations as well as many other training programmes. (By the 1980s, "traditional education" and a "back-to-basics" three-Rs emphasis largely pushed these programmes aside, with notable exceptions.)

By 1974 the actual term "people skills" had come into use.

Educational Importance/impact

A significant portion of the deaths in the United States can be attributed to psychosocial deficits in people skills for stress management and supportive social connection. Business, labour and government authorities agree that wide-ranging people skills are necessary for 20th-century work success in the SCANS report. At least one foundation, Alliances for Psychosocial Advancements in Learning (APAL), has made support of SCANS-related people skills a major priority.

UNESCO research found that young people who develop speaking/listening skills and getting to know others have improved self-awareness, social-emotional adjustment and classroom behaviour; self-destructive and violent behaviour also were decreased. The Collaborative for Academic Social and Emotional Learning (CASEL) has identified 22 programmes in the US that are especially comprehensive in social-emotional learning coverage and effective in documented impacts.

Soft Skills

Soft skills is a sociological term relating to a person's "EQ" (Emotional Intelligence Quotient), the cluster of personality traits, social graces, communication, language, personal habits, friendliness, and optimism that characterize relationships with other people. Soft skills complement hard skills which are the occupational requirements of a job and many other activities. Soft skills are personal attributes that enhance an individual's interactions, job performance and career prospects. Unlike hard skills, which are about a person's skill set and ability to perform a certain type of task or activity, soft skills relate to a person's ability to interact effectively with coworkers and customers and are broadly applicable both in and outside the workplace.

A person's soft skill EQ is an important part of their individual contribution to the success of an organization. Particularly those organizations dealing with customers face-to-face are generally more successful, if they train their staff to use these skills. Screening or training for personal habits or traits such as dependability and conscientiousness can yield significant return on investment for an organization. For this reason, soft skills are increasingly sought out by employers in addition to standard qualifications.

It has been suggested that in a number of professions, soft skills may be more important over the long term than occupational skills. The legal profession is one example where the ability to deal with people effectively and politely, more than their mere occupational skills, can determine the professional success of a lawyer.

Soft Skills are *behavioural* competencies. Also known as *Interpersonal Skills,* or *people skills,* they include proficiencies such as communication skills, conflict resolution and negotiation, personal effectiveness, creative problem solving, strategic thinking, team building, influencing skills and selling skills, to name a few.

Hard Skills

Hard skills are any skills relating to a specific task or situation. These skills are easily quantifiable unlike Soft skills which are related to one's personality.

Hard skills are specific, teachable abilities that may be required in a given context, such as a job or university application.

Examples of hard skills include:

- facility with spreadsheets
- typing
- proficiency with software applications
- operating machinery
- software development
- speaking a foreign language
- calculus

Assessing Industry Demand for VET Courses

Vocational education and training is fast emerging as an important area of focus as Germany and India enhance their strategic bilateral partnership. One of India's biggest challenges as well as advantages is its growing young population. The average Indian will be only 29 years old in 2020. India targets creation of 500 million skilled workers in 2022, and Germany is one of its strong partners for this.

Germany's dual system of vocational education and training (VET) is a very simple and cost-effective model.

Enlarge image Training centre of Bosch in India (© Bosch) The practical training (approx. 70 percent of training duration) takes place in companies, in the real processes of business and production. This training is based on a compulsory curriculum, which is adapted to the conditions of the training company and is monitored and controlled by the respective Chambers, who also arrange for the interim and final examinations (comparable to Sectoral Skill Councils). This in-house training is guided and imparted by certified corporate trainers.

The 'apprentices' undergoing training sign a vocational training contract with the company (legally equivalent to a labour contract under labour laws) and are paid a training salary by them.

The theoretical part of the training (approx. 20 percent of training duration) is taught in vocational schools, run by the state governments.

The system proves advantageious for all stakeholders.

- The government does not need to equip the vocational schools with expensive machinery necessary for practical training suited to industrial needs. It has to only guarantee a fitting theoretical training in vocational schools with well-trained teachers. This saves the cost of investing into equipment and machinery just for training purposes.
- Companies train students in real working processes, within the actual production cycle. The competitive business scenario makes it essential that companies be well equipped with state-of-the-art machinery. They also need to redevelop procedures of production at all times. Therefore the companies already have the equipment, which would be too expensive for vocational schools only for training purposes. Companies also have to train and employ certified corporate trainers within the company. All costs incurred by companies engaged in VET are considered an investment. While the students are trained, they also become more productive and contribute to the creation of wealth; and the company can look to getting an early return on investment. Additionally, after the examinations, companies who take in their apprentices have well-trained and educated workers who know the company and are skilled according to its needs.
- The companies engaged in VET are also constantly involved – through the vocational training departments of the Chambers – in the process of upgrading and modernisation of curricula.
- Young people get training that fits the needs of the industry. At the same time, vocational studies foster the pride of being involved in crafts amongst the students (approximately 67 percent of young people in Germany enjoy vocational education & training).
- The unions also play their part in the field of vocational training. They take part in developing and redeveloping professions and curricula, they negotiate the training salaries as part of

collective contracts for an industry, and the elected works councils also keep an eye on the practical training within the company.

Indo-German cooperation in vocational education & training (VET) has a long history. Till 2007, it was part of development cooperation. Now it is led by a bilateral working group, which was set up in 2008. Led by the Indian Ministry of Labour and Employment, the Indian side includes members from the two major industry associations – Federation of Indian Chambers of Commerce & Industry (FICCI) and Confederation of Indian Industry (CII). The German side is led by the Ministry of Education and Research (BMBF). Members include representatives of the chambers of crafts and industries, the Federal Institute for Vocational Education and Training (BIBB), iMOVE, the ministry's promoter of 'Training – Made in Germany', and trade unions. The bilateral working group on VET meets on an annual basis alternatively in India and Germany.

Skill Development Initiatives: Private-Public Partnership and Private Initiatives in India

Government-owned and managed ITIs (under the jurisdiction of the central government's Ministry of Labour) have been the main instrument for children completing class 8 or 10 in school to obtain vocational training. ITIs offer courses lasting 1-4 years all across the country, though they tend to be concentrated in the more industrialized southern and western states of India.

The 11th Five Year Plan, which for the first time had a whole chapter devoted to skill development, essentially had two ways of promoting vocational training through the ITI system in India. First, 500 of the 1896 ITIs (in 2007) were chosen as Centres of Excellence, in which only one or two trades of the 10-15 that are normally offered, were selected for the purposes of promotion as Centres of Excellence on a PPP basis. Of the 500 Centres of Excellence (CoE) to be created in ITIs, 100 are being supported by the Government of India and 400 by the World Bank. Second, the remaining 1396 ITIs were not to give any special focus on any particular trade, but were to receive Central Government funding for improving the infrastructure for skill development across all trades. For both the Centres of Excellence as well as the remaining ITIs the PPP mode took the following forms: new Institutional Management Committees (IMCs). New Institutional Management Committees consisting of both the ITI Principal as well as private sector industrial representatives were to participate in managing the ITIs. The experience with IMCs in the last three years has left a lot to be desired, as was found in a nation-wide study of ITIs conducted by the Institute of Applied Manpower Research (IAMR) in 2010-11. "The role of IMC in the management of the CoEs did not appear to be very encouraging. Most of the CoEs surveyed during the study reported that in terms of starting new trades, up-gradation of new trades, placement support and training support, the role of IMCs was mostly either 'good' or 'fair' (on a 5-point scale, which went up to 'Excellent' and 'Very Good'). On the other hand, in providing financial support, its role was described as 'poor'. The greatest problem faced by almost all the CoEs was the shortage of teachers."

Private Industrial Training Institutes

In 2007 when the Government of India decided to initiate a Skill Development Initiative there were just under 2000 private ITIs in the country. However, in the wake of the Government's focus on skill development in the 11th Five Year Plan, there took place a rapid increase in the number of private ITIs to nearly 6498 within three years. While this quantitative expansion of vocational training providers (VTPs) increased the availability of facilities for skill up-gradation in the country, the quality of training being imparted by these thousands of new VTPs could be open to question. The number of trades offered by private ITIs, as we found in the recent IAMR study cited above, is usually under five; in contrast, government run ITIs offer anywhere between 10-15 trades in their programmes. The private ITIs are also not professionally managed nor regulated well by government.

The Private Partners of NSDC

As part of the Government of India's Skill Development Initiative (which started in 2007 with the 11th Five Year Plan), three institutions were created: the Prime Minister's Skill Development Advisory Council, the National Skill Development Coordination Board (chaired by the Deputy Chairman, Planning Commission), and the PPP-based National Skill Development Corporation (NSDC). The NSDC is jointly funded by the private sector, and the Government of India (51% private equity owned mainly by Confederation of Indian Industry, Federation of Indian Chambers of Commerce and Industry, Association of Chambers of Commerce, and 49% equity owned by the Ministry of Finance).

The NSDC is the operational arm of the 3-tier management structure of the government's Skill Development Initiative. Since the second quarter of 2010, when NSDC acquired a Chief Executive Officer (CEO), NSDC has been rapidly supporting the creation of companies that are providing vocational training all across the country, on a profitable basis. The business model is as follows: NSDC finances the company start-ups through a combination of debt and equity, the debt part of which is to be re-paid by the business venture-cum-VTP over a number of years by providing vocational training to youth on a fee-paying basis. As many as 26 companies have started providing such training, all of which are required by agreement with NSDC to ensure 70% of their trainees get placed in industry.

National Vocational Education Qualification Framework (NVEQF) and the Private Sector

The Ministry of Human Resource Development (MHRD) has since late 2010 been engaged in an exercise to widen the scope of vocational education in government schools and the higher education system. Two specific initiatives of MHRD in this regard are notable: one, the vocational education provided to higher secondary school students run by the government is to be expanded by increased plan funding for the vocational education stream, which has been available in higher secondary schools since 1986. Second, the MHRD created an expert group in early 2011 to prepare a blue print radically transforming vocational education in the secondary and higher secondary school system of India to be called the NVEQF. The NVEQF has already been agreed too, in principle, by State Education Ministers in June, 2011. The NVEQF is now in the process of being piloted in Haryana State. It involves the extension of vocational education to secondary level (classes 9-10), in addition to higher secondary level in government schools (classes 11-12). In addition, it involves the creation of National Occupation Standards by the private sector by Sector Skill Councils (to be created by NSDC), so that in the entire country all vocational stream students in secondary and higher secondary education, as well as in polytechnics and engineering colleges, will be trained by using common curriculum across the country, which will be based on these National Occupation Standards (NOSs). These NOSs must be accompanied by a competency-based curriculum which has to be developed by private sector industry, in collaboration with, at the central level, the Central Board of Secondary Education (CBSE), and at the state level the State Directorates of Technical Education.

Moreover, certification for these courses and trades offered in the vocational stream of schools, polytechnics and engineering colleges, will all be jointly done by government and the private sector, so that youth can then be easily employed by industry. In other words, there has already begun a process which will lead to an expansion of training along these lines, which will gather the momentum over the years.

Skills Development: Attitudes and Perceptions

Without positive attitudes and perceptions, students have little chance of learning proficiently, if at all. There are two categories of attitudes and perceptions that affect learning: (1) attitudes and perceptions about the *learning climate* and (2) attitudes and perceptions about *classroom tasks.* A basic premise of the Dimensions of Learning model is that effective teachers continually reinforce attitudes and perceptions in both these categories. The master teacher has internalized techniques and strategies for enhancing these attitudes and perceptions to such a degree that the techniques are frequently transparent: they have become part of the fabric of instruction and are barely noticeable to the undiscerning eye.

Employers' Perceptions of Key Skills

Key Skills combine two main features. Firstly, they focus on a set of skills which relate to a person's ability to operate in a workplace, alone or with others. Working with others, improving own performance, problem solving and the oral part of communication fall into this category. Secondly, a distinction has to be made between basic and Key Skills. Basic skills can be defined as the fundamental techniques of literacy and numeracy. The acquisition of basic skills does not necessarily mean a person can apply them in a practical way. It is this application which Key Skills address.

Knowledge of Key Skills

Around half the employers interviewed had heard of Key Skills. However, only two-thirds of these could name any of the Key Skills. There was some confusion over the terminology. Some employers were confused about the distinction between basic and Key Skills. Others talked about their own internal skill frame-works, defining skills which were essential to their own organisation. These usually included both generic and occupational specific skills. There was, however, considerable overlap between the generic skills mentioned, and Key Skills.

Despite the relatively low level of knowledge of Key Skills, and confusion over the terminology, employers were generally sympathetic with the overall aims of Key Skills. They welcomed an initiative which would better prepare young people for working life, and provide a set of skills which would enable them to adapt to changing labour markets.

The Need for Key Skills

Employers reported a high level of need for all six Key Skills, for young workers and for all employees. On a scale where 1 was 'not at all important' and 5 was 'very important', the average scores ranged from 3.3 to 4.7. Working in a team, learning and oral communication were rated very highly. They were most likely to be reported 'very important' for successful employment.

Written communication and the use of numbers were reported to be important, but they were of less wide-spread importance. These skills were more likely to be needed in certain jobs, rather than throughout an organisation. The use of numbers was, in particular, reported to be more of an occupational, rather than a generic, skill.

IT received the least emphasis. One-quarter of employers reported that IT was 'not very important' or 'not at all important' for all employees, and just over one-third reported a similar lack of importance for young workers.

People with sound Key Skills are argued to perform better, and to be essential to modern organisations. At senior levels, a wider range and depth of Key Skills is needed. Sound Key Skills help people progress, where opportunities for promotion exist. Those with good Key Skills are also in a stronger competitive position in the labour market more generally.

Satisfaction with Key Skills

Employers expressed fairly high levels of satisfaction with the Key Skills of employees. Average scores for all Key Skills, and for both young workers and all employees were above 3.0 (the 'satisfactory' point on the scale). It should, however, be emphasised that questions were asked about satisfaction with the skill levels of employees, rather than with skills available in the labour market more generally.

Despite the overall levels of satisfaction, some differences do emerge. Employers were slightly less satisfied with the skills of young workers. However, although recruiting from what is reported to be an unsatisfactory pool, it seems that employers were generally able to find young people who were satisfactory. Employers were developing selection criteria which identified those not just with the best Key Skills, but those exhibiting potential to develop these skills. Many were also putting considerable effort into training and developing employees in these skills. Furthermore, competence in many Key Skills increases with experience and, in some cases, maturity.

The Key Skill Units in Detail

A major aim of this study was to explore employers' views on the content of the Key Skill units. Broadly each Key Skill has been broken down into a number of components, or elements, and each of these is defined at four different levels. The lower levels are straightforward, involving being able to conduct a task and to do it accurately. The higher levels are more demanding, involving reviewing and monitoring an activity, and generally taking responsibility for driving things forward. These levels have been developed to allow progression, and aim to meet the needs of different employers and occupations. Simplified versions of each unit were constructed and discussed with employers during the in-depth interviews.

Several themes emerge which were common to all, or many of the Key Skill Units:

- Progression between levels — the difference between Levels 1 and 4 was clear to employers. However, the progression between individual levels was frequently not clear.
- The relatively low level of need — employers reported that their greatest need was for employees at the lower levels within each unit. It was mostly those with managerial and professional roles who were expected to take on responsibilities included in Levels 3 and 4.
- The specificity of need — employers could not always easily relate to the generic units. They had specific needs for the application of each Key Skill, whether these were particular to their organisation or an occupation.
- Confusion between how the Unit differed from basic skills which, it was felt, should be acquired through schooling. For example, how did communication differ from literacy, and the application of number from numeracy?
- Some misunderstanding of the role of Key Skills — Key Skills do not aim to develop occupational specific skills, and there

was some confusion about the distinction between generic and specific skills. For example, the IT unit aims to improve the skills of IT users; it does not aim to increase the supply of IT specialists.

Other comments were specific to particular Key Skills. These included:

- Communication — It was felt that the oral aspects of communication were dealt with too formally and the unit did not properly describe the many facets involved in verbal communication.
- Working withothers — It was felt that this placed too much emphasis on the role of the individual in a team, rather than addressing the more dynamic and interactive aspects of working with others.
- Improving own learning and performance — it was questioned whether learning and performance should be treated together. It was commented that they often involve different targets, motivations and actions.

Omissions and Additions

Employers identified several groups of skills which were important to them in a generic sense, and which they did not feel were fully recognised in the Key Skill units. There included:

- personal and interpersonal skills and abilities
- customer service and understanding quality
- business awareness
- personal and staff management.

Recruitment

The way people present themselves through an application form or CV is very important. It is not just what is said, but how the information is presented. This is often taken as an indicator of broader abilities and attitudes. The recruitment interview remains the main form of assessment. Many employers are formalising their interviewing and trying to be more precise about the criteria used in assessing people. However, subjective assessment is still relied on to a considerable extent. Employers are not always looking for well developed Key Skills, especially in young people, but evidence of the potential to develop them. Attitudes and personality are usually seen as the most important indicators of such potential.

Can Key Skills be Developed?

Literacy, numeracy and IT were all seen as teachable, although it was recognised that some people do have stronger aptitudes than others, particularly with numbers and IT. Sound skills in communication and the application of number do require good basic literacy and numeracy skills.

Views varied about the extent to which the other three Key Skills, and oral communication, as well as a range of personal and interpersonal skills which are seen to underlie them, could be developed. Some argued that good Key Skills depend on natural ability; others that innate ability plays a role, but that a person's early experiences, background and socialisation are most important. However, many employers do believe that Key Skills can be improved through training and development. Employees do need to be receptive to training, and different people will be capable of progressing to different extents.

Technical and Vocational Education and Training for Industrialization

Technical and vocational education and training (TVET) is back on the development agenda of many African countries after years of benign neglect, instigated by a complex set of reasons that included budgetary constraints and criticisms of the World Bank in the early 90's on its direction and focus. The World Bank had argued at the time that the cost of technical and vocational education was too high compared with the returns to the economy, that the quality of training was poor and that there was considerable mismatch between training and the needs of industry. Simply put, the delivery of vocational education and training was not cost-effective. However, since the beginning of the new millennium, a fresh awareness of the critical role that TVET can play in economic growth and national development has dawned among policy makers in many African countries and within the international donor community. The increasing importance that African governments now attach to TVET is reflected in the various Poverty Reduction Strategy Papers that governments have developed in collaboration with The World Bank. In its poverty reduction strategy document, Cameroon for example intends to develop vocational and professional training to facilitate integration into the labour market; Cote d'Ivoire talks about strengthening vocational training; Ghana links vocational education and training with education of the youth and the development of technical and entrepreneurial skills; Lesotho and Rwanda focus on linking TVET to businesses while Malawi emphasises the need to promote self-employment through skills development. Other countries that have prioritised TVET initiatives in their national development policy documents include Chad, Ethiopia, Guinea, Senegal, Sierra Leone, Uganda and Zambia.

One of the most important features of TVET is its orientation towards the world of work and the emphasis of the curriculum on the acquisition of employable skills. TVET delivery systems are therefore well placed to train the skilled and entrepreneurial workforce that Africa needs to create wealth and emerge out of poverty. Another important characteristic of TVET is that it can be delivered at different levels of sophistication. This means that TVET can respond, not only to the needs of different types of industries, but also to the different training needs of learners from different socio-economic and academic backgrounds, and prepare them for gainful employment and sustainable livelihoods. A skilled workforce is a basic requirement for driving the engine of industrial and economic growth, and TVET holds the key to building this type of technical and entrepreneurial workforce.

The term "TVET" as used in this paper follows the 1997 UNESCO International Standard Classification of Education definition, which is education and training to "acquire the practical skills, know-how and understanding necessary for employment in a particular occupation, trade or group of occupations or trades." It is important to note that TVET is not only about knowing how to do things but also understanding why things are done in a particular way. The conceptual definition of TVET cuts across educational levels (post-primary, secondary, and even tertiary) and sectors (formal or school-based, non-formal or enterprise-based, and informal or traditional apprenticeship). It is therefore important to keep in mind the transversal and longitudinal nature of TVET as we attempt to highlight the importance of this type of education and training. In order to place the discussion in the right perspective, we shall first examine the current training and socio-economic environment within which TVET systems in Africa operate.

Current Status of TVET in Africa

TVET systems in Africa differ from country to country and are delivered at different levels in different types of institutions, including technical and vocational schools (both public and private), polytechnics, enterprises, and apprenticeship training centres. In West Africa in particular, traditional apprenticeship offers the largest opportunity for the acquisition of employable skills in the informal economy. In Ghana, the informal sector accounts for more than 90 percent of all skills training in the country.

In all of Sub-Saharan Africa, formal TVET programmes are school-based. In some countries, training models follow those of the colonial power. In general however, students enter the vocational education track at the end of primary school, corresponding to 6 – 8 years of education as in countries like Burkina Faso and Kenya, or at the end of lower or junior secondary school, which corresponds to 9 – 12 years of what is called basic education in countries like Ghana, Nigeria, Mali and Swaziland. In many countries, the vocational education track has the unfortunate reputation of being a dead-end, so far as academic progression is concerned and fit for those pupils who are unable to continue to higher education.

The duration of school-based technical and vocational education is between three and six years, depending on the country and the model. Some countries like Ghana, Senegal, and Swaziland in an attempt to expose young people to pre-employment skills have incorporated basic vocational skills into the lower or junior secondary school curriculum. However, this approach has met with some scepticism. The sceptics argue that technical and vocational education for employment is unlikely to be effective when delivered concurrently with general education in junior secondary schools. This is because employment-oriented training requires inputs in human (qualified instructors) and material resources that are not available or are too expensive to provide in all junior secondary schools in a country or even in a cluster of secondary schools. Vocationalisation of the junior secondary school curriculum should therefore be viewed with caution. A good basic education provides a solid foundation for a good technical and vocational education. The only cases in which vocationalisation may be helpful is probably in the use of computers, general agriculture or farming, and entrepreneurship. Computer literacy is relevant to all occupations while the teaching of basic agriculture and entrepreneurship is not capital-intensive or too costly.

What type of governance structures do we have for managing TVET in Africa? In many countries, oversight responsibility is shared in general between the ministries responsible for education or technical education and labour or employment, although some specialised vocational training programmes (e.g. in agriculture, health, transport, etc.) fall under the supervision of the sector ministries. In spite of the large variety of training programmes, from hairdressing to electronics and automobile repair, the place of TVET in the overall school system in many countries is marginal both in terms of enrolment and number of institutions.

The socio-economic environment and the contextual framework in which TVET delivery systems currently operate on the continent may be described by the following groups of indicators:

Weak National Economies Characterised by Low job Growth, High Population Growth, and a Growing Labour Force: The per capita income of most Sub-Saharan African countries (outside South Africa) is less than US$400. Although the economy in a few countries, including Botswana, Ghana and Kenya, is growing at a respectable rate of more than 5%, the annual real growth rate in many countries is less than 2%, limiting the prospects for employment creation. On the other hand, it is estimated that about 500,000 young people add to the labour force each year in Kenya, as many as 700,000 in Tanzania and 250,000 in Zimbabwe. Globally, African economies face the daunting task of finding productive employment for 7 to 10 million annual new job seekers into the labour market over the next few years. This huge deficit in the employment statistics is not unrelated to the high population growth rate of African countries and the increasing number of school leavers arising out of national initiatives of the past decade or two to achieve universal primary education.

Shrinking or Stagnant Wage Employment Opportunities Especially in the Industrial Sector: Apart from Botswana, Ivory Coast, Ghana and South Africa, the industrial labour force is less than 10% in most African countries. The vast majority of the workforce is in the services and agricultural sectors. In many African countries, with the notable exception of South Africa and Mauritius, about 85% of the workforce is in the informal, non-wage employment sector.

Huge Numbers of Poorly Educated, Unskilled and Unemployed Youth: Although some progress has been made, the illiteracy rate in many countries is still high at over 50%. Of significance to TVET is the fact that enrolments at the secondary school level, where TVET is normally provided, is also low with only a few countries having a gross enrolment rate of over 50%. The average school completion rates in Africa are such that many young people drop out of the school system before they have acquired any practical skills and competences for the world of work. Average completion rates are 80 – 90% for primary school; 30 – 40% for lower or junior secondary school; and about 20% for senior secondary school. And only 1 – 2% of the college age group actually enter the universities and other tertiary institutions. In Ghana, for example, 49.1% of the total workforce is illiterate and only 3.9% have had any vocational or technical training. In Tanzania, less than five percent of the labour force is educated above primary school level.

Educated but Unemployed College and University Graduates: In almost all countries in Africa, large numbers of graduates coming out of the formal school system are unemployed, although opportunities for skilled workers do exist in the economy. This situation has brought into sharp focus the mismatch between training and labour market skill demands. Critics argue that the lack of inputs from prospective employers into curriculum design and training delivery in universities and colleges is partly responsible for the mismatch. Another reason that is often cited for the incidence of high unemployment among graduates is the absence of entrepreneurial training in the school curriculum.

Uncoordinated, Unregulated and Fragmented TVET Delivery Systems: Except for a few countries (notably, South Africa, Botswana, Mauritius, Tanzania, Malawi, Zambia, and Namibia), TVET provision in Africa is spread over different ministries and organisations, including NGOs and church-based organisations, with a multiplicity of testing and certification standards.

This situation has implications for standardization of training, cost-effectiveness, quality assurance, recognition of prior learning, and the further education of TVET graduates, because of the absence of a framework for mutual recognition of qualifications. In the informal sector, traditional apprenticeship, which is often the only means for the rural poor and the economically disadvantaged to learn a trade is marginalised, unregulated, and lacks government support and intervention.

The diverse TVET management structures and the sharing of supervisory responsibilities by various government bodies and ministries account for some of the inefficiencies in the system, like duplication and segmentation of training, and the absence of a common platform for developing coherent policies and joint initiatives. Such fragmented governance structures do not promote effective coordination, sharing of resources, and articulation within the system.

Low Quality: In general, the quality of training is low, with undue emphasis on theory and certification rather than on skills acquisition and proficiency testing. Inadequate instructor training, obsolete training equipment, and lack of instructional materials are some of the factors that combine to reduce the effectiveness of training in meeting the required knowledge and skills objectives. High quality skills training requires qualified instructors, appropriate workshop equipment, adequate supply of training materials, and practice by learners.

Geographical, Gender and Economic Inequities: Although access and participation in TVET in Africa reflects the gender-biased division of labour (justifying therefore the current efforts of gender mainstreaming in vocational education and training), we should not lose sight of the economic and geographical inequities. Economic inequity is a greater barrier to participation in technical and vocational education than gender. In many African countries, children of poor parents are unable to afford the fees charged by training institutions. Invariably, the good technical and vocational schools are located in the big towns and cities, thereby limiting access to rural folks.

Poor Public Perception: For many years, technical and vocational education in Africa has been considered as a career path for the less academically endowed. This perception has been fuelled by the low academic requirements for admission into TVET programmes and the limited prospects for further education and professional development. Worse, the impression is sometimes created by governments that the primary objective of the vocational education track is to keep dropouts and "lockouts" from the basic and secondary school system off the streets, rather than project this type of training as an effective strategy to train skilled workers for the employment market. The term "lockouts" refers to students who are unable to move up the educational ladder, not because of poor grades but because of lack of places at the higher level.

Weak Monitoring and Evaluation: Current training programmes in many countries are supply-driven. TVET programmes are very often not designed to meet observed or projected labour market demands. The emphasis appears to be on helping the unemployed to find jobs, without any critical attempt to match training to available jobs. This situation has resulted in many vocational school graduates not finding jobs or finding themselves in jobs for which they have had no previous training. Non-targeted skills development is one of the major weaknesses of the TVET system in many African countries. Training institutions also do not track the employment destination of their graduates. Consequently, valuable feedback from past trainees on the quality of the training they have received and the opportunity for their experience-based inputs to be factored into the review of curricula and training packages are lost. In other words, the use of tracer studies to improve the market responsiveness of training programmes is currently absent in many countries.

Inadequate Financing: Only a few governments in Africa are able to finance TVET at a level that can support quality training. Ethiopia spends only about 0.5 percent of its education and training budget on TVET while Ghana spends only about 1 percent. It must be recognised that TVET is expensive on a per student basis. In 1992, Gabon spent as much as US$1,820 per TVET student. Unit costs are necessarily expected to be higher in TVET institutions than in primary and secondary schools because of smaller student-to-teacher ratios, expensive training equipment, and costly training materials that are "wasted" during practical lessons.

Public Versus Private Provision of TVET: TVET in Africa is delivered by both government and private providers, which include for-profit institutions and non-profit, NGO and church or faith-based institutions. School-based government training institutions are generally fewer in number than those in the private sector, although Kenya with its over 600 Youth Polytechnics is a notable exception. In Ghana, government TVET institutions include 23 technical institutes under the Ministry of Education with a total enrolment of about 19,000 students and 38 National Vocational Training Institutes run by the Ministry of Manpower Development and Employment. There are an estimated 500 private establishments of diverse quality that enrol over 100,000 students. The Catholic Church is the single largest private provider of TVET in Ghana, enrolling about 10,000 students in its 58 technical and vocational training institutions.

In almost all countries, non-government provision of TVET is on the increase both in terms of number of institutions and student numbers. This trend is linked to the fact that private providers train for the informal sector (which is an expanding job market all over Africa) while public institutions train mostly for the more or less stagnant industrial sector. Private providers also target "soft" business and service sector skills like secretarial practice, cookery, and dressmaking that do not require huge capital outlays to deliver. On the other hand, the first choice of students is the public vocational schools because of the lower fees charged and the perception of better quality. Women constitute the majority of students in private institutions (76 percent in Ghana; 60 percent in Tanzania and Zimbabwe; 55 percent in Senegal). For obvious reasons, for-profit private providers are often concentrated in the urban centres, while Church-based institutions tend to be based in rural and economically disadvantaged locations.

In Tanzania, public institutions account for only 8 percent of the total number of institutions, while enterprise-based training (at 22 percent), for-profit institutions (at 35 percent), and Church/NGO providers (at 31 percent) make up the bulk of the private sector institutions. In Zambia, public TVET provision is at 18 percent, while Church, NGO and for-profit providers take up 18 percent and 36 percent, respectively. It is important to distinguish within the private providers, in-company or enterprise-based training that is often dedicated to the sharpening of specific skills of company employees or is designed to train potential employees to perform professional tasks related to the company's activities.

State support for non-government providers vary from country to country. In Ghana, government support is currently limited to the payment of salaries of selected key management and teaching staff and small grants for administrative purposes. In some francophone countries (Cote d'Ivoire and Mali), non-government providers receive much more substantial support.

Threat of HIV/AIDS: The impact of HIV/AIDS on the labour force in Africa (and hence its potential effect on vocational and technical training and skills development strategies) is considered alarming in a number of countries. According to the United Nations AIDS Prevention Agency (UNAIDS), an estimated 3.8 million adults and children in Sub-Saharan Africa became infected with HIV during 2000, bringing the total living with HIV/AIDS to 25.3 million. However, information is scarce on how African governments have factored the threat of HIV/AIDS into their TVET programmes. Yet the technical and vocational training environment, because of the inevitable use of sharp cutting tools and machines for training, presents a constant danger for the spread of the disease and puts the trainees at risk.

The current status of TVET in Africa is not all about weaknesses. TVET systems in a growing number of countries are undergoing or have undergone promising reforms that are designed to build on the inherent strengths of the system and respond to the needs of industry and the challenges of the 21st century. Some of these African and international best practices in TVET delivery can be adapted and adopted by others for rapid industrialisation.

International and African best Practices and Strategies

The primary objective of all technical and vocational education and training programmes is the acquisition of relevant knowledge, practical skills and attitudes for gainful employment in a particular trade or occupational area. The need to link training to employment (either self or paid employment) is at the base of all the best practices and strategies observed world-wide. In recent years, in view of the rapid technological advances taking place in industry and the labour market in general, flexibility, adaptability, and life-long learning have become the second major objective of vocational and technical training. The third objective, which is particularly important for African countries, is to develop TVET as a vehicle for rapid industrialization, as well as economic empowerment and social mobility of the individual.

Invariably, effective vocational and technical training begins with the formulation of a national policy and the establishment of a national implementation body, either as a semi-autonomous body or as an agency within a designated government ministry. Such agencies or National Vocational Training Authorities have been established in many countries, including Botswana (Botswana Training Authority – BOTA), Mauritius (Industrial and Vocational Training Board – IVTB), Namibia (National Vocational Training Board – NVTB), Tanzania (Vocational Education Training Authority – VETA), and Zambia (Technical Education, Vocational and Entrepreneurship Training Authority – TEVETA). Ghana has also recently passed an Act of Parliament that establishes a Council for Technical and Vocational Education and Training (COTVET) which will have overall responsibility for skills development in the country. The Council is expected to establish an Apprenticeship Training Board to link non-formal and informal vocational training to the formal TVET sector. Private training providers, including NGOs and Church Based Organisations (CBOs) are represented on the Council. In general, Training Authorities, through their various specialised organs and occupational advisory committees, have the responsibility to develop national vocational qualification frameworks and proficiency levels as well as standards for validation of training, certification and accreditation of training institutions.

From outside Africa, two training models stand out for mention: the centralised Singaporean model and the dual system practiced in Germany. In Singapore, a National Manpower Council ensures that training is relevant to the needs of the labour market. Training also includes the inculcation of shared cultural values and attitude development. The dual system of vocational training in Germany allows for learning to take place in a vocational school and in an enterprise concurrently. Approximately, 70% of all school leavers, aged between 15 and 19 years undergo training under the dual system. The dual system promotes the linkage of vocational training to the world of work. It is doubtful, however, if the industrial fabric in Africa is sufficiently developed and versatile to support the German dual system type of training.

Strategic Policy Framework

How then can technical and vocational training be promoted in Africa in order to achieve the strategic policy goal of stimulating industrial and economic growth? In my opinion, five broad strategic objectives will have to be met. These are: enhancing the quality of training, assuring relevance and employability of trainees, improving coherence and management of training provision, promoting flexibility of training and life-long learning, and enhancing the status and attractiveness of TVET.

Enhancing the Quality of Training: Training for high-quality skills requires appropriate training equipment and tools, adequate supply of training materials, and practice by the learners. Other requirements include relevant textbooks and training manuals and qualified instructors with experience in enterprises. Well-qualified instructors with industry-based experience are hard to come by, since such categories of workers are also in high demand in the labour market. But they could be suitably motivated to offer part-time instruction in technical and vocational schools.

Technical education is expensive and quality comes at a price. There is no substitute for adequate funding when it comes to delivering quality vocational education and training. In this regard, a training fund can be established to support TVET from payroll levies on employers. Training levies are in effect taxes imposed on enterprises to support skills development. Although the tax level is generally less than 2 percent of the enterprise payroll, the cooperation of employers is necessary for the successful implementation of such a scheme.

Training levies are in operation in several African countries, including Cote d'Ivoire, Mauritius, Mali, South Africa, and Tanzania.

Competency Based Training (CBT) can also enhance quality. The concept of competency-based training is not new to Africa. Traditional apprenticeship, particularly as practiced in West Africa, is competency based. A competency is the aggregate of knowledge, skills and attitudes; it is the ability to perform a prescribed professional task. CBT is actually learning by doing and by coaching. It is necessary to incorporate the principles and methodology of CBT into the formal technical and vocational education system.

However, since the development and implementation of competency-based qualifications (involving standards, levels, skills recognition and institutional arrangements) are very costly in terms of training infrastructure and staff capacity, piloting of the CBT approach in a few economic and employment growth areas is recommended, rather than a wholesale training reform strategy. Vocational students should be encouraged to build a portfolio of projects undertaken or items produced during training as evidence of proficiency and proof of ability to perform prescribed professional tasks.

Quality should be seen as "fit for purpose", rather than as measuring up to an ill-defined standard. Quality that is fit for purpose is dynamic and improves as the purpose or the job to be done moves up to a higher plane.

A decentralised and diverse TVET system that includes school-based training, enterprise-based training, and apprenticeship training (both non-formal and informal) requires a strong regulatory framework for overseeing training curricula, standards, qualifications and funding. A suitable qualifications framework and inspection system will provide the necessary quality assurance and control mechanism within such a diverse system.

Assuring Relevance and Employability of Trainees: Assuring the employability of trainees begins with effective guidance and counselling of potential learners in the choice of training programmes in relation to their aptitude and academic background. Employability presupposes the acquisition of employable skills that are related to the demands of the labour market. Labour market information systems and tracer studies which track the destination of graduates in the job market can provide useful feedback for the revision of training programmes so as to enhance the employability of trainees.

Improving Coherence and Management of Training Provision: In order to ensure coherence and management of training provision, it will be necessary to establish a national agency or body to coordinate and drive the entire TVET system. Depending on the country, this agency could be under the umbrella of the ministry of education and vocational training or stand on its own as an autonomous body. In either case, the coordinating agency should include representation from all relevant stakeholders, including government policy makers, employers, public and private training providers, civil society, alumni associations, and development partners.

Strengthening the management and coherence of training provision cannot be complete without a National Vocational Qualifications Framework (NVQF) that ensures the transfer of learning credits and mutual recognition of qualifications within the entire system. The South African National Qualifications Framework provides such a mechanism for awarding qualifications based on the achievement of specified learning outcomes prescribed by industry. The framework allows for accumulation of credits and recognition of prior learning, which promotes the culture of life-long learning. The development of a qualifications framework is not an easy task. It involves the active involvement of industry practitioners, teachers, and policy makers. Some countries have a single qualifications framework that embraces both vocational and general education and extends beyond vocational qualifications. As an example, Tanzania is developing a 10-level national qualifications framework (NQF), ranging from craftsman qualifications (level 1 – 3) through technician, diploma, and bachelors degree qualifications to masters degree (level 9) and doctorate degree award at level 10. It is, however, too early to evaluate the Tanzanian experience or recommend it to other countries.

***Flexibility of Training and Life-long Learning*:** Life-long learning has a beneficial effect on the development of a high quality TVET system. This is because the skills of the workforce can be continually upgraded through a life-long learning approach. This also means that learners who have had limited access to training in the past can have a second chance to build on their skills and competences. Life-long learning also involves the recognition of prior learning, whether in the formal or non-formal system. A National Qualifications Framework can provide the needed flexibility and coherent framework for life-long learning within the entire TVET system through the creation of equivalent qualifications across all the sub-sectors of vocational and technical training: formal, non-formal and informal.

Status and Attractiveness of TVET: Enhancing the status and attractiveness of TVET will involve changing perceptions and attitudes of the public about technical and vocational education. For this to happen, the use of role models in TVET and the involvement of successful entrepreneurs in motivation campaigns, especially in schools, will be necessary. An embarrassing shortage of role models is one of the banes of TVET. Technical and vocational education should be seen as a valid passport to a good job and not as a second best choice or the only educational route for the academically less endowed.

The status of technical and vocational education can also be enhanced by upgrading polytechnics and polytechnic-type non-university institutions to offer technical or "skills" degrees. The trend world-wide is to strengthen polytechnic institutions and their role in industrial and technological development, re-engineer their training programmes for greater relevance and higher quality, and generally raise their status and attractiveness as higher institutions of choice for senior secondary school leavers. Japan, Korea and Singapore have been awarding "skills" degrees for many years now and Ghana has recently granted accreditation to two of its polytechnics to start offering degree programmes in a few technological areas. The Kenya Government has also decided to follow this positive trend of revitalizing polytechnic education and promoting skills training to the highest level possible.

The Impact and Challenge of Globalisation

Like every aspect of human endeavour today, the forces of globalisation have not overlooked technical and vocational education and training. Tony Blair, the British Prime Minister once had this to say about globalisation:

> *"You have no choice, this is inevitable. These forces of change driving the future don't stop at national boundaries, don't respect tradition. They wait for no one and no nation. They are universal."*

Globalisation is characterised by the increasing integration of national economies around the world. The process of globalisation is driven by the ease of information exchange, capital flows, and the migration of people, labour, goods, and services across national boundaries. The challenge of globalisation for TVET in Africa is the tension it has created between developing skills for poverty eradication and skills for global economic competitiveness. Although the primary objective of technical and vocational training in Africa is to support economic growth and wealth creation for poverty alleviation through the acquisition of employable skills, a strategic approach to skills development on the continent cannot ignore the effects of globalisation.

For this reason, the acquisition of "industrial" skills is as important to Africa as the basic vocational and technical skills. In the advanced developing countries like Singapore and Malaysia, the rise to economic prominence was supported by the development of high level technical skills. However, the experience of these countries also shows that their industrial lift-off was preceded by high stocks of literacy and basic skills. The sheer lack of skills of all sorts in Africa and the demands of poverty alleviation mean that African countries must pursue the development of skills at all levels of the spectrum (basic, secondary, and tertiary levels), with each country emphasizing the skill levels that correspond best to their current stage of economic development and the needs of the local labour market. At the same time, the important requirement of building a society imbued with high stocks of basic numeracy and literacy skills cannot be ignored.

Modern society is characterised by the increasing application of information and communication technologies. ICT education therefore must form a strong component of all levels of skills training. In the globalising labour market, employees are regularly required to update and upgrade their knowledge and skills in order to remain abreast with the rapid technological advances in the workplace. Globalisation reinforces the imperatives of quality, relevance, flexibility, technology-mediated learning, and life-long learning. These attributes constitute the education and training bench-marks for skilled human resource development in the knowledge-driven economies of today.

Interestingly, globalisation can offer Africa opportunities for high-level technical skills training through the process of technology transfer. In effect, technology-rich trans-national corporations, if suitably motivated, can become important private sector training providers of high-level industrial skills within the TVET system of their host countries. This is because a major dimension of globalisation is foreign direct investment (FDI) and the implantation of trans-national corporations in developing economies. FDI inflows, accompanied by top-grade technical expertise and modern manufacturing machinery can trigger a process of technology transfer, skills accumulation and industrialisation in the receiving country. Although the debate is still on as to whether globalisation helps or hurts, a country can upgrade its industries and increase the skills stock of its technical workforce through FDI and the operations of technologically advanced multinational companies in the country. The activities of such companies may be directly or gently steered by government policy to include provision of high-level skills training and the establishment of collaborative practical research and innovative training programmes with the country's higher education institutions, particularly the universities and polytechnics.

However, globalisation can also hurt the development of indigenous technology. The downside effect of globalisation on technical and vocational education and training in Africa is the flooding of local markets with all manner of cheap goods and technology products from foreign countries. What is the market for a locally produced wooden chair when the imported plastic version is cheaper? Again, how competitive is the cost of a locally sewn dress against cheaper imported second-hand clothes? National policies should therefore take into account these and other globalisation-induced factors in designing TVET programmes and courses for industrialisation in an increasingly inter-connected world economy.

Key Policy Issues

What are the key policy issues and strategies involved in the re-engineering of an effective technical and vocational education system for industrialisation, economic growth and wealth creation? To my mind, there are five policy issues that cannot be ignored.

Linkage with Other National Policies and Strategies: Since technical and vocational education constitutes only one item of many on a country's development agenda, it will be necessary for each country to define and specify clear articulation lines between TVET and other sectors of the national economy in order to effectively link its TVET policy to other national strategies and policies in the area of education and training at all levels, employment, and socio-economic development. This means that national TVET strategies in Africa must give priority to training in areas such as agriculture, ICT, and modern infrastructure development. An efficient transport and communication network, a reliable energy and water supply system, adequate housing, and national food security are basic requirements for industrialisation.

Linkage with Regional and International Policies: In the inter-connected world of today, no country is an island. It is therefore important for national TVET policies to create room for possible dovetailing into existing regional and international education and training policy frameworks and protocols. National TVET strategies should take into account the education and training protocols of regional groupings like ECOWAS, SADC, and COMESA (where they exist), and those of acknowledged international agencies involved in education and skills training, such as UNESCO, ADEA, and ILO.

Linkage With the World of Work: Since the ultimate objective of TVET is employability and employment promotion, it is necessary to link training to the needs of the labour market. TVET must be relevant and demand-driven, rather than supply-driven and a stand-alone activity. In order to do this, data is required on the actual employability of TVET graduates, available job opportunities, and the evolving skills demands on the labour front. Determining the demand for skills is best achieved through country-specific Labour Market Information Systems (LMIS) and other survey instruments. The function of a labour market information system or labour market "observatory" is to collect, process and make employment projections from information provided by employment ministries and agencies and from demographic surveys, tracer studies that track the employment destination of TVET graduates, labour market related reports produced by economic think-tanks, and feedback from employers. An effective LMIS will be difficult to establish and operate now in many African countries for the simple reason that there is a paucity of data and information from which labour market trends can be captured, as well as lack of trained research staff with adequate technical expertise to run the system. In the short term, however, indicative labour market information can be gathered from trade and employer associations, NGOs, employment agencies, as well as large public and private sector employers. Training institutions can also conduct local labour market surveys in and around their localities. Information so gathered and analysed would then serve as inputs for the development of new or revised courses and training programmes, equipment and learning materials selection, instructor formation, and guidance and counselling of students and trainees.

Instructor Training and Professionalisation of TVET Staff

The professional and pedagogical competence of the technical teacher is crucial to the successful implementation of any TVET strategy. Governments should therefore make conscious efforts, not only to train but also to retain technical teachers in the system.

Technical teachers may be suitably motivated through equitable remuneration packages and incentive schemes that may include government subventions and loans to teacher associations and special credit facilities for the teachers to acquire cars, houses, etc.

The delivery of quality TVET is also closely linked to the building of strong management and leadership capacity to drive the entire system.

TVET system managers, professionals and policy deciders will therefore also have to be trained and their skills upgraded to enable them confidently drive the system with its various implementation structures, including qualifications framework, accreditation standards, assessment guidelines, quality assurance and accountability frameworks.

Funding and Equipping TVET Institutions

On a per student basis and compared with other levels of education, in particular primary and secondary education, TVET is much more expensive to deliver. There is need therefore to spread the funding net as wide as possible to include:

- *National Governments:* Governments should allocate a respectable percentage of their national budgets to the TVET sector
- *Employers: Employers,* both public and private, should contribute to a training levy based on a percentage of their enterprise payrolls.
- *Development Partners:* The World Bank and the African Development Bank, for example, can support country-specific projects, multinational projects, and micro-financing schemes.
- *Trainees:* Equitable cost-sharing mechanisms and fees paid by students and trainees should help offset their training costs
- *Training Providers:* Training providers and institutions can raise funds internally through the operations of their production and commercial units
- *Community:* Local communities can make cash and non-cash contributions in the form of land and through community fundraising activities.
- *Donors:* Individuals or groups (e.g. wealthy individuals, churches or faith-based organisations, NGOs) can support TVET through donations and endowments.

Policy Roles and Recommendations

Effective technical and vocational education and training for industrialisation can only happen if all the relevant stakeholders play their part. Governments, training institutions, parents and guardians, development partners and employers, all have important roles to play.

Governments

- Develop and support implementation of national TVET policies;
- Improve coherence of governance and management of TVET;
- Introduce policies and incentives that will support increased private sector participation in TVET delivery;
- Improve capital investment in TVET;
- Establish TVET management information systems for education and training, including labour market information system;
- Institute measures to reduce gender, economic, and geographical inequities in TVET provision;
- Introduce sustainable financing schemes for TVET;
- Increase funding support to the sector;
- Build leadership and management capacity to drive TVET system;
- Mainstream vocational education into the general education system, so that the vocational track is less dead-end;
- Introduce ICT into TVET
- Constantly monitor and periodically evaluate the performance of the system and apply corrective measures accordingly.

Educational Institutions and Training Providers

- *Provide training within national policy framework;*
- *Deliver a flexible and demand-driven training;*
- *Develop business plans to support training activities;*
- *Establish strong linkages and collaboration with employers and industry;*
- *Mainstream gender into training activities and programmes;*
- *Introduce ICT into training*
- *Institute bursary schemes for poor trainees;*
- *Strengthen guidance and counselling services to trainees;*
- *Network and bench-mark with other training providers;*

- *Involve community, parents and guardians in training activities.*
- *Training institutions should be encouraged to be profit-oriented and to become active operators in the training market;*

Parents and Guardians

- Support children and wards to choose the vocational education track;
- Reject perception that TVET is for the less academically endowed;
- Lobby politicians in favour of TVET;
- Support activities of educational institutions and training providers.

Donors and Development Partners

- Support development and implementation of national TVET policies and strategies;
- Fund small business development research;
- Fund acquisition of training equipment;
- Support post-training employment support services for TVET graduates, including business start-ups;
- Support capacity building in TVET sector – instructor training, management training, technical assistance, etc.
- Help in identifying and disseminating best practices in TVET;
- Support TVET advocacy initiatives, motivation campaigns and programmes.

Employers

- Deliver workplace training to employees
- Contribute financially to national training fund
- Provide opportunities in industry for TVET teachers to regularly update their workplace experience;
- Provide opportunities for industrial attachment and internships for trainees
- Contribute to the development of national skills standards.

Bibliography

Aron, L. Y., & Zweig, J. M.: *Educational Alternatives for Vulnerable Youth: Student Needs, Program Types, and Research Directions*, Urban Institute, Washington, DC, 2008.

Burkam, D. T., Lee, V. E., & Dwyer, J.: *School Mobility in the Early Elementary Grades: Frequency and Impact from Nationally-representative Data*, National Research Council, Washington, DC., 2009.

Carlson, D., Reder, S., Jones, N., & Lee, A.: *Homeless Student Transportation Project Evaluation*, Washington State Transportation Center, Seattle, WA, 2006.

de la Torre, M., & Gwynne, J.: *Changing Schools: A Look at Student Mobility Trends in Chicago Public Schools since 1995*, Consortium on Chicago School Research, Chicago, 2009.

Gibbons, S., & Telhaj, S.: *Mobility and School Disruption,* Centre for the Economics of Education, London, 2007.

Hartman, C.: *Rights at risk: Equality in an Age of Terrorism,* Citizens' Commission on Civil Rights, Washington, DC, 2002.

Jacob, B., & Ludwig, J.: *Improving Educational Outcomes for Poor Children*, National Bureau of Economic Research, Cambridge, MA, 2008.

Jason, L. A., Danner, K. E., & Kurasaki, K. S.: *Prevention and School Transitions*, The Haworth Press, New York, 1993.

Jason, L. A., Weine, A. M., Johnson, J. H., Filippelli, L. A., & Turner, E. Y.: *Helping Transfer Students: Strategies for Educational and Social Readjustment*, Jossey-Bass, San Francisco, 1992.

Killeen, K. M., & Schafft, K. A.: *Handbook of Research in Education Finance and Policy*, Routledge, New York, 2008.

Larson, A.: *Homeless and Highly Mobile Students: A Description of Students from three Minnesota Districts,* Center for Advanced Studies in Child Welfare/Minn-LInK, St. Paul, MN, 2009.

Lee, V. E., & Burkam, D. T.: *Inequality at the Starting gate: Social background Differences in Achievement as Children begin School*, Economic Policy Institute, Washington, DC, 2002.

Paik, S., & Phillips, R.: *Student Mobility in Rural Communities: What are the Implications for Student Achievement?,* North Central Regional Educational Laboratory, Chicago, 2002.

Ream, R. K.: *Uprooting Children: Mobility, Social Capital, and Mexican American Underachievement*, LFB Scholarly Publishers, New York, 2005.

Ron Miller: *Self-Organizing Revolution*, Holistic Education Press, 2008.

Rumberger, R. W., Larson, K. A., Ream, R. K., &. Palardy, G. J.: *The Educational Consequence of Mobility for California Students and Schools,* Policy Analysis of California Education, Berkeley, CA, 1999.

Sanbonmatsu, L., Kling, J. R., Duncan, G. J., & Brooks-Gunn, J.: *Neighborhoods and Academic Achievement: Results from the Moving to Opportunity Experiment,* National Bureau of Economic Research, Cambridge, MA, 2006.

Schafft, K. A., & Killeen, K. M.: *Assessing Student Mobility and its Consequences: A 3-district Case Study,* Education Finance Research Consortium, Albany, NY, 2007.

Schafft, K. A.: *Poverty, Residential Mobility and Student Transiency within a Rural New York School District*, Penn State University, University Park, PA., 2005.

Tierney, W. G., & Rhoads, R. A.: *Faculty Socialization as a Cultural Process: A Mirror of Institutional Commitment,* The George Washington University Graduate School of Education and Human Development, Washington, D.C., 1994.

Wadsworth, E. C.: *A Handbook for New Practitioners,* New Forums Press and the Professional and Organizational Development Network in Higher Education, Stillwater, OK, 1988

Wheeler, D. W.: *Face to Face: A Sourcebook of Individual Consultation Techniques for Faculty/Instructional Developers,* New Forums Press, Stillwater, OK, 1988.

Wilkerson, L., & Lewis, K. G.: *A Guide to Faculty Development: Practical Advice, Examples, and Resources,* Anker Publishing, Bolton, MA, 2002.

Index

M

P

S

T

U

V

❑❑❑